EX AUDITU

An International Journal of Theological Interpretation of Scripture

Volume 17 2001

Ex Auditu is published annually by Pickwick Publications, 215 Incline Way, San Jose, California, 95139-1526, USA.

Subscriptions
Individuals:
U.S.A. - $17.00
Canada - $15.00 (in U.S. Funds)
All other countries - $18.00 (in U.S. Funds)
Students - $12.00

Institutions:
U.S.A. - $30.00
Canada - $25.00 - (in U.S. Funds)
All other countries - $30.00 (in U.S. Funds)

This periodical is indexed in the *ATLA Religion Database,* published by the American Theological Library Association, 250 S. Wacker Dr., 16th Flr., Chicago, IL 60606, E-mail: atla@atla.com, WWW: http://www.atla.com/; *Internationale Zeitschriftenshau für Bibelwissenschaft*; *Religion and Theological Abstracts;* and *Old Testament Abstracts.*

Please address all subscription correspondence and change of address information to Pickwick Publications.

ISSN 0883-0053

EX AUDITU

An International Journal of Theological Interpretation of Scripture

KLYNE R. SNODGRASS, *Editor*
NORTH PARK THEOLOGICAL SEMINARY
3225 WEST FOSTER AVENUE
CHICAGO, ILLINOIS 60625-4987
USA

Tel: (773) 244-6209
Fax: (773) 244-6244
e-mail: ksnodgrass@northpark.edu
web site: http://www.northpark.edu/sem/exauditu

THE EDITORIAL BOARD MEMBERS AND CONSULTANTS represent various disciplines and denominations. Theological Interpretation of Scripture is a task to be taken seriously by scholars who are committed to the Christian faith and tradition. However, as one editorial consultant stated: "let people gradually get used to the idea that a sane hermeneutics is both oriented in advance toward agreement/consent and is simultaneously exigent, discriminating, critical."

EX AUDITU

Volume 17 2001

CONTENTS

Announcement of the 2002 Symposium

North Park Theological Seminary in Chicago, Illinois, is pleased to announce that the eighteenth Symposium on the Theological Interpretation of Scripture will take place September 26-28, 2002. The Symposium will start at 7:00 p.m. on September 26 in Nyvall Hall and will extend through a Saturday afternoon worship service on September 28.

The theme in 2002 will be Spiritual Formation. The following persons have agreed to make presentations:

Sam Balentine, Baptist Theological Seminary at Richmond	Old Testament
Michael Dash, Interdenominational Theological Center	Ministry and Context
John Endres, Jesuit School of Theology at Berkeley	Old Testament
Stephen Kang, Wheaton College	Christian Formation and Ministry
Eugene Peterson, Regent College	Worship Leader
Ephraim Radner, Ascension Episcopal Church, Pueblo, CO	Theology
Stephen Rasor, Interdenominational Theological Center	Sociology of Religion
David Scholer, Fuller Theological Seminary	New Testament
Loren Stuckenbruck, University of Durham	New Testament
C. John Weborg, North Park Theological Seminary	Theology

Persons interested in attending the sessions should write before September 1 to:

Ms. Guylla Brown
North Park Theological Seminary
3225 W. Foster Avenue
Chicago, Illinois 60625

Meals may be taken at North Park and assistance can be provided in finding nearby lodging.

ABBREVIATIONS

Amp.	Amplified Bible
BibInt	*Biblical Interpretation*
HES-CR	Human embryonic stem-cell research
JJS	*Journal of Jewish Studies*
JSOT	*Journal for the Study of the Old Testament*
JSOTSup	Journal for the Study of the Old Testament: Supplement Series
NIDOTTE	*New International Dictionary of Old Testament Theology and Exegesis*
NTS	*New Testament Studies*
R & T	*Religion and Theology*
TDOT	*Theological Dictionary of the Old Testament*

PUBLISHER'S STATEMENT

Since 1990, North Park Theological Seminary has ably hosted the annual symposium on Theological Interpretation of Scripture, with one of its faculty members serving as editor of EX AUDITU. All the papers presented at the symposia were published by Pickwick Publications.

Age has crept up to tell us that it is time for us to seek another theological institution to undertake both the symposia and its annual publication of EX AUDITU. The journal has received a very positive response from all over the world and has become a self-supporting project.

At this time, therefore, we invite any theological seminary with genuine interest in continuing what the late professor, Ben F. Meyer called "an issue of the greatest importance," to respond to this invitation and write for the details of this offer to:

Dikran Y. Hadidian
Pickwick Publications
215 Incline Way
San Jose, CA 95139

INTRODUCTION

The terrorist attacks on the World Trade Center made the discussion of biblical ethics stunningly relevant. Doubt existed at first whether North Park's Symposium on the Theological Interpretation of Scripture would even take place. Could people get flights from places like Washington, D.C.? None of us involved in planning for a discussion of biblical ethics had any idea how pertinent the topic would be. Suddenly we were not having a polite discussion about ideas but found ourselves wrestling with dilemmas quite similar to those faced by Dietrich Bonhoeffer, whose ethics just happened to be the subject of the first paper. We were all reminded quickly why our tasks as exegetes, theologians, and ethicists is important. Either our world will be an ethical world, or it will be a tormented world. That is true whether we speak of the world of financial accounting and the Enron fiasco, of the world of ethnic conflict, or the worlds of racism, poverty, injustice, and violence.

Precisely here American Christianity in virtually all of its manifestations has made a fatal error. Christians have concluded that their religion is primarily about what one believes and, although ethics are discussed, in the end actions are optional or at least not at the heart of this religion. In some traditions such thinking is grounded in the desire to avoid any notion of salvation by works. In other traditions it is grounded in the assumption of the inability of humanity to accomplish what is right and/or the confidence that God will forgive our sins anyway. But surely all this is to tear thinking from being and living.

When we read the Bible, how such erroneous thinking has become so prevalent is a mystery. The Bible—whether the various parts of the OT, the teaching of Jesus, or the writings of Paul and other early Christian leaders—seeks to describe and motivate *action* in keeping with the purposes of God. Certainly the Bible is not about rule keeping or action for its own sake. But, undeniably the Bible is about identity formation; it both tells us who we are and what we are to *do* because of who we are. Much of the Bible is explicitly about how God's people are to act, and for the NT how followers of Jesus Christ should shape their lives to his and what they should do because they believe. The Bible is largely about ethics.

Being biblical, however, is no easy task. True, much of what God expects of his people is obvious and beyond serious debate. At the same time many issues are debated and what one should do is by no means clear. Further, the Bible is an ancient document and sometimes not immediately transferable to the modern world. On many issues it does not say enough or address the complexity of our world. On other issues the Bible says nothing directly on the topic at hand. How is one to discern what elements are culturally or contextually limited in application? How pertinent is the OT for Christian living? Many of the debates in the modern church are explicitly debates about the application of ethical texts and especially the way the OT commands are to be appropriated in a Christian context. The papers collected here discuss these issues, particularly the importance of biblical ethics, what the goal is in pursuing biblical ethics, and ways of being biblical, even regarding issues the Bible does not discuss. What the journal cannot reflect adequately is the depth and energy of the discussions of each of the papers.

Thanks is expressed to each of the presenters and respondents, particularly for those who had to travel in uncertain circumstances. Special thanks is expressed to Sondra Wheeler, not only for her paper, but also because she agreed to provide a response to Marion Soards' paper on the stem cell debate. The request for her response came as a result of her contribution to the discussion at the symposium. Thanks is also expressed to Miroslav Volf and Eerdmans Publishing for permission to reprint his article "Theology for a Way of Life," which was originally published in *Practicing Theology: Beliefs and Practices in Christian Life* (eds. Miroslav Volf and Dorothy C. Bass, 2002, 245-263). Since this article has been reprinted without change, references in the article to "this volume" (as in n. 7) refer to the Eerdmans volume, not the current issue of *Ex Auditu.*

Klyne R. Snodgrass
The Editor

DIETRICH BONHOEFFER'S THEOLOGICAL INTERPRETATION OF SCRIPTURE FOR THE CHURCH

GEFFREY B. KELLY AND F. BURTON NELSON

The problems that Dietrich Bonhoeffer addressed during his brief career as a teacher, ecumenist, catechist, pastor, director of an illegal seminary, conspirator against a criminal government, and, finally, a martyr, were many. All these roles reflected aspects of his devotion to Jesus Christ and the Christian Church. He spoke and wrote extensively on peace, poverty, the idolatry of national security, the Jewish question, the struggle against the heretical Reich Church, the no compromise demands of the Sermon on the Mount, freedom and justice, the denunciation of government malevolence, the reform of the church, and no excuses obedience to the teachings of Jesus Christ. Decisions to be made on each of these issues were risky under a government whose *modus covivendi* was conformity, coercion, and hasty, barbaric punishment of every deviation from its dictates. Each issue in turn required the kind of spiritual discernment in which Bonhoeffer placed himself in the power of God's Word now become decisive for him through the attractive, persuasive movement of the Holy Spirit. His life became an unending effort to convince others, particularly those who were called to be the moral leaders of the community, to obey the will of Jesus Christ, not the will of Adolf Hitler, in countering the systemic injustice in which the churches seemed to acquiesce or to resist in only a halfhearted way. For this purpose he attempted to derive a spiritual, pastoral meaning from the scriptural word, an approach more dependent on faith in the teaching power of the Holy Spirit than in the less soul-nurturing rules of historical criticism. He read the Bible as a Word of God aiding human beings to discern what should be done in the concrete situation of confronting governmental evil headlong and defending the victims of the national heartlessness.

THE SPIRITUAL INTERPRETATION OF THE BIBLE

Bonhoeffer had, in fact, decided early on in his student days that the Scripture was a guiding light for a way of life and not a jousting arena for scholars to show off their brilliance in textual exegesis. One of his student essays announces his intentions to use the Bible pastorally. The paper was entitled, "Can a Distinction Be Drawn Between a Historical and a Pneumatological Interpretation of the Scriptures, and How Does Dogmatic Theology Regard This?" The paper unnerved his mentors at Berlin University, suspicious, as they were at the time, of Karl Barth's pungent challenge to the liberal theology for which Berlin was noted. The idea of separating the scientific exegesis more in vogue in his classes at the university from the spiritual, pastoral interpretation that might more directly nourish one's faith was an attraction that Bonhoeffer wished to pursue in preparing himself for life after academe. The historical approach that searched out the most accurate text as well as the original intention of the writer construed through use of all the tools of historical criticism and rational, scientific exegesis appears to be secondary in importance in Bonhoeffer's analysis. The study was turned in on July 31, 1925. It was not well-received by his mentor, Reinhold Seeberg, who had sniffed out the Barthian influence and assigned the paper only the mediocre grade of "satisfactory."

The opening words of Bonhoeffer's essay directly expose his problem. Does one read the Scriptures in a purely scientific mode or—what he will signal as his preference—does one read the Bible in a spirit of prayer and faith with the mind opened to what God, and not the skilled scientific exegetes, may be saying? "The Christian religion," he wrote, "stands or falls by belief in the divine revelation that became historically real, tangible and visible—that is, to those who have eyes to see and ears to hear—and thus in its very essence contains the question that we ask ourselves today about the relationship between history and spirit, or applied to the Bible, between letter and spirit, Scripture and revelation, man's word and God's."[1] By the time Bonhoeffer had typed those words, his interest in the exciting new theology of Karl Barth had captivated him and left him disgruntled with the textual criticism in which he had acquired enough expertise to satisfy his teachers, Adolf von Harnack and Karl Holl, neither of whom were friendly to Barth's mode of searching the Scriptures with what they had seen as an a priori pastoral bias. For someone like Reinhold Seeberg, the teacher for whom this paper was written, the essay appeared to be open rebelliousness on the part of the university's most promising young student, now in danger of being "seduced" by Barthianism. Bonhoeffer countered his critics with the assertion that the textual criticism then in vogue left only "rubble and fragments."[2] He felt at the time that historical criticism had failed to appreciate the biblical sources as agents of revelation and sacred canon, not to be merely handled as a literature to be picked apart and finely honed for textual accuracy. He did not repudiate the historical critical method; in fact, he insisted it was still necessary.

For Bonhoeffer, however, the scientific approach had to give way to the pneumatological which inevitably became "prayer . . . supplication to the Holy Spirit which alone, as it pleases, gives it the hearing and understanding without which the most highly intellectual exegesis is nothing. Textual understanding and interpretation, preaching, that is the realization of God, is contained in the prayer: *Veni creator spiritus* [Come, creator spirit]."[3] Bonhoeffer appeared to be struggling at this time between the lure of academe and his personal attraction to the Bible as a guiding word in which God makes God known through the enlightening inspiration of the Holy Spirit speaking God's truth to the human hearer of the Word. Bonhoeffer seems to have collapsed into one the once vigorously debated Protestant distinction between inspiration and illumination. The historians at the university would surely not be comfortable with Bonhoeffer's acerbic judgment of their efforts at textual accuracy: "For history, scripture is only a source; for pneumatology, it is testimony."[4]

The testimony of which Bonhoeffer wrote in that student essay would soon become for him the commands of Jesus Christ given to Christians to obey and the judgments of God against human idolatries and pretentiousness. His use of the Scripture would be thoroughly centered on Jesus Christ. It is Jesus who speaks through the Bible. His Word cuts through all the human efforts to control and manipulate the God in whom Christians profess to believe. It is Jesus Christ who in the Scripture stands as a bracing reminder to Christians that he, not human projections or human pretenders, is the Word of God incarnate in the little ones calling out to Christians to embody for them the very compassion of their Father God (Matt 5:43-48; 6:2-4; 25:31-46; Luke 6:32-36; John 15:11-17; 1 John 4:7-21).

THE SCRIPTURAL MANDATE TO LEARN OF AND TO FOLLOW JESUS CHRIST

In his doctoral dissertation, published as the book, *Sanctorum Communio*, Bonhoeffer distilled his definition of the church, not from any of the definitions then floating about in systematic theology, but from what he saw as the overall thrust of the Christian Scriptures. He could then write that the church is "Christ existing as the church community."[5] From that point on in both his dissertation and his *Habilitationsschrift* the measure of the church's fidelity to its vocation became for Bonhoeffer its conformity with Jesus Christ and its willingness to teach and even to suffer for the sake of the gospel truth. For him, Jesus Christ is both the fact of the church and the ideal toward which the church must always strive; at the same time, Jesus is the never ending prophetic challenge to the church to represent the presence of Jesus Christ in one's everyday social world. We see here traces of Bonhoeffer's earliest written appreciation of Christ's central relationship to people within the specifically Christian congregation as well as within the wider world. Structured by Jesus Christ, the "communion of saints" is declared to be the locus of that solidarity with people that Bonhoeffer would later see both as the attractive life of a church and the strength and test of Christian faith. He is emphatic in his declaration that, in Christ, God has not only entered human history, as the Bible attests, but has in a striking way shaped that history in ways more extensive than even the Bible or Christian imagination could ever acclaim.

In effect, as the biblical story of creation relates and as Bonhoeffer reiterates in *Sanctorum Communio*, God's life has become inescapably bound up into human life. Bonhoeffer depicts Christ's role in this history in the formation of one's personal and social existence by standing as our representative at the point where human community has been disrupted by sin and healed by God. Jesus Christ is the Lord through whom God's love, the basis and bond of all community, overcomes sin and brings about the reconciliation of individuals with themselves and of people with each other. In *Sanctorum Communio* we see, too, a statement of the ideal ground of those actions on behalf of the oppressed that would become the pulse of Bonhoeffer's own resistance to Nazism and of his role in the conspiracy. Bonhoeffer writes glowingly of Christ's vicarious action as the basis of that communion of people whose oneness would be structured by "agapeic" love, their living and acting for others rather than for themselves. It is self-sacrificing love, not necessarily aimed at receiving love or acknowledgement in return, that shapes the community into concrete resemblance to Jesus Christ.

Bonhoeffer's reading of the Scriptures will thus be focused on the meaning he derives from his relationship with Jesus Christ. A pattern thus emerges in the examination of his collected writings. He begins with the a priori that the church is "Christ existing as community." That community is, as Jesus was described in the Gospels, a prophetic savior who preached salvation and freedom through the faith that expresses itself in acts of love and caring for the needy of societies in which Christian faith is embodied (Matt 5:1-10; 25:31-46; Luke 6:20-26). Bonhoeffer's Jesus is, following John's Gospel, the way, the truth, and the life. But Jesus' way is a life of compassion for the least of Jesus' brothers and sisters. Jesus' truth is the gospel mandates that are to be obeyed, and Jesus' life is the call to be God's witness against all the forms that evil and untruth can take within one's person, one's community and one's nation. He refuses to become entangled in the exegetical debates about form criticism and demythologization then raging in the universities.

Bonhoeffer states at the outset of his Christology lectures, for example, that he refuses to dwell on the distinction between the Jesus of history and the Christ of faith; for him, they are one and the same. Nor does he want to slip into the theological quagmire of speculative analyses into how the incarnation was possible, into the makeup of the Trinity, or into the exact demarcation between the divine and human in Jesus. Points of departure like these, he declared to his students, would either die the death of abstraction or meander into the dead end of those dull doctrinal formulations so ideal for avoiding a confrontation with the disturbing challenges of Jesus' life. Instead of asking how one is able to think out the distinctiveness of the two natures in the one person, Bonhoeffer posed to his students what he felt to be the more relevant question: "Who is this man of whom it is testified that he is God?"[6] In some ways this quotation from Luther that Bonhoeffer repeated at several junctures in his Christology lectures also echoed Luther's declaration that if one had been a villager in Nazareth and had seen Jesus fetching a bucket of water at the town well, one could have said, "there goes Jesus carrying water," or just as equally true, "there goes God carrying water."

This approach gave Bonhoeffer the opening to declare that Jesus could very well be the worker on the factory floor or the Jew victimized by the anti-Jewish legislation. In the summer of 1933, to suggest that Jesus could be the Bolshevik or the Jew was extremely daring, given the ways in which the Nazis had managed to demonize both groups within Germany. In an attempt to move his students to probe more deeply into the mindset of the "poor worker" (read: Bolshevik), he tells his students: "The poor worker does not say, 'Jesus is God.' But when he says, 'Jesus is a good man,' he is saying more than the bourgeois say when they repeat 'Jesus is God.' God is for them something belonging to the church. But, Jesus can be present on the factory floor as the socialist; at a political meeting, as an idealist; in the worker's world, as a good man. He fights in their ranks against the enemy, capitalism."[7] Throughout these lectures Bonhoeffer emphasizes the humanity of Jesus on the one hand and his compassion for and identity with the poor and lowly of German society. He criticizes those religionists who think that in proclaiming Jesus as God and enthroning him in gaudy splendor they have honored him adequately. Jesus, he says, craves no such theology of glory. He enters the murky world of sin and death, not as a king, but hidden in the world "in weakness and not to be recognized as God-man." Bonhoeffer goes on to say that in this way Jesus provokes "contradiction and hostility. He goes incognito, as a beggar among beggars, as an outcast among outcasts, as despairing among the despairing, as dying among the dying."[8]

Bonhoeffer makes the connection between Jesus and the church as between a *theologia crucis* and a *theologia gloriae*. The church, too, must be the humbled church, but not glorying in its purported humility and certainly not boasting of its power and its influence. Instead, the church must humbly confess its sins and not see Jesus Christ, the beggar and the outcast, as "the stumbling block to its own hopes and wishes." That would be taking scandal from Jesus' way of life and his teachings on making common cause with the castaways of Germanic society (See Matt 12:2-6, especially v.6 where Jesus declares those blessed who do not take scandal in his compassionate outreach to the blind, the lame, the lepers, the deaf, and the poor).

These lectures were exciting to his students. Bonhoeffer was praised by them for turning theology into a search for personal meaning.[9] The twist he gave to Christology was not something new to him. As early as his pastoral internship in Barcelona, he depicted the essence of Christianity as more than its religious trappings and even more than its embodiment in a church, even though Christianity needs the church because the church bears the message of God's ways in the cross of Jesus Christ. But the true essence of Christianity, he insists, lies not in its human structures and institutional settings but in the very way the cross of Jesus Christ becomes "the light of eternity [that] shines down on those who are ever neglected, insignificant, weak, ignoble, unknown, inferior, oppressed, despised; here it radiates over the houses of prostitutes and tax collectors . . . . Here the light of eternity has been cast on the toiling, struggling, and sinning masses." He adds that this same light is stymied before the houses of the prosperous and the smugly knowledgeable. He ends with the remarkable conclusion from the ways of Jesus Christ: "Christianity preaches the unending worth of the apparently worthless and the unending worthlessness of what is apparently so valuable. The weak shall be made strong through God and the dying shall live."[10]

In an Advent sermon from that same Barcelona period, he uses the judgment scene from Matthew's Gospel (Matt 25:31-46) to remind the people that Advent means more than preparing to welcome the cuddly babe of Bethlehem. To his congregation he preached that Advent must be an everyday event in which they must face up to the shocking reality that Jesus may be standing at their door asking them "for help in the form of a beggar, in the form of a ruined human being in torn clothing. He confronts you in every person that you meet. Christ walks on the earth as your neighbor as long as there are people." He wanted his people to notice that other seamy side of Barcelona where the grubby poor lived and where Christ was asking them for the help that they in the everyday spirit of Advent were called on to give.

In one of his major talks during the church's "Week of Repentance" after returning from a year as a Sloane Fellow at Union Theological Seminary, Bonhoeffer returned to the same theme, but this time after delivering a lengthy, at times sarcastic complaint that the church had become otherworldly because that provided it with an easy accommodation with the forces of secularism then sweeping the country. It was ironically a deceptive way for the church to evade God. But the evasion is doomed and churches become less than Christlike should they take the facile escape route into otherworldliness in its ceremonies and practice. His theme was the petition from the Lord's prayer, "Thy Kingdom Come" (Matt 6:10). The church is called to witness to that Kingdom. But, Bonhoeffer cautions the people, "Christ . . . does not lead us in a religious flight from this world to other worlds beyond; rather, he gives us back to the earth as its loyal children."[11] The church must coexist with the state, to be sure, but its function is not to cave in to the state and withdraw within its sacred ceremonialism. The church confronts the state; it too serves the people, but in the manner of Jesus Christ. "The Kingdom of God," he concludes, "is not to be found in some other world beyond, but in the midst of this world . . . . God wants us to honor God on earth; God wants us to honor God in our fellow man and woman and nowhere else." That, he says, is the practical gist of Jesus' Sermon on the Mount and the Last Judgment scene in Matthew's Gospel. The church must be alert not to evade the demands that Jesus makes in the incognito of the hungry, the thirsty, the sick, the imprisoned, the dying.

The same theme will reappear in Bonhoeffer's *Ethics* in which he addresses the practical problems of a nation and of churches seemingly without any moral bearings while under the control of a government engaged in genocide and a bloody war of aggression that had caused worldwide anguish. He speaks of conforming oneself with Jesus Christ, of preparing the way for the restoration of the peace of Jesus Christ. His scriptural moorings are embedded in the passages that speak of the role of the Baptist, smoothing out the rough ways (Matt 3:1-17), and of Luke proclaiming that God will bring down the powerful and lift up the lowly (Luke 1:46-55). But his attention turns also to the valleys of human wretchedness, human bondage to evil, poverty, and ignorance that have despoiled the church of its moral credibility and hindered the coming of Jesus Christ in their troubled world. Although he will build his ethics up to the point where he asks that people stop dividing their lives into the two distinct spheres of secular-profane and religious-sacred, at this juncture he also traces the malaise of the people to the church's failure to prepare the way for the coming of Christ anew into a world where the war will yield to a lasting peace. There is an immense responsibility that has been neglected with the consequence that faith has withered and Germany was set up for the advent of the ruthless, immoral ideology of Nazism. "The hungry need bread and the homeless need a roof; the dispossessed need justice and the lonely need fellowship; the undisciplined need order and the slaves need freedom. To allow the hungry to remain hungry would be blasphemy against God and one's neighbor, for what is nearest to God is precisely the need of one's neighbor. It is for the love of Christ, which belongs as much to the hungry as to myself, that I share my bread with them and that I share my dwelling with the homeless. If the hungry do not attain to faith, then the guilt falls on those who refused them bread. To provide the hungry with bread is to prepare the way for the coming of Grace."[12]

These are the practical actions that Bonhoeffer claims were not done by Christians and their churches with the kind of consistency that might have prevented the accession to power of Adolf Hitler with all the evil consequences that resulted. The manner in which Hitler gained absolute power would create the moral dilemma of tyrannicide which Bonhoeffer also addresses in his *Ethics* in a consequential approach to a decision which would be sinful no matter what course of action they choose. But his ire in the beginning of his book is directed against the church for neglecting its mandate to care for and defend the dispossessed in the manner of Jesus Christ. In his prison letters he will put it more graphically: The church stands up only "for the church's cause but [it has] little personal faith in Christ." As a result, he added, "'Jesus' is disappearing from sight." The church had become "the church on the defensive, [not] taking risks for others."[13] In the *Ethics* he takes the scriptural mandate that Jesus gave his followers and subsequently his church to follow him in the way of the beatitudes and the cross as a basis for demanding that the church confess its guilt as an accomplice in the evil perpetrated against innocent peoples in the Nazi era (cf. Matt 5:1-12; Mark 8:34-37). Earlier in the *Ethics* he had written that the basis of ethical thinking lies in conformity with Jesus Christ. Now he turns on the church and reminds it of its acquiescent role in the atrocities of the Nazi government. He held the churches responsible because they were either silent or a disappointing opposition to those who had accepted the challenge to deliver their nation from evil. The conspirators were forced to act in isolation from their churches. The church, he declared in this disturbing passage from the *Ethics*, was by its silence "guilty of the decline in responsible action, in bravery in the defense of a cause, and in willingness to suffer for what is known to be right."

Bonhoeffer's words ring with the regret at his church's having shared in the national guilt through lack of compassion and the desire not to become involved. "It has stood by while violence and wrong were being committed under cover of this name Christ." Because of this he asked the church to confess "that it has witnessed the lawless application of brutal force, the physical and spiritual suffering of countless innocent people, oppression, hatred, and murder, and that it has not raised its voice on behalf of the victims and has not found ways to hasten to their aid." His poignant confession included a powerful phrase which could itself serve as a model for acknowledgement of the church's responsibility in the Holocaust: "It is guilty of the deaths of the weakest and most defenseless brothers and sisters of Jesus Christ."[14]

What is remarkable about this confession of guilt is that it was composed, not in the gloom of the collapse of Hitler's Reich, but at the very zenith of Nazi military success—the fall of France. While the people of Germany, including many prominent church people, were milling about the streets hailing the victories of their army and the enlightened, fearless leadership of their Führer, and church bells were gonging their joyous acclaim, Bonhoeffer was privately lamenting the church's guilt in the suffering on which the Nazi military success fed.

THE SCRIPTURAL MANDATE TO BE A WITNESS FOR PEACE AGAINST WAR

Something dramatic happened to Bonhoeffer during his year of studies at Union Theological Seminary in New York; he became a pacifist. This significant shift in his life came about as a result of his close friendship with the pacifist Jean Lasserre, founder of the "Movement for Reconciliation" in his native France. Encouraged by Lasserre to face the gospel's insistence on universal brotherhood and sisterhood in Jesus Christ, Bonhoeffer came to understand more personally the absurdity of Christians killing people for the sake of national pride or territorial ambitions. Lasserre motivated his German friend to reread and reexamine the challenges of Jesus' Sermon on the Mount in which peacemakers are blessed. Bonhoeffer began to recognize the need to transcend the national setting of his faith and loyalty. It was a struggle with his own attachment to Germany, but eventually the struggle wrung from him a deeper commitment to Jesus' Sermon on the Mount and a firm devotion to the cause of world peace.

Speaking before the German Student Christian Movement in Berlin in 1932, for instance, he linked following Christ with becoming witnesses for peace. Bonhoeffer jolted his youthful audience with his sharp, uncompromising insistence on uniting a professed faith in Christ with the issue of how they might bring peace about. He dismissed the phoniness of so many peace treaties where considerations of national security dominated the more important issues of human dignity and the gospel demands. He rejected the politically expedient ethic that in time of war one is justified in side-stepping the command of God, "you shall not kill," and the word of Jesus, "love your enemies." "This," he says, "makes grace cheap."[15] Here Bonhoeffer uses Scripture as a command to be obeyed, nothing less. The commands of Jesus Christ are given simply to obey.

The vehemence of Bonhoeffer's resistance to the glorification of war is seen further in a sermon on the Day of National Mourning. Taking as his text the apocalyptic verses of Matt 24:6-14, Bonhoeffer spoke to a congregation gathered to commemorate the war dead and with several of those in attendance wearing their military uniforms bedecked with medals of honor. In unmistakable language he proclaimed the daring words that, in the name of Jesus Christ, Christians must reject war as one of the insidious powers attempting to wipe the spirit of Jesus Christ and his commands from Christian consciousness and to replace that spirit with the language of political expediency. Knowing that soldiers can be thrilled by allusions to Christ as their leaders pep them up to shed their blood "for God and country," Bonhoeffer called the deceitful tactic a confusion of fighting "in the name of Christ against the true Christ." That, he says, is when the "powers of the world are revealed" as those who deny Jesus Christ, wanting only "to snatch the disciples from him, . . . to show them that it is madness to go with him, that Christ has no power or authority, only words; that they, the powers of reality, speak the language of facts and this language is more convincing than the language of Christ. The world bands together against the spirit of Christ, the demons are enraged; it is a revolt against Christ. And the great power of the rebellion is called—war!"[16] Bonhoeffer thus used the church service to expose the fraud behind the political propagandizing of soldiers to the extent that in the call to arms the teachings of Jesus Christ have utterly no relevance. He was aware that church acquiescence in war gave the impression that Christians could purge their minds of Jesus Christ in order to support the murderous work of the army in battle, a triumph of patriotism over God's word.

Bonhoeffer put the cost of achieving peace on earth most forcefully in a sermon delivered at the ecumenical conference held in Fanø, Denmark. The setting was a morning chapel service in which Bonhoeffer, taking as his text Ps 85:8 ("Let me hear what God the Lord will speak: For God will speak peace to God's people, and to God's faithful"), asked the assembled church leaders not to miss a serious opportunity to act as the one church of Jesus Christ in addressing an issue so clear as the promotion of peace and the condemnation of war. He pushed those present to abandon their usual staidness and stop couching their resolutions in inoffensive, polite and easily ignored platitudes. In his sermon Bonhoeffer attacked attempts to downplay or ignore the teachings of Jesus Christ on peace by appealing to national security needs or legitimate defense of one's country. God was not to be identified with the idol of national security—he had denounced the idolatry of national security in an earlier ecumenical address in Gland, Switzerland, in 1932. The church, to be true to its claim to radiate the presence of Jesus Christ to the world, had to be either in the vanguard of the peace movement or risk falsifying the gospel.

Bonhoeffer went on to point out that "this church of Christ exists at one and the same time in all peoples, yet beyond all boundaries, whether national, political, social, or racial." In prison Bonhoeffer would speak of an "unconscious Christianity," a concept that has its scriptural counterpart in Acts 17:24-31.[17] When nations take up arms against one another they are in reality taking up arms against Jesus Christ who lives in the German, the English, the French, and in all those who are the targets of militarized annihilation. And so he beseeched the ecumenical council to speak out, "so that the world, though it gnash its teeth, will have to hear, so that the peoples will rejoice because the church of Christ in the name of Christ has taken the weapons from the hands of their sons, forbidden war, proclaimed the peace of Christ against the raging world." A significant sentence from that sermon remained forever emblazoned in the memories of Bonhoeffer's students: "Peace must be dared; it is the great venture."[18] The effect of Bonhoeffer's words on that congregation of eminent church delegates was electrifying. One of his students remarked that "Bonhoeffer charged so far ahead that the conference could not follow him."[19] After the war the famed ecumenical leader, Wim Visser t'Hooft, would remark that this was Bonhoeffer's way of calling the church back to its true mission.[20]

DISCIPLESHIP AND THE CROSS: FAITH, OBEDIENCE, AND THE COST OF FOLLOWING CHRIST

At the outset of his spiritual classic, *Discipleship*, Bonhoeffer declared that he wanted to get behind the battle cries and catchwords of the church struggle and turn to the one person who ought to be the center of their concerns. He appeals to the scriptural word and asks questions that will set the tone for all the disturbing passages that follow. "What did Jesus want to say to us? What does he want from us today? How does he help us to be faithful Christians today?" As if in partial answer to his own questions and a caution against what the average German was hearing in church pulpits throughout the land, he concluded in this opening section: "It is not ultimately important to us what this or that church leader wants. Rather, we want to know what Jesus wants."[21]

What Jesus wants of Christians and their churches becomes in this inspiring book the basis for his confronting his seminarians—the book itself began as a series of lectures to the seminarians he was directing in the illegal Confessing Church seminary in Finkenwalde—with the uncushioned challenges of Jesus' own words and with the exhortations of Saint Paul. Bonhoeffer probes the seemingly "impossible demands" of Jesus' Sermon on the Mount; they are not to be ignored. Jesus' commands become, in fact, the guidelines of every chapter. Jesus' words and example hold for him the only promise of liberating the churches of Germany from their thralldom with Hitler and Nazism's law and order kingdom in order to undertake those responsible deeds necessary for the rejuvenation of Christian faith in keeping with what a genuine following of Jesus Christ was exacting of them.

The opening passages of Bonhoeffer's book expose his deeply felt chagrin at the church's watering down of Jesus' teachings and example. He shares his conviction that too many church leaders had cheapened themselves and misled their parishioners. He plunges straightaway into what he views as the real source of the crisis generated by the collapse of any effective resistance to the anti-Christian ideology of Nazism. "Cheap grace is the mortal enemy of our church. Our struggle today is for costly grace."[22]

Bonhoeffer then moved at a breathtaking pace to the problem of following Jesus Christ when so many churches and their parishioners lived comfortably in thrall to a seductive political dictator. Faith in Jesus Christ and Christian life in church communities were, he said, at a crossroads where the direction Christians took would determine whether or not they and their churches were true or false followers of Christ. In the typical church life which had permeated the parishes of Germany Bonhoeffer detected only "cheap grace." As he put it, "Cheap grace is that grace which we bestow on ourselves. Cheap grace is preaching forgiveness without repentance; it is baptism without the discipline of community; it is the Lord's Supper without confession of sin; it is absolution without personal confession. Cheap grace is grace without discipleship, grace without the cross, grace without the living, incarnate Jesus Christ."[23]

This "cheap grace" had, in Bonhoeffer's opinion, reduced Christianity to a system of facile conformism with the material world in which faith became mere intellectual assent to orthodox doctrine and Christian life became adapted to the world's standards of the successful citizen. The churches had been lured into the ecclesiastical "bargain basement" way of living one's faith: baptism without commitment to live as Christ, forgiveness of sins without sincere repentance, and church life without the semblance of genuine community. In this ambience of "cheap grace" Christian life was hardly distinguished in its mediocrity from the rest of the world.

Bonhoeffer laments in *Discipleship* the loss of a sense of Jesus' presence in the churches. During the crisis years of the Hitler era, Christians had become, in Bonhoeffer's caustic judgment, "like ravens . . . gathered around the carcass of cheap grace," imbibing "the poison which has killed the following of Jesus."[24] He detects a further complication in the modern day rejection of Christian discipleship: the failure to take Jesus Christ at his word, still less to obey Jesus' commands in all their forthrightness and simplicity. The question Bonhoeffer hoped to resolve through a renewed sense of what it means to follow Jesus Christ was how to bring one's self-seeking and self-centeredness under the authority of Jesus Christ and his beatitudinal standards of Christian conduct in the Sermon on the Mount (Matt 5:1-12). Single-minded obedience to Christ was, for him, the essence of being Christian. He used as an example the faith of Jesus' followers who were willing to leave everything to join Jesus (Mark 1:16-20). But, he reminds his readers, their faith is truly liberating only if coupled with the obedience to Christ's word that paradoxically appears to limit one's freedom to do as one pleases. Hence Bonhoeffer's injunction: "Only the believers obey and only the obedient believe."[25] He never loses his insistence that faith demands obedience to Jesus' commands or it means nothing. He uses the apostles' eagerness in answering the call of Jesus to expose the subterfuges and rationalizations of those who avoided the call. Uppermost in his intentions is to restore the biblical connections between the life, death, and resurrection of Jesus and the present-day call to a new life of genuine Christian discipleship. He shared his conviction that what is needed desperately in the Hitler era is to recover true communion with Jesus Christ, to commit oneself solely to Jesus. At the same time he acknowledged that following Christ in full obedience to the gospel call is to endure suffering patterned after Jesus' own experience of rejection, condemnation, and the cross. In unforgettable, sobering words Bonhoeffer told his seminarians that every Christian worthy of the name must bear the cross. "Whenever Christ calls us his call leads us to death."[26]

Bonhoeffer's many years of interaction with and reflection on the Sermon on the Mount reach their fullest expression in those sections of *Discipleship* that challenge Christians and their churches to follow Christ wherever they may be led because they belong to the community of the crucified. Bonhoeffer's biblical understanding of faith being bonded to the sufferings of Jesus Christ extends not only to the ultimate sacrifice of one's life but to the daily acts of renunciation that define discipleship, the Beatitudes (see Matt 5 and Luke 6). He declares at the outset of his commentary that the Beatitudes are the point of convergence where discipleship and the cross, the sufferings of Jesus and the Christian community come together. Jesus proclaims his followers to be blessed in what the world would call misery: poverty, meekness, sorrowing, rejection, sufferings, persecution, even death. This is the paradox of joy in suffering, life in death, that only intimacy with Jesus, not any political or social program, can bring about.

To give but one striking example, Bonhoeffer depicts the death of Jesus paralleling the death to self endured by those who would be compassionate. In Bonhoeffer's spiritual outlook following Jesus to death entails a renunciation even of one's own personal dignity. Those who enter on the beatitudinal way of compassion, he says, "share in other people's need, debasement, and guilt." As he is quick to note, Christians join the ranks of the disenfranchised by their making common cause with those reprobated and marginalized by their criminal government. He praises those who, in face of their own needs, "have an irresistible love for the lowly, the sick, the suffering, for those who are demeaned and abused, for those who suffer injustice and are rejected, for everyone in pain and anxiety."[27] Even more painful than the sacrifice of their lives, the followers of Jesus give away their greatest possession, "their own dignity and honor," in order to be compassionate. In many ways, this passage from his lectures constitutes a description of the vocation to be church in a nation where people are hurting. Bonhoeffer assured his seminarians, some of whom had already experienced the indignity of being branded unpatriotic, disloyal Jew lovers or enemies of the Nazi party, that God takes on their shame and eventually delivers them from evil.

As Bonhoeffer continues his analysis of Christian discipleship as it is lived in church, he turns to the Apostle Paul's teachings on the need for Christians to live and die in Christ (Gal 2:19-20; Phil 3:7-11), conscious of their baptismal consecration. Here, as elsewhere, Bonhoeffer's analysis is inspirited with a theology of the cross that blends Paul's preaching only Christ crucified and Luther's declarations that Christ's death on the cross, not the glory of pompous triumphalism and celebratory ritualism in Rome, was the source of God's grace infusing goodness into individual Christians and their churches. Bonhoeffer makes it clear that those who follow Jesus Christ must live immersed in the world only to be summoned by Christ to live in the kind of worldliness that casts a critical judgment on human pretentiousness, particularly its fascist form in Nazi Germany. He views the Sermon on the Mount as a worldly document, not a retreat from Christians' visible witnessing in and to the world (Matt 5:13-16). In effect, Bonhoeffer sees himself on solid scriptural ground as he offers Christ's mandate to break with any civil rule that denies the dignity of people for whom Jesus Christ died and with whom Jesus Christ has identified as his brothers and sisters.

Despite the risks of defying Nazism's threats against dissenters, including clergy who dared criticize official government policies, Bonhoeffer never backed down from his demand that Christians and their churches step up their visibility in witnessing to Jesus Christ. He who died in naked ignominy on the cross commissioned his followers to be a light to the world, not a guardian of bloodless dogma or a timid lookout for the safe way not to offend a vindictive government. Bonhoeffer acknowledged the presence of Jesus' body in the twentieth century community of his followers reaching out in word and sacrament to their fellow human beings as they would to their needy Lord.[28]

When Bonhoeffer published *Discipleship*, a majority in his nation had yielded their souls to the totalitarian yet wildly popular dictatorship of Adolf Hitler. Against the ideology that was sweeping the people, Bonhoeffer offered his readers the revolutionary values of Christ's Sermon on the Mount and the Pauline exhortations to Christians to allow the attitudes of Jesus Christ to become their own. The Christ who was obedient to his Father God even to his death on the cross now lives on in his twentieth century followers. Bonhoeffer closes *Discipleship* with a remarkable plea for Christians to be conformed to the image of Jesus Christ. He says that such conformity is not something we accomplish on our own; rather, it is the impact in our lives of God's design "to take shape within us."[29]

This form is as varied as the crucified Jesus undergoing again the pains of his followers and in their person crying out anew for deliverance from evil. Bonhoeffer sees in this widespread conformity Jesus' never ending solidarity with his marginalized and tormented brothers and sisters which bestows on them a dignity no human defilement could ever deny. "In Christ's incarnation," Bonhoeffer observes, "all of humanity regains the dignity of bearing the image of God. Whoever from now on attacks the least of the people attacks Christ, who took on human form and who in himself has restored the image of God for all who bear a human countenance."[30] This subtle reference to the Jewish victims of Nazi venom has far-reaching implications for the church's dialogue with Judaism after the Holocaust. For the moment in which he spoke those words his intent was to urge the church to live in the likeness of Jesus Christ by entering into solidarity with the least of the people then under attack by a ruthless, criminal government.

BONHOEFFER'S SERMONS ON TRUTH, FREEDOM, JUSTICE, AND HUMAN WEAKNESS: A CALL TO THE CHURCH

It is not surprising that Bonhoeffer chose John 8:32 for his text in a sermon he gave at the conclusion of the university semester in 1932. He began by telling the students assembled in the church that this passage was the most revolutionary statement in the NT but that it was understood by only a few revolutionaries. Too often freedom had become a mere slogan for the masses in their desire for a better life. Bonhoeffer wondered aloud who are the genuine revolutionaries of whom the gospel speaks. For him they are those set free by Christ's truth and who live in the truth of Christ's teachings. He pointed out that at times even an innocent child or a court jester can blurt out the truth that anxiety ridden adults try to hide through their polite conversations aimed at giving no offense even when confrontation may be called for. When one reads some of the German resistance literature, it is uncanny to note how so many opponents of the Nazi regime, including many church leaders, had to watch their words very carefully so as not to give offense to Nazi sympathizers. The ruthlessness and swiftness with which the Gestapo punished dissent enabled the Hitler government to enforce the denial of freedom of speech in Nazi Germany. Many churches and clergymen lived in that kind of anxiety, giving in to their fears instead of being faithful to their calling to be the voice of truth for those who have no voice against tyranny.

Bonhoeffer pointed out how ridiculously easy it was for people so glibly and so easily to speak of freedom in those times. But to speak of freedom as the Bible does is difficult. There the Word of God may indicate something less popular. There is so much that is less than the truth spouted in church, politics, and world views that the genuine "truth" by comparison can seem cold, disturbing, and even violent enough to arouse one's apprehension and worries. The clever ones of this world try to shield themselves from the truth by telling more refined lies and by polishing up their appearances. Soon enough, Bonhoeffer concluded, "they take their lies for the truth."[31] No one can deny, he argued, that political lies, social lies, self-serving lies exercise a domineering power over people. Sooner or later, often too late, people realize the impact of the duplicity into which their lives have sunk.

Deliverance into true freedom, Bonhoeffer told his congregation, comes not from one's deeds, personal strength, or courage, but only in God's liberating them from themselves. He then described the freedom that is the truth of Jesus Christ. "To be free does not mean to be great in the world, to be free against our brothers and sisters, to be free against God; but it means to be free from ourselves, from our untruth, in which it seems as if I alone were there, as if I were the center of the world; to be free from the hatred with which I destroy God's creation; to be free from myself in order to be free for others."[32] The love of which Bonhoeffer speaks here is God's own love, living in and from God's own truth. Its setting is the church which is called to embody the freedom and truth of Jesus Christ. But the church lacks the innocent freedom of speech of the child or the courage to be free enough or truthful enough to speak out against the evil that was threatening civil life within Germany.

Bonhoeffer's climactic statement was preached at a time when the Nazi propaganda machines were declaring that Hitler and the Nazi party were leading the way as revolutionaries to a better Germany for an unparalleled future glory of the German nation. Bonhoeffer's words are a direct contradiction of these Nazi claims. Not the followers of Adolf Hitler, but "the people who love, because they are freed through the truth of God are the most revolutionary people on earth. They are the ones who upset all values; they are the explosives in human society. Such persons are the most dangerous . . . . The disturbance of peace, which comes to the world through these people, provokes the world's hatred."[33] If we can extrapolate from these words in terms of their meaning for the church, it would be that churches, by their love, can be the true revolutionaries when, by their ability to disturb the smugness of the people, they succeed in exploding the lies that have seduced the people into un-Christlike behavior. Freedom in Bonhoeffer's sermon is ultimately the freedom that comes from being in communion with God's Word of truth which is Jesus Christ. Bonhoeffer's argument here is reminiscent of Luther's "On the Freedom of a Christian" where he insists that a Christian is perfectly free though that freedom may entail being subject to all those to whom Christians have committed themselves in a communion of caring and benevolent sharing. Living that freedom, which is a primary demand on the church community, is to follow Jesus Christ and to become the extension of Christ's compassion, peace, and love to those entrusted to one's care by the power of God's own truth.

Bonhoeffer's compassion for the poor comes through strongly in several of his sermons. In his ecumenical conference in Gland, Switzerland, for example, he linked the frustration of the poor peoples of the world with the violence that turned national security into an idolatry. He spoke there of the fallout in nations that neglect their poor: "millions hungry, people with cruelly deferred and unfulfilled wishes, desperate people who have nothing to lose but their lives and will lose nothing in losing them."[34] Bonhoeffer's defense of the poor appears most detailed and energetic in the one sermon that deals directly with their plight using as text the Lukan story of Lazarus and the rich man (Luke 16:19-31). The setting was Berlin, on the First Sunday after Trinity Sunday, May 29, 1932. Bonhoeffer challenged his congregation to permit themselves to be confronted with the revolutionary words of Jesus in this gospel. He asked that the churches put an end to the spiritualized distortions of this story. "We must put an end to this insolent and hypocritical spiritualizing of the gospel. Either take it for what it really is or hate it, but be honest about it."[35] Being honest demands that they and their churches reflect on their attitudes toward the Lazaruses of German society in 1932. It is speaking honestly, he stated, to admit "we really despise the multitude of Lazaruses among us and the gospel of the poor [because that gospel] stings our pride, pollutes our race, and weakens our power. We are rich but proud of it . . . ."[36] He went on to declare that it is too easy to scorn the multitudes of Lazaruses because they have no name. But can we really ignore the Lazarus who encounters us face to face in the many forms Jesus assumes and say that we deride this Jesus and his proclamation that the poor are indeed blessed and loved by God their Father. The poor, he said, have little need for the cynicism behind the pious phrases they are dealt or the lies beyond the miserly handouts of politicians and church leaders who are supposed to attend to their needs. Bonhoeffer then related care given to the poor, the paralyzed, the blind, the deaf, and the homeless to the part Christians contribute to the in-breaking of God's kingdom. It is difficult to miss here the later application of his words to the Nazi program for the eugenic cleansing of the Aryan race through euthanizing those deemed unfit for the new Germany.

On a more practical level, Bonhoeffer knew that the people to whom he was preaching were the same ones who had been exposed to the drum beats of the Nazi promises of a new millennium, a new world order of prosperity and glory. Jesus' message is just the opposite, he reminded the people. Jesus proclaims, not the promises of slick political leaders sanctioned by a weakling clergy afraid of losing their privileges, or the justification of violence done through hatred of the weak, the unproductive handicapped, and those considered of an inferior race, but the compassion that the rich person was unable to show to the leprous Lazarus. "Blessed are you outcasts and despised, you casualties of society, you men and women without work, you broken and ruined ones, you lonely and forsaken, you who endure violence and unjustly suffer, you who suffer in body and soul. Blessed are you since God's joy will come over you and will remain eternally with you. That is the gospel of the dawn of the new world, the new order, that is the world of God and the order of God. The deaf hear, the blind see, the lame walk, and the gospel is preached to the poor . . . ." (Matt 11:2-6; Luke 7:21-23).[37] Bonhoeffer's words are a direct exposé and contradiction of the deceitful tactics of those political leaders who proclaimed their ability to establish a "new world order," a utopian slogan far removed from Jesus' idea of how a church and a society should order themselves.

Social justice for the poor has everything to do with the protection believing Christians and their churches can offer to the weak brothers and sisters in the midst of nearly every society on earth. That Christian duty became the point of Bonhoeffer's London sermon delivered to a Reformed Church in London in 1934. Basing his sermon on 2 Cor 12:9 ("My strength is made perfect in weakness") Bonhoeffer began by stating that every philosophy has attempted to answer the question of what meaning weakness could have in this world. He admitted that everyone seems to have attitudes toward weakness and its problems though people would rather ignore the problem of dealing with the presence of the weak among them, lest it make them uncomfortable. But Paul's declaration opens the way for Bonhoeffer and his people to explore what Paul could have meant and, more important, what meaning can be derived from dealing with human weakness for the church in the 1930s.

He asked why the existence of weak, handicapped, destitute people seems so important. His answer is a series of rhetorical questions: "Have you seen a greater mystery in this world than poor people, old people, insane people—people who cannot help themselves but who have just to rely on other people for help, for care? Have you ever thought what outlook on life a cripple, a hopelessly sick man, a man exploited by society, a colored man in a white country, an untouchable [in India] may have?"[38] If they have ever thought of these very concrete examples of just what forms weakness may assume, he told them that, first of all, their own life is very qualitatively different; and secondly, they are all inseparably bound to the weak.

In fact, he informs them that Christianity was in its very origin a religion of and for the weak. Its identification with the miserable masses, the weak of this world, became at once its great attraction for Jesus' followers and a source of indignation and enmity for many others, including those who espoused an aristocratic philosophy of life in which strength, power, and violence were glorified. Bonhoeffer's comment on this is emphatic: "Christianity stands or falls with its revolutionary protest against violence, arbitrariness and pride of power and with its plea for the weak."[39] But he admitted to this congregation, Christendom has too easily slipped into the worship of power, and Christians and their churches have failed to take the initiative in doing what is necessary to help the weak of this world. He called for bold initiatives from Christians courageous enough to follow the lead of Jesus Christ. "Christians should give much more offence, shock the world far more, than they are now doing. Christians should take a stronger stand in favor of the weak rather than consider the possible moral right of the strong."[40] Christian churches are, in other words, called to be counter cultural, becoming persistent advocates on behalf of those who are powerless to escape their destitution.

At this point in his sermon Bonhoeffer urged those present to protest against those who minimize the crushing weight set by society upon the weaker citizens by exalting strength and heaping honors on the mighty of this world. Christians need to reverse their attitudes. There must be, he said, an overt preference given to those who are suffering and exploited. The strong, he said, should always look up to the weak. "Weakness is holy, therefore, we devote ourselves to the weak . . . . The weak need not serve the strong, but the strong must serve the weak, and not with any feeling of benevolence but with reverence and love." He concluded that ultimately "Christianity turns our human scale of values upside down, and establishes a new order of values in the sight of Christ."[41] His words here are very close to the convictions he shared with his congregation in Barcelona, that "Christianity preaches the unending worth of the apparently worthless and the unending worthlessness of what is apparently so valuable."[42]

BONHOEFFER'S MARTYRDOM, THE SUFFERINGS OF GOD IN THIS WORLD, AND NEW FORMS OF CHURCH

Dietrich Bonhoeffer had himself staked his life on the Sermon on the Mount and the gospel commands of Jesus Christ who was demanding of him, not the easy, cheapened Christianity of mere regular church attendance, or the purity of never tackling tough moral decisions, but a faith lived in undertaking an active responsibility to extricate his church and his nation from the evil war into which they were plunged. This was an unparalleled streak of worldwide violence in which millions were being killed on bloody battlefields and in hellish death camps.

In a letter from prison that his best friend, Eberhard Bethge, would treasure for its words of faith and courage, Bonhoeffer shared one of the sources of the faith that led ineluctably to his arrest by the Gestapo and his imprisonment and execution. To learn more fully what God has promised to those who love and serve God, he said, one had to "persevere in quiet meditation on the life, sayings, deeds, sufferings, and death of Jesus."[43] He went on to declare that living close to God and in the light of God's presence was an entirely "new life" because in God all things had become possible. He would add that it was certain that "danger and distress can only drive us closer to God. It is certain that we can claim nothing for ourselves, and may yet pray for everything; it is certain that our joy is hidden in suffering, and our life in death . . . ."[44]

Bonhoeffer was not speaking here of the unleashing of human potential for the grandiose, extraordinary deeds that are often invoked to judge human greatness and earn illustrious medals in ceremonies honoring the military heroes of a nation. Rather, he was coming to grips in Tegel prison with the fearful reality of his own death. The July 20, 1944, plot against the life of Adolf Hitler had failed, as had all the other numerous attempts. The noose of the Gestapo was being drawn ever more tightly around those of his band of conspirators, many of whom, though already in prison, were implicated in the assassination attempt. Soon Bonhoeffer would begin the long journey to the death camp at Flossenbürg and his execution.

In prison Bonhoeffer had come to experience more deeply the pathos of God's "weakness" and "foolishness" that Paul had made the leitmotif of his first letter to the Christians of Corinth. While the warring world was refining its malevolence and Christ was being tortured and crucified anew on Nazi Golgothas, Bonhoeffer was entering into the last phase of his young life, a prisoner whose final writings would inspire countless Christians to reexamine their own commitment to Jesus Christ and to renew their determination to live their faith in greater fidelity to the gospel. The extent of God's love for God's people, Bonhoeffer now saw, not in the power of God to eradicate systemic evil with a quick divine word and to permanently assuage all grief, but in the way God had made divinity itself vulnerable in the stark, unfathomable reality of Jesus' humanity. When hopes for his release from prison were dimmed, Bonhoeffer took comfort from the word of Mark 15:34 in which Jesus cries out in despair from the cross, "My God, my God, why have you abandoned me?" This passage had become a consoling message from God telling Bonhoeffer that not even Christ could avoid the human consequences of sacrificing oneself for the sake of others, sharing both the earthly blessings of God's providential care and the inevitable sufferings of God's people. "Like Christ," Bonhoeffer wrote, "Christians must drink the earthly cup to the dregs, and only in doing so is the crucified and risen Lord with them, and they crucified and risen with Christ."[45] Bonhoeffer firmly believed that Christ was not like a God who came to earth from on high, to remain supremely aloof except to intervene at certain dramatic moments with opportune miracles, and then depart virtually untouched by the world's harshness and life's tragedies. Christ experienced the absence of God at the very moment when he veritably ached for deliverance. In the gospel story of Jesus' fate Bonhoeffer could see that God does not offer any glib answers to the agonizing problem of human grief. Instead, from every vantage point of faith, God has freely chosen to suffer with those who suffer. This realization of God's eloquent silence in the midst of the sufferings of God's children and Jesus' brothers and sisters became at once Bonhoeffer's greatest consolation and most demanding challenge as he began to accept the reality of his own impending death.

In the London sermon on human weakness to which we have alluded, Bonhoeffer spoke words similar to what we read in the prison letters. There he attempted to take the experience of pain and suffering to a deeper level by declaring that suffering is holy. Why holy? "Because God suffers in the world through man and whenever he comes he has to suffer from man again." This is a daring statement, given the theology of the time which emphasized God's inability to suffer because God, being spirit and perfect in every way, is immune to the sufferings of mere mortals. To say that God suffers with his human creatures and because of them is to put an entirely new dimension on the problem of evil. But Bonhoeffer was adamant: In Jesus, the man for others, God suffered on the cross, and in Jesus' enfleshed solidarity with all peoples; therefore, all human suffering must be seen as sharing in God's own suffering and weakness. If we suffer, Bonhoeffer added, then God suffers much more intensely. "Our God is a suffering God," he proclaimed in a now famous quotation from his collected writings.[46] That line would be echoed in his prison letters when he wrote, "the Bible directs us to God's powerlessness and suffering; only the suffering God can help." In the next letter he wrote of sharing in God's sufferings in one's secular life.[47] To the biblical affirmation that God is love Bonhoeffer added that, because of love, God is one who suffers.

The implications of these insights for the church are unmistakable. Bonhoeffer's fundamental discontent with his church as well as his hopes for the future in a reformed, revitalized church are brought out with added vehemence in the prison letters. The church that proclaimed so eloquently its belief in resurrection seemed fearful of following Jesus to the cross. "The church," he urged in these letters, "must come out of its stagnation. We must move out again into the open air of intellectual discussion with the world, and risk saying controversial things, if we are to get down to the serious problems of life."[48] To Bonhoeffer the church had become a stagnant pond of general resolutions, pious devotions, and "prayerful" nonactivity—all a conscience-saving cover for its feckless complicity in the war.

When he had given up hope for release from prison, short of a total and destructive allied victory, Bonhoeffer began a project that would take "complete stock" of the church, probe deeply into the real meaning of Christian faith, and draw conclusions for the future life of that church if it could finally be restored to credibility in the post-war world. Only the outline of this project along with a few sentences survived the war. This manuscript enables us to appreciate the exciting new shape he would have given the church had he lived to implement his vision. Certainly his own project encompassed far more than the bland, conservative church revival of the postwar era. Thomas Day is perceptive in his portrayal of Bonhoeffer's intent as one of "clearly planning to lay the conceptual explosives within the walls of the ecclesiastical establishment, and in this way to perform a service for the future of the church."[49]

To begin, he insisted that a church hesitant to take risks for the sake of alleviating suffering in the world was a poor imitation of Christ. If Christ is "the man for others," then "the church is the church only when it exists for others."[50] What Bonhoeffer has said of the this-worldly involvement of the church to protect the weakest and most defenseless of the brothers and sisters of Jesus Christ and of a coming era of a "religionless Christianity" can be summed up in this expression. The church in the new era he saw dawning for Christianity would be a servant church defined by its Christic other-centeredness. He asked that the Christian community give radical proof of its conformation to Christ in the modern world by divesting itself of all its wealth and traditional privileges. "To make a start, it should give away all its property to those in need. The clergy must live solely on the free-will offerings of their congregations, or possibly engage in some secular calling. The church must share in the secular problems of ordinary human life, not dominating, but helping and serving. It must tell people of every calling what it means to live in Christ, to exist for others."[51] The future of the church, he held, depended on whether it had the courage to participate in the full life of Christ in the world. The life of Christ reaches people not only through the church's explicit proclamation but also by the force of example whereby the person of Jesus Christ encounters people through the community of believers. Bonhoeffer envisioned a totally new form of church that would shed forever those religious trappings and empty rituals so often mistaken for authentic faith.

CONCLUSION

Bonhoeffer's willingness to enter into solidarity with those branded by such modern ideologies as less than fully human was inspirited by the example of Jesus Christ who dared his followers—in later years his church—to search for him not in the clouds of heaven, or on the thrones of earthly majesty, or the banquet tables of the affluent, but in the places where hurting people can only cry out to God in their distress. To be one with those oppressed by Nazi brutality, as Bonhoeffer was, made him a sharer in God's own vulnerability. The mystery of personal suffering is not that God permits it, but that God suffers in the loneliness, anguish, and tragic deaths that scream out their denial of any belief in a God who cares. In their pain those who suffer call out to the Spirit of Christ in those who hear, not the lament of strangers, but the heart-rending cry of brothers and sisters who may otherwise be as remote as the despised psychotic on death row or the maggot-laden untouchable on the stinking streets of Calcutta gasping out his dying breath. God's communion with people is never so intense, nor is a church ever more the church of Jesus Christ, than when human suffering is alleviated by the compassion of those who exhibit the qualities of the loving God in whom a church continues to trust.

Ultimately the challenge of Dietrich Bonhoeffer to the Christian Church is to renounce its addiction to its privileges, pomp, and perquisites, and, in all truth, to believe in the Christ whom it never fails to preach and integrate Jesus' gospel into church policies and church action, particularly the Sermon on the Mount and the Last Judgment scene that Matthew's Jesus proclaims, and to share in God's own compassion. The personal gifts of Christians and their churches are always in the service of Jesus Christ in whom they confess their faith. These gifts are often placed at the disposal of the most needy and, at times, the least grateful. The face of Jesus Christ is often hidden in the incognito of the less than attractive beggar or the psychotic criminal, the neurotic, and the handicapped through all sorts of illnesses. The challenge to the Christian church is to combat the multiple causes of suffering, to live on the edge where one does not compromise with evil, to embrace the pathos and persecution of the prophet, all the while working with courage and renewed faith for the peace, justice, and freedom that are Jesus' legacy to his followers.

AFTERWORD

The discussion of this paper at the symposium raised several questions about Bonhoeffer's own struggle in deciding to participate in the assassination atttempt on Hitler. This "afterword" is a reflection on that discussion.

It is almost axiomatic that researchers into the life and theology of Dietrich Bonhoeffer will run into frustrating dead ends if their sole method is to classify him neatly according to prefixed identifying categories. Bonhoeffer has been called a theologian, an ethicist, a pastor, a prophet, and a spiritual writer of note. If he was a theologian, he was hardly systematic; he never developed a consistent theology in the mode of Barth and Tillich. What he wrote was "on the move," always in critical reaction to crisis events in his nation and church. If he was a loyal pastor in his church, how can we explain his sharp repudiation of his own church on the issue of its alleged complicity in an evil ideology? So strong was his critique that some commentators believed he had intended to leave the church. If he was an ethicist, how can we overlook the huge gaps in his published ethics where he attempted to address problematic situations with fragmentary, less than neat ethical solutions? If he was a spiritual writer, how can we find any logical order in the eclecticism that drives his scattered comments on God, Christ, church, faith, ethics, and religion?

We have, for our part, rejected attempts to reduce Bonhoeffer to his philosophical, theological, and ethical influences. We have refused to identify him with any one category. We believe that, too often, critics evade his challenges by invoking strong objections to the selective ways he uses Scripture, or by carping on the shifting inconsistency in his ethics of resistance to systemic injustice, or by picking apart his Christology for its failure to highlight the creedal statements about Jesus Christ, or by rejecting his more spiritual writings on the grounds of his simplistic, prophetic idealism. It is too easy, we believe, to say that Bonhoeffer jumps over the textual and the historical to the existential in his use of the Scriptures and thus his exegesis is flawed. Is that the main issue or is the issue how one draws inspiration from a liberating biblical word in order to respond to the sufferings of Germany's *Untermenschen*? It is too easy to criticize Bonhoeffer's ignoring of the powerful exegesis of von Harnack and other scriptural scholars in Berlin in order to follow the tendentious biblical interpretations of Karl Barth. Where was von Harnack coming from? What was his agenda compared to that of Karl Barth with whom Bonhoeffer was so impressed? Who better speaks prophetic outrage to the powerful who wreak cruel destruction on a vulnerable people?

If there is one unifying thread in Bonhoeffer's life and theology, it is his enduring love of Jesus Christ and his wholehearted commitment to Jesus' beatitudinal teachings in the Sermon on the Mount. Out of his relationship with Jesus Christ came his solidarity with the poor and oppressed and his unwavering embrace of the cause of justice, his pacifism, his defiance of civil authority, his angry criticism of his church for huckstering cheap grace, his prophetic denunciation of governmental repression of the Jews, his invective against the idolatry of national security, his appeal to the ecumenical church to reject every resort to war, and finally his joining a conspiracy mired in ethical dilemmas. In all these difficult twists and puzzling turns in his life, Bonhoeffer preached and taught with a confidence born of his having immersed himself in the Word of God in daily meditation, a practice he also urged for his seminarians. At the height of the war years he wrote of the importance of this practice to them: "Daily quiet attention to the Word of God which is meant for me, even if it is only for a few minutes, will become the focal point of everything which brings inward and outward order into my life."[52] If Bonhoeffer sounded like the prophets of old in extending the difficult demands of Jesus Christ to his students, seminarians, congregations, and church leaders, he was, in turn, inflamed, like Jeremiah, with the uncompromising demands of Jesus that had burned their way into his very heart.

Bonhoeffer was conscious, too, that he was, like Jesus Christ, held in the power of the Spirit. God's biblical Word had become God's Word for him. Until he was caught up in the deceptions of the conspiracy he spoke his mind publicly as a servant of the church, but primarily, as a servant of Jesus Christ and out of pastoral concern for the victims of Nazism for whom the church was responsible. To a church, proud of its synodal accomplishments in the Hitler era, he could ask the annoying question: "Where is Abel your brother?"[53] To church leaders deciding by majority vote to leave church resistance to Nazism's control of the churches to individual pastors, he would utter the disturbing words: "When will Confessing Church synods ever learn that majority decisions in matters of conscience kills the spirit?"[54] In his *Ethics*, he would indict his church and the churches of Nazi Germany for complicity in the atrocities, declaring the churches guilty by their silence of the blood of the innocent.

It was this unflinching love of Jesus and deference to the irresistible impulsions of the Holy Spirit that drove Bonhoeffer to confront head-on the troublesome decision to abandon his pacifism and to join the conspiracy. He gradually became the moral backbone of the plot to assassinate the head of state. The neat ethical systems in which he had been schooled no longer were of help as he then had to cope with the moral dilemma of engaging in deception, in plotting the overthrow of the government, and encouraging the assassination of Adolf Hitler. His four efforts to craft an ethics for an era of unbelievable immorality were also destined never to be completed. Yet his fragmentary ethical reflections always come back to the central person of Jesus Christ. How do Christians conform themselves to Jesus Christ and not to some seductive earthly lord in the murky world in which millions were being slaughtered on the battlefields and death camps where atrocities were commonplace? Why have Christians compartmentalized their lives, separating their secular tasks from their faith, shutting off Jesus' words of love, forgiveness, and compassion?

The questions he raises in his ethical reflections continue. Can Christians refuse their God-given responsibility to do what they can to rescue the brothers and sisters of Jesus Christ from the horrors of a world at war and genocidal extinction? Does not Jesus understand the fellowship of sinners and guilt in which he and his fellow conspirators had been cast? Can Christians not trust in the forgiving love of God as they do the sinful deed? Should not the conspirators beg pardon of God for the blood they will have shed? And thus his ethics of imitating Jesus merged into his weighing the consequences of not acting. "Christians," he wrote to the conspirators, "must have some share in Christ's large heartedness by acting with responsibility and in freedom when the hour of danger comes, and by showing a real compassion that springs, not from fear, but from the liberating and redeeming love of Christ for all who suffer. Mere waiting and looking on is not Christian behavior."[55] For Bonhoeffer it is unchristian to remain safely on the sidelines or hiding in a feckless silence when the hour of danger for the sake of

Jesus Christ comes. He lamented in his letters from prison that he saw a lot of church energy put into its self-preservation but "little personal faith in Jesus Christ. . . Jesus is disappearing from sight."[56] He wondered why the church that preached resurrection was so seemingly afraid of crucifixion. If God allowed God to be edged out of the world onto the cross, cannot Christians who proclaim their communion with Jesus Christ enter into his fellowship of suffering?

Ultimately, Bonhoeffer put himself in harm's way for the sake of Jesus Christ. That is why he has been revered as a Christian martyr and why fascination over his life and heroic death continue to this day. German theologian Dorothee Sölle proclaimed Bonhoeffer the one theologian capable of leading Christians and their churches into the twenty-first century. Abandoning his pacifism would profoundly disturb Bonhoeffer. It was sinfully to leave behind the call of Jesus to be non-violent in resisting evil. But all his choices seemed fraught with sin at every turn. He chose to embrace the guilt of the conspiracy in the hope of saving untold millions from their fate and especially of rescuing his helpless Jewish brothers and sisters. "Who will speak up for those who have no voice?" became his searing question to the church.[57] The difficult sayings of Jesus continued to haunt him in the crisis years of the church struggle with Nazism. He who lamented the cheap, facile pandering of the churches to the baser instincts of the people would himself embrace the costly grace of the cross, losing in the process what he said was the cost of the beatitudinal call to compassion: his pacifism and his reputation. In his book, *Discipleship*, he had taught that, to reach out to the victims of Nazi injustice, Christians must even surrender "their own dignity and honor."[58] Bonhoeffer would die a traitor's death but at the end would utter his last words in full communion with his crucified Lord: "This is the end; for me, the beginning of life."[59]

Today Christians continue to look to Bonhoeffer for inspiration. He proclaimed peace against Hitler's clarion call for war. He preached forgiveness of enemies as Hitler promised vengeance. He preached another kind of love of country while Hitler demanded uncritical, blind patriotism. He preached trustful abandonment to God's compassionate care even of sinners while Hitler appealed for homage to the idol of national security. Today Christians are called again not to lay aside the teachings of Jesus Christ even as they face the terrible choices of how best to respond to the terrorist attack on the United States. Have we reached the point where violence and revenge alone can make up for the loss of American lives and the tragic disturbance to the "American way of life"? Can we still follow the path of peace through reaching out to those people who rage against this country? Bonhoeffer asked the churches gathered for an ecumenical discussion to forbid war. Are his words still valid today?

There are no clear parallels between the depth of ideological evil in Nazi Germany with its euthanizing of the non-productive, Gestapo terror, expansionistic war, and genocide and the present day acts of terrorism against innocent American civilians. "Terrorism," it has been said, "is the atomic bomb of the poor." What is clear is that we as Christians need to commit ourselves more earnestly to Jesus Christ and to biblical ethics. We must renew our calling as baptized Christians to be ministers of that world-wide reconciliation which alone can bring about peace on earth.

In the midst of a world seething with the hatred against enemies aroused by Hitler's tirades against those who had wounded Germany and hurt Germans militarily, economically, and emotionally, Bonhoeffer in a dramatic sermon urged his congregation to forgiveness. His words in 1938 bear repeating as Americans contemplate their proclaimed war against terrorists with calls for retaliatory bombing of nations said to harbor terrorists. His words are a commentary on Rom 12:17-21.

> God gave God's life, God's all, for your enemies; now you, too, give them what you have: bread if they are hungry, water if they are thirsty, aid if they are weak, blessing, compassion, and love for your enemy. Are they worth it? Who indeed could be more worth our love, who could stand in greater need of our love than those who hate? Who is poorer than those who are more in need of help, who is more in need of love than your enemy? Have you ever looked upon your enemies as those who, in effect, stand destitute before you and, without being able to voice it themselves, beseech you: "Help me, give me the one thing that can still help me out of my hate; give me love, God's love, the love of the crucified Savior"? All the threatening and showing of fist is really the result of this poverty: it is essentially a begging for God's love, for peace, for community. When you reject your enemy, you turn the poorest of the poor from your door.[60]

These were words spoken out of Bonhoeffer's close relationship with Jesus Christ who himself forgave even his executioners. The writings of Dietrich Bonhoeffer—pastor, teacher, catechist, spiritual director, defender of the oppressed, and martyr—will continue to challenge us even today, and will continue to do so all throughout the years of this twenty-first century.

NOTES

1. Dietrich Bonhoeffer, *Dietrich Bonhoeffer Werke* (ed. by Eberhard Bethge et al., 16 vols.; Munich: Chr. Kaiser, 1987-99), 9:305-306.
2. Ibid., 9:307.
3. Ibid., 9:322.
4. Ibid., 9:320.

5. Dietrich Bonhoeffer, *Sanctorum Communio: A Theological Study of the Sociology of the Church* (ed. By Clifford J. Green; vol. 1 of *Dietrich Bonhoeffer Werke*; Minneapolis: Fortress, 1999), 140-141, 190, et passim.

6.Dietrich Bonhoeffer, *Christ the Center* (San Francisco: HarperSanFrancisco, 1978), 35-39.

7. Ibid., 36.

8. Ibid., 107.

9. Geffrey B. Kelly and F. Burton Nelson, *A Testament to Freedom: The Essential Writings of Dietrich Bonhoeffer* (San Francisco: HarperSanFrancisco, 1995), 80.

10. Ibid., 52

11. Ibid., 89.

12. Dietrich Bonhoeffer, *Ethics* (New York: Macmillan, 1965), 137.

13. Dietrich Bonhoeffer, *Letters and Papers from Prison* (ed. by Eberhard Bethge; New York: The Macmillan Company, 1971), 381.

14. Bonhoeffer, *Ethics*, 114.

15. Kelly and Nelson, 94-95.

16. Ibid., 202.

17. See Geffrey B. Kelly, "'Unconscious Christianity' and the 'Anonymous Christian' in the Theology of Dietrich Bonhoeffer and Karl Rahner," *Journal of Philosophy and Theology* 9 (1995): 117-149.

18. Kelly and Nelson, 228-229.

19. Eberhard Bethge, *Dietrich Bonhoeffer: A Biography* (ed. and revised by Victoria Barnett. Minneapolis: Fortress Press, 2000), 389.

20. Willem A. Visser t'Hooft, "Dietrich Bonhoeffer and the Self-Understanding of the Ecumenical Movement," *The Ecumenical Review* 28 (April 1976), 201-203.

21. Dietrich Bonhoeffer, *Discipleship* [formerly *The Cost of Discipleship*] (ed. by John D. Godsey and Geffrey B. Kelly; vol. 4 of *Dietrich Bonhoeffer Werke*; Minneapolis: Fortress, 2000), 37.

22. Ibid., 43.

23. Ibid., 44.

24. Ibid., 53.

25. Ibid., 63.

26. Ibid., 87.

27. Ibid., 106.

28. Ibid., 233.

29. Ibid., 285.

30. Ibid.

31. Dietrich Bonhoeffer, *Gesammelte Schriften* (ed. by Eberhard Bethge; 6 vols; Munich: Chr. Kaiser, 1958-1974), 4:83.

32. Kelly and Nelson, 206.

33. Ibid.

34. Ibid., 104.

35. Bonhoeffer, *Gesammelte Schriften*, 4:55.

36. Ibid.

37. Kelly and Nelson, 205.

38. Bonhoeffer, *Gesammelte Schriften*, 4:179-180.

39. Ibid., 4:180.

40. Ibid., 4:181.

41. Ibid.
42. Kelly and Nelson, 52.
43. Bonhoeffer, *Letters and Papers from Prison*, 391.
44. Ibid., 391.
45. Ibid., 337.
46. Bonhoeffer, *Gesammelte Schriften*, 4:182.
47. Bonhoeffer, *Letters and Papers from Prison*, 361.
48. Ibid., 378 (translation slightly altered).
49. Thomas I. Day, *Dietrich Bonhoeffer on Christian Community and Common Sense* (New York and Toronto: Edwin Mellen Press, 1982), 203.
50. Bonhoeffer, *Letters and Papers from Prison*, 382.
51. Ibid., 382-383 (translation slightly altered).
52. Kelly and Nelson, 457 ("Circular Letters in the Church Struggle," March 1, 1942).
53. Ibid., 28 ("Editors' Introduction").
54. Ibid., 465 (Letter of August 11, 1938, to the Old Prussian Council of the Brethren, Berlin).
55. Ibid., 483-484 ("After Ten Years: A Letter to the Family and Conspirators" at Christmas, 1942).
56. Bonhoeffer, *Letters and Papers from Prison*, 381 ("Outline for a Book").
57. Geffrey B. Kelly, "Bonhoeffer and the Jews: Implications for Jewish-Christian Reconciliation," in *Reflections on Bonhoeffer: Essays in Honor of F. Burton Nelson*, (ed. Geffrey B. Kelly and C. John Weborg; Chicago: Covenant, 1999), 149. See also Eberhard Bethge, "Dietrich Bonhoeffer and the Jews," in *Ethical Responsibility: Bonhoeffer's Legacy to the Churches* (ed. John D. Godsey and Geffrey B. Kelly; New York and Toronto: Mellen, 1981), 69.
58. Bonhoeffer, *Discipleship*, 106 ("Editors' Introduction").
59. Kelly and Nelson, 44 ("Editors' Introduction").
60. Kelly and Nelson, 287-288 ("Sermon from 23 January, 1938").

“ALL THESE I HAVE KEPT SINCE I WAS A BOY” (LUKE 18:21): CREATION, COVENANT, AND THE COMMANDMENTS OF GOD

IAIN PROVAN

An interesting religious custom was described to me during an OT Ethics class during the Fall of 2000—how new or old it is, I do not know. It is allegedly the habit of some Christian folk in at least one part of the U.S.A. to place in their front yard a replica stela inscribed with the Ten Commandments. It is apparently intended to accomplish for the yard that which the bumper sticker or the fish accomplishes for the sanctified motor vehicle: it marks it off as Christian territory. The implicit belief underlying the practice seems to be that the Ten Commandments represent some kind of distinctively Christian summation of what is important in life—a digest of the basic rules of the human game, now abandoned in large measure by the surrounding culture but boldly proclaimed in public view by the Christian householder. Here, at least, God’s standards will be adhered to. The belief itself still frequently finds expression also among post-Christian people of an older generation, who may not have much practical faith to speak of, but when asked about the guidelines according to which they live their lives, will often make reference to the Ten Commandments as their moral compass. “These, at least, have I kept since I was a boy”—and it would be better for society in general if everyone else did the same. There is indeed an entire intellectual stream within conservative, Calvinist Protestantism in the U.S.A., commonly referred to as Theonomy, that holds not only to the centrality of the Ten Commandments for Christian faith and life, but also to the centrality of much of the remainder of OT Law; for “until heaven and earth disappear, not the smallest letter, not the least stroke of a pen, will by any means disappear from the Law until everything is accomplished” (Matt 5:18). In such a way of thinking, it is not just the Ten Commandments that represent God’s timeless absolutes for the ordering of human existence, but whatever else in OT Law has not been specifically rescinded by Jesus or the writers of the NT. The Ten Commandments rightly belong in the Christian front yard, and much else besides. They belong not only in the front yard, in fact, but in every other public space as well—for as God is God of the whole universe, so also God's law should be the standard not only for personal life, but also for public life. (This "Theonomic" position is well outlined, for those interested in pursuing this topic, in G. L. Bahnsen, *Theonomy in Christian Ethics*, 2d ed.; Phillipsburg, Pa.: Presbyterian and Reformed, 1984).

In favor of such an approach to the OT, it can be said that it at least takes these ancient Scriptures seriously as Scriptures, which is not something that can be said with any confidence about vast reaches of the remainder of the twenty-first century Christian church. In Western culture, in particular, the word "old" does not have particularly positive connotations. "Old" entities are likely to be marginalized or disposed of in favor of what is new. Perhaps this has something to do with the declining use of the OT in churches; for declining use there certainly seems to be, accompanied by a declining authority in matters of faith and life. The very idea that one might turn to the OT for guidance on *ethical* matters, as a Christian, is one that is scarcely countenanced by many. It is the NT that guides the Christian on the pathway through life—a NT that has itself left the OT behind.

It is the impossibility of this stance of which Theonomists and those of similar view remind us. Any casual reading of the NT will in fact reveal to us the centrality of the OT to the thinking of both Jesus and the apostles on a whole range of issues, including ethical issues. For Jesus himself, the OT Scriptures represented God's authoritative revelation of himself, his own character, and also of the pattern for human conduct. Time and again in the course of his teaching and disputes he prefaces what he is about to say with statements such as "It is written" (e.g., Mark 14:27; Matt 11:10). Time and again he bases his teaching or arguments on the OT (e.g., Mark 12:28-31 [virtually quoting Deut 6:4-5 and Lev 19:18]; Mark 7:9-13 [quoting Exod 20:12; 21:17]); and as we have already seen, he explicitly says in the Sermon on the Mount that these same OT Scriptures have a lasting validity (Matt 5:17-20). The OT was fundamental to Jesus. He did, of course, frequently interpret the OT in ways that his contemporaries did not like, and the Gospels do tell us that in certain respects the OT is no longer binding on followers of Jesus. But that is not the same thing as saying that Jesus left the OT behind as a whole. He certainly did not.

It is unsurprising that we find the same perspective among the apostles. The Apostle Paul, for example, often applies the Ten Commandments to the various ethical situations with which he is confronted in the churches (Rom 7:7; 13:9; Eph 6:2-3); and taking his lead from Jesus, he applies Lev 19:18 to what is left untouched by these commandments (Rom 13:9; Gal 5:14). In other places too he depends directly upon the OT for ethical guidance (e.g., the injunction that two or three witnesses are necessary to establish a matter, 2 Cor 13:1, quoting Deut 19:15). Second Timothy 3:16 may or may not have been written by Paul himself, but it certainly reflects his attitude and the attitude of the whole NT to the OT—"All Scripture is inspired by God and profitable for teaching, for reproof, for correction and for training in righteousness."

It does not appear to be open to followers of Christ, then, to dispense with the OT and to retain only the New as our ethical guide. It is a suggestion at which the apostles themselves would have been amazed, given that none of them thought that they were in the process of composing a *replacement* set of Scriptures for the church, rather than merely exegetical reflections on the Scriptures of the church.

And yet, the question remains as to how, exactly, Christians are to read the OT for ethical guidance. Which is the appropriate way to go? Is the OT Law truly to be taken over into the modern Christian context in the large measure advocated by the Theonomists? Are the Ten Commandments, which lie at the heart of that Law, indeed to be regarded as timeless moral absolutes that encapsulate the essence of the good life? As we read on in Matthew's Gospel, beyond Matt 5:18, we find some scriptural reason to ask further questions even about the latter (and therefore also about the former, one assumes). For in due course, we read of Jesus' encounter with the rich young ruler, recorded for us in all three Synoptic Gospels (Matt 19:16-30; Mark 10:17-31; Luke 18:18-30). Here is a man who has kept the commandments; but he is also a man who has fallen short of the kingdom of God. He has kept the commandments, but his Christian discipleship is deficient—for he has failed in generosity to the poor. This raises a very interesting question about the nature of the Ten Commandments in respect of the kingdom of God that Jesus has come to inaugurate. It does not, after all, appear that these commandments, which fail to enjoin generosity, can be quintessentially (or at least exhaustively) Christian; it does not, after all, appear that we can have in these commandments a synopsis of the Christian life. But more than that, the story of the rich young ruler raises an interesting question about the nature of the Ten Commandments in respect to the remainder of the *OT*. For other sections of the OT, if not the commandments, *do* enjoin or commend generosity to the poor (e.g., Ps 112:5; Prov 11:25; 22:9); and it is surely this kind of scriptural material that lies in the background of Jesus' instruction to the rich young ruler to "sell everything you have and give it to the poor" (Luke 18:22). The question is this, then: are the Ten Commandments rightly regarded as expressing the quintessence of what the *OT* has to say about the virtuous life? Or has much of the Christian debate about the OT and Ethics gone awry right from the beginning by failing to understand what the OT truly has to say about such an issue—by failing to set the commandments, and indeed OT Law more generally, within a much wider OT scriptural context, and to understand them in that context? It is to reflection on such matters that the present paper will devote itself, moving toward an answer to this question: how *should* Christian readers read the OT, when it is ethical guidance that they are seeking from these Scriptures? How is the word of truth, in this area, rightly to be interpreted?

THE COVENANT AND THE LAW OF MOSES

The Ten Commandments do not float above the realm of history, nor are they devoid of literary connections. They are historically located, and they have a literary context, or rather, two literary contexts. They are found in Exod 20:1-17, in the midst of the Exodus narrative and just prior to the so-called covenant law code of Exod 20:18-23:19, and in the long prologue to the legal prescriptions of Deuteronomy, in Deut 5:1-21. Good exegetical practice demands that their historical and their literary locatedness must play their part in determining their meaning and significance.

Analysis of the commandments in context reveals, first of all, that they are clearly marked off from the surrounding "commands, decrees, and laws," as Deut 5:31 and 6:1 describe them. These ten "words" (the literal translation from the Hebrew, reflected also in the Greek-inspired term for the commandments, "Decalogue") are words spoken directly to the people of Israel by God, who proclaimed them "in a loud voice to your whole assembly there on the mountain" (Deut 5:22). They are to be distinguished from the many other words from God that were passed on to the people through the mediation of Moses, who was delegated by the fearful people to "go near and listen to all that the LORD our God says," beyond the ten words (Deut 5:27; cf. Exod 20:19). The form of the Ten Commandments is correspondingly different from that of the other "commands, decrees, and laws." The other legal material in both Exodus and Deuteronomy is largely casuistic in form: it relates to particular cases, to which particular instructions apply and attached to which are often particular penalties. We may note, for example, Exod 21:2 and Deut 13:1-3:

> If you buy a Hebrew servant, he is to serve you for six years. But in the seventh year, he shall go free, without paying anything.
>
> If a prophet, or one who foretells by dreams, appears among you and announces to you a miraculous sign or wonder, and if the sign or wonder

> of which he has spoken takes place, and he says, "Let us follow other gods" (gods you have not known) "and let us worship them," you must not listen to the words of that prophet or dreamer.

The Ten Commandments are, by contrast, apodictic in form. They are generalised rules of behavior, usually employing "you shall not" language (the exception is the sixth commandment) rather than "if" language, that have no particular penalties prescribed for the persons who disobey them. The words that God himself speaks thus have a different shape to the words that Moses speaks on God's behalf. They are marked off from their literary context not merely by the content of the passages in which they occur, but by their very form. It is not surprising, then, that the remainder of the OT tradition should also regard the ten words as "marked off" from the remainder of OT Law and should return to these words on numerous occasions as foundational words for community life—as principles of conduct which stand above and behind all the specific guidelines given by God through Moses to enable stable community life to continue. So it is that we find the opening lines of the Decalogue alluded to in Ps 81:9-10:

> You shall have no foreign god among you; you shall not bow down to an alien god. I am the LORD your God, who brought you up out of Egypt.

We find the seventh, eighth and ninth commandments alluded to in Ps 50:18-20:

> When you see a thief, you join with him; you throw in your lot with adulterers. You use your mouth for evil and harness your tongue to deceit. You speak continually against your brother and slander your own mother's son.

Hosea 4:1-2 describes eighth-century Israel in similar terms:

> There is no faithfulness, no love, no acknowledgment of God in the land. There is only cursing, lying and murder, stealing and adultery; they break all bounds, and bloodshed follows bloodshed.

Jeremiah 7:9 reads a later Israel against the background of the same "ten words," just as 1 Kgs 21:1-16 echoes their content in cataloguing the earlier sins of Ahab and Jezebel.

That the Ten Commandments are distinct in significant ways, then, from much of the rest of OT Law is already clear enough. To our observations thus far, however, we may add the following (or rather, draw out an implication in the preceding discussion): that the Ten Commandments clearly portray *ideals* of behavior for the community of God's people in a way that much of the remainder of OT Law does not obviously portray such ideals. Much of the remainder of OT Law (where it is not concerned with ritual rather than ethical matters—ritual matters that do not directly concern us in this paper) focuses on dealing with a community in which relationships have already broken down, and persons have already damaged others by their wicked behavior. It is not concerned with inculcating ideals, but with limiting the damage already caused by behavior that falls well short of the ideal, and with providing some kind of recompense to the victim, or some kind of sanction for the perpetrator.

For example, Deut 22:23-29 provides us with a number of rules about illicit sexual conduct. Since betrothal is tantamount to marriage in ancient Israelite society, it is regarded as a case of adultery if the betrothal contract is breached through sexual intercourse between the betrothed woman and an outsider. The man in both cases where betrothal is involved (vv. 23-27) is therefore put to death, but the woman is not put to death if the act took place in the country (and thus no one knows whether or not she, as *unwilling victim*, cried out for help, vv. 25-27). She is only executed if she failed to cry out for help in a town (and is thus presumed to have consented, vv. 23-24). It is not much of a choice that is offered to the woman in the town, if she truly did *not* consent to the act: the death penalty on the one hand (because she kept quiet in the face of the assault), or, on the other hand the risk of further violence or death at the hands of the assailant (because of her attempts at noisy resistance to rape). The final case (vv. 28-29) underlines, though, that these are not laws drawn up with the rights of women particularly in mind or with more than certain aspects of her interests in view. For rape of an unbetrothed, unmarried woman the fine for the man is only fifty shekels of silver. The woman, however, suffers not only the trauma of rape but the further trauma of having to live with the man who raped her. We may note that the fine is paid to the father to compensate him for the damage to his property, and not to the woman. The woman has no say in the matter, not being a legal person under Israelite law.

We are not reading in this passage of OT ideals with respect to male-female relations. We are a long way here, in fact, from the vision of Gen 1-2, which speaks of mutuality and intimacy in marriage between two people who are both made in God's image, and from the vision of the Song of Songs, which exegetes the Genesis reality. We are also a long way from the ideal reflected in the tenth commandment, which forbids the coveting of persons or property that belong to the neighbor—in this case, to the prospective groom or to the father. Deuteronomy 22:23-29 is not about ideals at all. It is about dealing with wickedness, in concrete societal circumstances, in ways that at least mitigate some aspects of the consequences of wickedness: the unbetrothed woman is at least guaranteed a home and sustenance, rather than cast out to fend for herself in a society in which this was virtually impossible for a woman. It is also about providing at least some deterrent to men who are tempted to abuse women by threatening the prospective perpetrator with either the death penalty or lifelong responsibility for his actions. But it is not about ideals of behavior.

Thus far it is evident, then, that the Decalogue does stand apart from much of the remainder of OT Law, offering principles of conduct that come directly from the mouth of God rather than guidance mediated through Moses as to how to handle specific cases of moral and legal infraction. Yet the question remains: is the Decalogue to be regarded as an *exhaustive* account of the morally upright life? Granted that it provides us with important principles of conduct, is it to be regarded as articulating all the principles that truly matter? The answer to this question appears certainly to be "no." It is not just that specific moral principles that are thought to be important elsewhere in the OT do not come to expression in the Decalogue, thus revealing its non-exhaustive nature (although this is true, as the already-mentioned example of generosity to the poor illustrates). More than this, however, it should be noted that the form of the Ten Commandments is predominantly negative. Various activities are selected for prohibition: the worship of other gods, the making of images, misusing God's name, working on the Sabbath, murder, adultery, stealing, giving false testimony, and coveting that which belongs to one's neighbor. Important as it may be that one should avoid such activities, it is difficult to see how the good life can truly be defined only in terms of negatives. Here are some things that one should *not* do; but what is it that one should *do*?

To ask the question is immediately to see that the Ten Commandments cannot represent a summation of all that is important about the ethical life; and indeed, the more predominant note struck by the OT is positive and not negative. For example, Hos 6:6 expresses God's heart in this way: "For I desire mercy, not sacrifice, and acknowledgment of God rather than burnt offerings." Here the negatives are juxtaposed with positives: God does not desire sacrifice/burnt offerings, but he does desire mercy towards one's neighbor and acknowledgment of himself. Similarly, Mic 6:8 speaks in these terms: "He has showed you, O man, what is good. And what does the LORD require of you? To act justly and to love mercy, and to walk humbly with your God." Leviticus 19:18 famously combines another pair of negatives and positives: "Do not seek revenge or bear a grudge against one of your people, but love your neighbor as yourself." Finally by way of example, the Decalogue in Deut 5 is closely followed by the Shema of Deut 6:4-5, which sets the larger context within which the Decalogue is to be observed:

"Hear, O Israel: The LORD our God, the LORD is one. Love the LORD your God with all your heart and with all your soul and with all your strength." God is one, and the human vocation is to love God with every aspect of the human being, responding in unity of being to the unity of God. The various specific commandments that also come from God are to be understood and obeyed within this larger context.

Seen within this larger context, the Ten Commandments are revealed to contain, not an exhaustive summation of the godly life, but rather only selected examples of the kinds of things that loving God and one's neighbor involves, and then only in terms (mainly) of negatives to be avoided rather than positives to be embraced. Not everyone will in fact possess manservants or maidservants or oxen and donkeys and other animals, and not everyone will find himself hosting a sojourner within the gates (Deut 5:12-14). Not everyone can express love for God and neighbor, therefore, by ensuring that these fellow creatures rest on the Sabbath. This commandment has particular people of power in mind. In contrast, everyone can seek to refrain from stealing (Deut 5:19); but from an OT perspective, one's duty to one's neighbor is not in fact exhausted by refraining from stealing. It also involves seeing that justice is done to that neighbor and that generosity is extended to him. There is more to that which is good than can be expressed in an injunction not to act in a certain way. There is a larger vision of life within which negative injunctions must be understood and embraced.

It is thus apparent that the Ten Commandments are themselves somewhat like the case law of the OT after all, in the sense that all the material we have been reviewing thus far must be read as a selective rendering of principles of conduct that lie behind it, designed to show by way of example what it means in practice to love God and neighbor, or to act justly, to love mercy, and to walk humbly with God. The Ten Commandments do this in the expression of what we might call "second-order principles"—selected ideals for behavior that mark out in a general (though not exhaustive) way the religious and ethical territory, as it were, within which the Israelite is to live. Loving God and neighbor certainly means refraining (mainly) from these specific activities, even if it means much more than this. The biblical case laws also reflect, but in a different way, what it means for a community to take seriously the love of God and of neighbor. They, too, are presumably selective—we cannot possibly have recorded in the OT all the cases that ever came before a legal authority in Israel. Rather, we are provided with a number of these that reveal to the reader the various ways in which a particular community dealt with the reality of community life when it came into conflict with the ethical vision—the ways in which the attempt was made to approximate to the ethical vision in specific cases.

Such is the nature of covenant law in the OT then, but we are not finished with what the OT has to say about ethics just because we are finished with covenant law. Just as the Decalogue has a larger context within the Law that is important for its proper understanding, so also covenant law has a larger context within OT creation theology, and it is important that we examine that context too if we are to gain a clear understanding of what an "OT Ethics" truly looks like.

CREATION AND ETHICS

It is an intriguing fact about the OT, which has often been obscured by an overemphasis on covenant as *the* governing and organizing theme of these Scriptures, that it clearly does not root its ethical vision only in the law that was given to Israel at Sinai, but also in the created order, which in different ways is itself thought to "declare the glory of God . . . proclaim the work of his hands" (Ps 19:1). No great gulf is set, in fact, between covenant and creation as contexts within which the will of God may be ascertained and the right pathway through life identified.

We may begin here with the Prophets, who are correctly regarded by Jewish tradition as the great interpreters of the covenant, and yet nonetheless are also found to place covenant and creation in close connection to each other. Amos 1-2 provides an excellent example. The opening chapter records a number of oracles against foreign nations, each of which shares a common structure. They begin with the formulaic "For three sins . . . , even for four, I will not turn back my wrath" before proceeding to describe the crimes of the nation in question and to announce divine judgment. The series builds to a crescendo with the surprising introduction into it, first of Judah (Amos 2:4-5) and then of Israel (Amos 2:6-16). The basis for Amos' condemnation of Israel and Judah is, unsurprisingly, their rejection of "the law of the LORD" and "his decrees" (2:4). The other nations, however, are just as roundly condemned for wrongdoing, even though they were never given any law at Mount Sinai. It is simply presupposed that they know the difference between right and wrong and therefore know very well that their war-crimes (for that is the focus of Amos' indictment) are wicked. Whether knowledge has been gained at Mount Sinai or simply from conscience or a sense of common humanity, however, genuine knowledge of ethical principles is assumed to be prevalent.

Even when dealing with Israel's sins, though, the prophets can move easily between covenant and creation as bases for ethical standards and judgments. There is throughout the prophetic corpus a profound sense that there is an order in nature itself that is worthy of imitation by human beings, whether

Israelites or not. Thus Isa 1:3 observes, "The ox knows his master, the donkey his owner's manger, but Israel does not know, my people do not understand." Jeremiah 8:7 notes, "Even the stork in the sky knows her appointed seasons, and the dove, the swift and the thrush observe the time of their migration. But my people do not know the requirements of the LORD." Other creatures know their place in the universe and adapt themselves to its true nature. Israel, on the other hand, has no understanding of a similar kind—even though Israel possesses Torah. Sin, in this way of thinking, is not so much the breaking of a commandment as the embrace of cosmic nonsense—a refusal to be sane, and the requirements of the Law are understood to be nothing other than the requirements for sensible living within the cosmos—for the God who creates the cosmos and the God who makes covenant are one and the same. Amos 6:12 reflects on Israel's sins, which are at the same time an expression of insanity: "Do horses run on the rocky crags? Does one plow there with oxen? But you have turned justice into poison and the fruit of righteousness into bitterness."

Moral norms are built into the nature of things, and not just into the Law given at Mount Sinai. Indeed, a considerable number of the references to sin that are found in the prophetic writings are not strictly speaking based on the Law at all. The prophets can be found assailing drunkenness, political error, and pride, for example—none of these attacks relating to the Law, but depending on ethical ideals deriving from other sources.

A similar perspective on ethics can be found in the biblical wisdom literature, especially Proverbs and Job. Here the language of covenant and law is entirely lacking. We are in fact not in the world of special revelation and mighty acts of God in Israel's history at all in these books, but much more in the world of what we might call natural theology (God's general revelation) and pragmatic religion. And knowledge of God here is derived from the ordinary things of life, and from the experience of those who are older and wiser in the ways of the world—from within the created order as it continues to function in its normal and harmonious ways. The good life which stands as the goal of the wise person in Proverbs is a long life characterized by good health, an abundance of friends and children, and sufficient possessions to get through life without too much hardship. It is the attainment of this good towards which Proverbs seeks to guide its readers, and certain things stand out as the means by which the good life is achieved and the bad life avoided. The good life is bound up with such things as obedience to parents, (e.g., 13:24; 20:30; 23:13-14); self control in speech (e.g., 13:3; 25:11-12, 23; 29:20); self control in subordinating the passions (e.g., anger in 14:29-30; 16:32; 29:11); marrying the right person (18:22; 19:13-14; 21:9, 19); generosity (14:31; 21:26; 25:21-22), and the absence of excessive wealth (30:7-9). The bad life is associated with sexual misconduct (5:1-6, 20-23); drunkenness (23:19-21, 29-35); laziness (6:10-11; 10:4-5; 26:14-16); misuse of the tongue (6:16-19; 10:18, 18:6-8); and other dark things (e.g., pride in 15:25-26; 16:5; greed in 15:27; 28:25; 29:4). The person who follows the path to the good life is wise, and the one who does not is a fool—because tradition, experience, and observation of the way in which the world works clearly suggests the right way in which to go. Even the ant knows something about this (6:6).

The book of Job also has the good life as its backdrop and goal, even though Job himself does not see much of it during the greater part of the book. The book opens with a picture of a man experiencing the life in all its fullness which is described in the book of Proverbs. It presents us with a man who is renowned for fearing the Lord (cf. Prov 9:10) and is consequently blessed by God. The question, however, is whether Job's righteousness would survive hardship, whether it is only self-serving and self-interested. A period of extreme difficulty for Job follows in which his moral integrity is tested, and in the end, as at the beginning, we find that Job is blessed in life because he is indeed righteous. The particular interest of the book from our point of view lies in how Job's righteousness is described, and here chapter 31 is most helpful. In this chapter Job himself provides us with a long list of sins that he considers that he has not committed, and at least two things are striking about this list. First, it is a list that reflects Job's ethical ideals, and those ideals far transcend the requirements of the Law, even with respect to the Ten Commandments. The Decalogue forbids adultery, for example, but Job claims not even to have looked lustfully at a girl (31:1). The Decalogue forbids stealing, but Job claims to have done much more for his neighbor than avoiding stealing from him (31:16-23):

> If I have denied the desires of the poor or let the eyes of the widow grow weary, if I have kept my bread to myself, not sharing it with the fatherless—but from my youth I reared him as would a father, and from my birth I guided the widow—if I have seen anyone perishing for lack of clothing, or a needy man without a garment, and his heart did not bless me for warming him with the fleece from my sheep, if I have raised my hand against the fatherless, knowing that I had influence in court, then let my arm fall from the shoulder, let it be broken off at the joint. For I dreaded destruction from God, and for fear of his splendor I could not do such things.

Reverence for God has led Job to radical love for his neighbor; and this involves actions beyond those specified by the Law. Examples such as these demonstrate beyond doubt the truth of our earlier contentions: that even the Decalogue does not exhaustively represent the ethical ideals articulated in the OT, and that indeed, the negative commands of the Decalogue are themselves only partial expressions of yet higher ideals that come to expression elsewhere in the OT.

The second thing that is striking about Job 31 is found in vv. 13-15. For the most part the chapter does not reveal to us where its moral norms are grounded, if it is not in the law given at Mount Sinai, which is not explicit in these verses. Job claims through his rhetorical question in v. 13 always to have ensured that his male and female slaves received justice when they have a grievance against him. The notion that slaves might legitimately have a grievance against a master is itself remarkable enough, but the ground that Job provides for treating them well in this way is even more astonishing (v. 15): "Did not he who made me in the womb make them? Did not the same one form us both within our mothers?" It is the common origin of both master and slave in God's creative activity that provides the imperative that Job should treat his slaves well and allow them even to bring a complaint against him. One is reminded of the insistence in Gen 1 that all human beings are made in the image of God, and indeed of the exegesis in Gen 9:6 of this reality in terms of the inherent sacrosanctity of human beings, such that for the life of any and every person, God will demand an accounting from a fellow human being who has shed blood. What we find here is a creation ethic that lies beneath and behind any covenant ethic that is expressed in the OT and which to some extent must be understood as making the latter relative. It is precisely this kind of ethic that already comes to expression in the prophetic corpus as the prophets preach the God of all creation to an Israelite community that has too narrow a view of God and of ethics, and has in particular forgotten that there may well be a considerable gap between Law and ethics—between what God has proclaimed and permitted at Sinai, on the one hand, and what may be the ideals of God's kingdom on the other. The prophet Malachi is on this track, for example, when he reminds his readers, even though he must know that divorce is permitted by Mosaic law, that divorce is nonetheless hateful to God (Mal 2:13-16):

> Another thing you do: You flood the LORD's altar with tears. You weep and wail because he no longer pays attention to your offerings or accepts them with pleasure from your hands. You ask, "Why?" It is because the LORD is acting as the witness between you and the wife of your youth, because you have broken faith with her, though she is your partner, the wife of your marriage covenant. Has not the LORD made them one? In flesh and spirit they are his. And why one? Because he was seeking godly offspring. So guard yourself in your spirit, and do not break faith with the wife of your youth. "I hate divorce," says the LORD God of Israel, "and I hate a man's covering himself with violence as well as with his garment,"

> says the LORD Almighty. So guard yourself in your spirit, and do not break faith.

This grounding of covenant ethics within the larger framework of creation ethics is not surprising, of course, when it is remembered that Israel is only called out by God to be a special people in the OT so that God will in the end bring blessing to the whole of creation. Abraham is brought from Ur, in response to the disasters of Gen 1-11, specifically so that "all peoples on earth will be blessed through you" (Gen 12:3), and the covenant that is made with him is made for that very long term purpose. The subsequent covenant at Sinai with all of Abraham's descendants retains that universalist perspective (Exod 19:6): "Although the whole earth is mine, you will be for me a kingdom of priests and a holy nation."

It is the task of priests to mediate God's blessing to others. Since it is thus the one God who created the universe who now calls out a people and makes covenant with them in order to bless the whole of creation, we would not expect to read covenant ethics outside of the context of creation ethics and without an eye to the larger story. Nor do our biblical writers encourage us to do so.

"HE HAS SHOWED YOU, O MAN, WHAT IS GOOD; AND WHAT DOES THE LORD REQUIRE OF YOU?"

What does this review of OT texts touching on ethics suggest to us about how Christian readers should read the OT, when it is ethical guidance that they are seeking from these Scriptures? It suggests above all that we must read individual OT texts within their broad biblical context.

The largest context is set by the theological theme of creation. God has created all things for right relationships with himself and among themselves, such that all creation knows his blessing (Gen 1-2), and right relationships involve a whole number of things, from a human point of view, which all of God's human creatures are called to embrace. A right relationship with God involves, for example, worship and trust in divine goodness. It is indeed in a distrust in divine goodness that we find the first human step away from God and into moral darkness, as Adam and Eve chose to accept the serpent's characterization of God as a God of unreasonable prohibition ("You must not eat from any tree," Gen 3:1) in place of an accurate characterization of God as a God of generosity and freedom ("You are free to eat from any tree," Gen 2:16). It is the God of generosity and freedom who is truly the God of creation, however, and he calls his image-bearers to be like him in relating to their fellow human beings and to the creation over which they have been given dominion. The first step in reading OT texts ethically, then, is to locate them within this largest creation context and to ask: how does this text relate to the creation will of God and to God's desire that all his image-bearers should be like him, should act justly, love mercy, and walk humbly with your God? It is within this creation context that covenant law can then be understood; it is law that partly reflects God's creation will for all people, including Israelites, but partly (perhaps even largely) does not. For covenant law does more than simply reflect ideals of human behavior in a God-created world. It is also designed to enable Israel, specifically as Israel, to function well within the world that she inhabits—a world in which she is to be a distinctive people in order to fulfil God's purposes, and a world in which moral darkness continually presses in upon human community and threatens to extinguish the light. Covenant law thus requires to be read through the lens of creation theology, if its relevance to the wider, non-Israelite world is to be established.

I suggest that this is precisely the kind of reading of the OT that we find widely practised in the NT. In the Sermon on the Mount, for example, Jesus first describes to his listeners the shape of the blessed life, which involves positively embraced actions and attitudes, rather than abstinence from action (e.g., showing mercy; making peace), before going on to teach them that various of the provisions of the OT Law, including two of the (negative) Ten Commandments, are not to be read as exhausting one's ethical responsibility to one's neighbor (Matt 5:1-48). Creation theology is specifically invoked in Matt 5:43-48 with respect to loving one's enemy (cf. Prov 25:21) and is later introduced to explain the teaching in Matt 5:31-32 about divorce (Matt 19:3-12: "Moses permitted you to divorce your wives because your hearts were hard. But it was not this way from the beginning"; cf. Mal 2:10-16). Job 31 with its own creation perspective lies in the background of Matt 5:27-30. There is a wider context within which specific texts are to be read, if they are to be understood properly. We have already seen the same move in the story of the rich young ruler, and we find it throughout the Gospels (e.g. Matt 23:23-24; Mark 2:23-28; 3:1-6; Luke 13:10-17).

The early church adopted the same approach to its OT reading, recognizing in the aftermath of Jesus' death and resurrection and in the new situation that these events created that still further questions required to be asked about the relationship between creation and covenant. Those aspects of OT Law that appeared to be specifically Israelite (Jewish) now increasingly came under scrutiny and were regarded as irrelevant to Christians (and especially Gentile Christians); for the period of history in which it was important for Jews to be distinct from Gentiles was now over, and all should be one in Christ. So it is that food laws, for example, come to be regarded as redundant for Christians, since there is a more fundamental theology about food that now, in the era of oneness in

Christ, reasserts itself (1 Tim 4:3-5): "They forbid people to marry and order them to abstain from certain foods, which God created to be received with thanksgiving by those who believe and who know the truth. For everything God created is good, and nothing is to be rejected if it is received with thanksgiving, because it is consecrated by the word of God and prayer."

At the same time, though, those aspects of OT Law that express something more than that which is specifically Israelite are retained in the NT and are regarded as undergirding Christian ethics. We have already noted the appearance of the Ten Commandments in various places in the NT, illustrating some of the things that loving God and neighbor mean in the NT period as in the Old. Another good example would be the way in which OT laws touching on homosexual practice are alluded to in NT teaching on this topic (1 Cor 6:9-10; 1 Tim 1:10; cf. Lev 18:22 and Lev 20:13), illustrating that even some of what is often called "purity law" was actually regarded as having a strongly ethical component. Finally, we may note the way in which the early church, thinking of itself as the same people of God as of old, applied to itself the Old Testament's economic ethics. There is the same concern in both testaments for the poor and needy (1 John 3:17) and the same ideal of equality among God's people, both economically (2 Cor 8:13-15) and indeed socially (James 2:1-7). If the ideal is fellowship, sharing, making sure that there is no one who is poor among you (Deut 15:4), then what we find in the early chapters of Acts is a body breaking bread and practising community of goods, making sure that there was indeed no poor among them.

There is thus in the NT both a "yes" and a "no" to OT covenant law, as it is read through the lenses of both creation and new creation. Christian readers of modern times should adopt the same approach in reading the OT ethically.

CONCLUSION

What are we to say, then, to those who were introduced in my opening paragraph, with their serious attachment to the law of Moses? We should certainly commend the seriousness with which they take the OT Scriptures. We should encourage them (and ourselves), however, to take them more seriously yet by setting covenant law more fully within the entire biblical context and understanding its nature more fully as a result. There is no question but that we shall derive a considerable amount of help, not only for our personal but also for our public lives, by reflecting on covenant law, as the Theonomists claim; but the precise implications of what we learn, both for our personal and for our public lives, will only be grasped by taking seriously both the creation and new creation contexts within which OT covenant law sits. As for those who do not go the whole way with the Theonomists but still hold the Ten Commandments in high regard, this is good! But do not identify the Ten Commandments with the complete will of God, and if you must display them in your front yard, at least lay out beside them all your worldly possessions, so that the poor can take them away after they have read the biblical text.

WHAT IS THE LAW OF CHRIST?

Graham Stanton

In recent years the ethical teaching of the NT writings has not been at the top of the agenda of most specialists. Yet the central issues must be taken seriously by those of us who want to practise theological interpretation of Scripture. Here are what I take to be some of the key questions.

(i) How is the ethical teaching of the NT writers related to their theological or christological concerns?
(ii) What is distinctive about the ethical teaching of the NT writings? How does it differ from the conventional Jewish and Graeco-Roman ethical teaching of the day?
(iii) What is the theological relationship between the ethical teaching of the OT and that of the NT? This latter question touches raw nerves today. For example, is it the case that the New Testament's teaching on love of enemy and reconciliation should be given priority over some strands of the OT in which retribution is prominent and in which capital punishment is enjoined in specific circumstances?[1]
(iv) To what extent should the teaching of Jesus be given priority in our theological reflection over Paul or other NT writers?
(v) How do we move from those first century writings to our own day? To what extent should we take on board the insights of the moral philosophers of our time—virtue ethics and all that? And what about the ethical teaching of the non-Christian religious traditions?

That is quite an agenda! How can we tackle parts of it, given the constraints of time and of my competence? I have decided to use one verse as my focal point. "Bear one another's burdens, and in this way you will fulfill the law of Christ" (Gal 6:2). To use but one verse as a way of addressing some of the questions in the agenda above will seem rash to many. But Gal 6:2 is one of the most interesting and difficult verses in Paul's most terse and profound letter. I hope I shall be able to show that a wide-ranging discussion of this one verse takes us to the heart of the ethical teaching of the NT writings and is relevant to some of the issues listed above. Perhaps too much discussion of NT ethics has dallied with generalities at the edge of the pool and has not plunged into the refreshing exegetical waters.

What is the law of Christ? As we grapple with this question, what should be our theological and hermeneutical presuppositions? I shall use what I now like to call "chastened historical criticism."[2] I am most certainly not prepared to abandon historical criticism, but, like many others, I am now more keenly aware of its limitations than I was twenty and more years ago. In particular, the tools of historical criticism can help us to recover Paul's intention and the circumstances which elicited his letter to the Galatian churches. But if we confine ourselves to historical questions, we are leaving Paul's letter back in the 50s on a shelf in one of the Pauline house churches somewhere in Asia Minor. In this symposium, however, we are concerned with the theological interpretation of Scripture for the ongoing life of the church today.

I accept that there is no such thing as presuppositionless exegesis, so I have no hesitation in taking as an initial assumption the conviction that Paul's ethical teaching can speak to us in our very different world. I take this assumption to be one of the main planks of theological interpretation.

I am convinced that theological interpretation of Scripture can be greatly assisted and stimulated by tracing some of the influences of the text on the life of the church in later centuries. This perspective, known as *Wirkungsgeschichte*, is just beginning to make an impact on Biblical scholarship in fruitful ways.[3] *Wirkungsgeschichte*, the history of the effects of the text, includes the history of the interpretation of the text in commentaries and sermons, but it may also trace the influence of the text on poetry and hymnody, on art and architecture, and on liturgy and doctrine. By attending to the influence of the text we may be forced to consider or to reconsider some awkward exegetical questions. If we believe, as I do, that in countless ways the Spirit has given life to the church through the bare bones of the text, then we may dare to hope and pray that this may happen in our own day. So I do not apologize for painting on a broader canvas than is customary for exegetes in a symposium paper. As compensation, I shall focus on just one verse!

I shall refer to a few of the ways the concept "the law of Christ" has been influential on the life of the church down through the centuries. My choice of examples is related to the main ways Gal 6:2 has been interpreted, but I shall not limit myself to explicit use of Paul's striking phrase.

THE LAW OF CHRIST AS THE TEACHING OF JESUS

I shall begin in an unexpected place, the important opening section of Justin Martyr's *Dialogue with Trypho*. Justin's Jewish opponent Trypho issues a strong challenge: Justin and his fellow-Christians claim to worship God, but fail to make their lives different from Gentiles in that they keep neither the feasts nor the sabbaths, nor have circumcision, nor carry out God's commandments (10:3). In short, Christians are law-less.

As a key part of his extended response Justin refers to Christ as *the new lawgiver* (*ho kainos nomothetēs*, 12:2 and 14:3), through whom "the poor have the gospel preached to them, and the blind receive their sight" (cf. Matt 11:5/ Luke 7:22). The sayings of Jesus are understood here as the gift of the new lawgiver.

Justin's most explicit statements concerning the sayings of Jesus occur in his account in the *Dialogue* of his conversion to Christianity which he dubs "philosophy safe and simple" (8:1). He tells Trypho that at the time of his conversion he experienced a passionate desire for the prophets and for those men who are the friends of Christ, presumably the apostles. He then expresses the hope that all people should be as keen as he is not to distance themselves from the Saviour's words (*mē aphistasthai tōn tou sōtēros logōn*), for they evoke *profound awe* (*deos*). Their innate power puts to shame those who turn aside from the right way, while pleasant rest (*anapausis*) comes to those who carry them out (8:2).

It is quite clear from this passage, and from Justin's well-known references to "the memoirs of the apostles," that for him the teaching of Jesus embedded in the Gospels is "the law of Christ."[4] Although Justin does not refer explicitly to Paul or to his letters, at numerous points he betrays knowledge of them. So it is possible that his understanding of Christ as the new lawgiver has been influenced by Gal 6:2.

Matthew's Gospel was probably an even more direct influence on Justin, even though it too is not named in Justin's writings. The evangelist intends to portray Jesus as the "new Moses" who gives the "new law" to his "new people." I am not suggesting that Matthew knew Galatians. Indeed, that is most unlikely. But the evangelist does view the teaching of Jesus as "the law of Christ," even though he does not use that phrase. Matthew has taken great care over the composition of his five discourses because he values the sayings of Jesus so highly. The sayings of Jesus are to be prominent in the missionary proclamation and catechetical instruction of the "new people" (28:18-20). The closing verses of the Sermon on the Mount emphasize strongly the importance of hearing and acting on the words of Jesus (7:24-27). For Matthew "the will of the heavenly Father" is equated with carrying out *the sayings of Jesus* (7:21, cf. Luke 6:46).

Matthew's Gospel provided the "new people" with a new set of authoritative traditions to be set alongside the law and the prophets. The evangelist does not spell out as clearly as his modern interpreters would like the precise relationship of "new" and "old." Matthew's Jesus does not repudiate the law: its continuing importance is affirmed very strongly (5:17-19). The love commandment of Jesus is singled out as expressing the very essence of Scripture (7:12; 22:37-39), but in no way does this contradict the law, any more than do the so-called antitheses in 5:21-48. I shall return to the love commandment below and insist that its use in Gal 5:14 must be allowed to play an important part in the interpretation of our key verse, Gal 6:2. Matthew hints—but no more—that the sayings of Jesus are the criterion for the interpretation of Scripture, but his primary emphasis is on the ways the sayings of Jesus strengthen and fulfill the law and the prophets.

The notion of Christ as the new lawgiver was all pervasive in the later tradition of the church. I shall now refer briefly to a handful of examples. First of all, the magnificent thirteenth century statue of Christ the lawgiver from the south side of Chartres Cathedral in France. For many years now a photograph of this statue has been prominently displayed in my study. Here Christ is depicted holding up one arm in blessing. His other hand is offering a beautifully bound codex which I take to be the Gospels. In other words, Christ is offering his own teaching as a new law. Protestants probably underestimate the powerful influence a statue such as this had on the on-going Christian tradition.

From the thirteenth century we jump to the sixteenth. Luther, Zwingli and Calvin wrote extensively on the Sermon on the Mount as "the law of Christ." They all insisted that Matt 5-7 represents the true interpretation of the law of Moses which had been obscured in Judaism. On the whole they emphasized the continuity between the "law of Christ" and the "law of Moses" more than their Catholic opponents.

Luther also discussed the Sermon in terms of "law" and "gospel." In some of his writings he emphasized that the Sermon is the "law of Christ" that makes people aware of the gospel of God's grace through Christ: "we are not able properly to fulfill one tittle out of our own strength . . . . but must always crawl to Christ." But in other passages Luther stated that the Sermon is not just the accusing law that points to sin: it is also "gospel." This is especially true of the Beatitudes (5:3-12). Christ "does not press, but in a friendly way entices and speaks: 'Blessed are the poor.'" (For further discussion see J. Pelikan, "Luther the Expositor," *Luther's Works, Companion Volume*, St. Louis: Concordia, 1959, 65-70.)

By referring in different passages in his writings to the Sermon both as "law" and as "gospel," Luther confused some of his later followers. Many Lutheran theologians have stressed that the Sermon is the law that awakens knowledge of sin. But some (notably J. Jeremias, *The Sermon on the Mount*, Philadelphia: Fortress, 1963) have claimed that the demands of Jesus in the Sermon are preceded by "gospel," that is, by his proclamation of the kingdom and by his encouragement to his disciples to share his own sense of sonship.

In many parish churches in England to this day two panels painted with Scripture texts hang behind the altar: the ten commandments on the left, and the Lord's prayer on the right. This practice goes back to the late sixteenth century, with even deeper roots in the medieval period. In the seventeenth and eighteenth centuries it became almost universal, though more recently some of these panels have been relegated to another part of the church building or placed in a dusty room beneath the tower. The setting up of these panels is related to the catechism in the 1552 Book of Common Prayer. Every person brought before the bishop for confirmation was expected to be able to recite the ten commandments and the Lord's prayer, as well as the brief explanations of both texts in the catechism. Perhaps the panels often acted as a crib for those with short memories!

The impact of this practice on the life of the church is clear. The ten commandments are singled out as the essence of the law of Moses, while the Lord's prayer is assumed to provide the essence of the "law of Christ." The theological instincts which lie behind the erection of those two panels of texts are profound, and in my view profoundly correct. They have a direct bearing on the theme of this symposium.

Here, then, is a very long and rich tradition of biblical ethics and of theological interpretation. While the phrase the "law of Christ" is not all that common, the *concept* is all but universal in the Christian tradition. It has two primary roots in the NT writings: Matthew's presentation of Jesus as the "new lawgiver," and a widely held interpretation of Paul's use of the phrase "the law of Christ" in Gal 6:2 (and in a related phrase in 1 Cor 9:21) as the teaching of Jesus.

We must now ask the hard question. What did Paul intend to convey by the phrase, "the law of Christ"? Given the strength of the tradition I have just sketched, it is no surprise to discover that Gal 6:2 has often been taken as a reference by Paul to the importance he attached to the teaching of Jesus. There have been several influential modern supporters of this interpretation. In his ICC commentary on Galatians (1921, p. 329) E. C. Burton wrote: " . . . this is one of the few passages in which the apostle refers to teaching of Jesus transmitted to him through the Twelve or their companions." Burton, however, failed to list the Jesus traditions which might have been in the apostle's mind.

C. H. Dodd was more specific, arguing in 1951 and 1953 that Gal 6:1-5 was an adaptation of Jesus' teaching in Matt 23:4 and 18:15-16.[5] At about the same time Dodd's pupil W. D. Davies was equally adamant. "When he (Paul) used the phrase *nomos tou Christou* (the law of Christ) he meant that the actual words of Jesus were for him a New Torah."[6] More recently R. N. Longenecker has defended a more sophisticated version of the same interpretation. He takes "the law of Christ" to refer to those "prescriptive principles stemming from the heart of the gospel (usually embodied in the example and teachings of Jesus), which are meant to be applied to specific situations by the direction and enablement of the Holy Spirit, being always motivated and conditioned by love."[7]

The difficulty with this general line of interpretation is that Paul alludes very rarely to sayings of Jesus, and refers explicitly to them even less often.[8] There is limited evidence in 1 Corinthians and in Romans 12-14, but even less evidence in Galatians. When the phraseology of Gal 6:1-5 is compared closely with the synoptic tradition, there are only two words in common, *barē* and *phortion*, and even they are not used in similar contexts.

Does this mean that we should cast aside the long tradition of Christ as the new lawgiver sketched above? By no means! Although I do not think that it is supported by Gal 6:2, the concept is a fair summary of Matthew's concerns in the Sermon on the Mount. But an important proviso must be added. For Matthew, and indeed for several early Christian writers, Christ is both the new lawgiver and is himself the new law: Christology and ethics are inseparable.

I shall give three examples, the first of which is from the evangelist Matthew. Jesus may be portrayed as a "new Moses," but the full significance of the Sermon on the Mount (and of the teaching of Jesus more generally) can only be discerned in the light of the conviction that Jesus is "God with us" (Matt 1:23). With his coming, in fulfillment of Isa 9:1, "light has dawned" (4:16). The Sermon on the Mount is proclamation of the good news of God's kingly rule (4:17, 22). It is both gift and demand; it is not a new set of rules and regulations.

My second example is from Justin Martyr, who also discerned the theological importance of the link between Christology and ethics. For Justin, Christ is not only "the new lawgiver," he is himself given by God as the final and eternal law (*Dialogue* 11:2, twice) and the new law (11:4, *ho kainos nomos*).[9] Justin elaborates his point in a splendid creedal passage in 43:1: by the will of the Father Christ was born Son of God by means of the Virgin; he was proclaimed by the prophets as about to come "as an everlasting law and a new covenant for the whole world." Justin insists that the law given by God to Moses at Mount Horeb is antiquated and belongs to Trypho and his fellow-Jews alone, whereas Christ, the new law, was given to all people (11:2). Justin does not believe for one moment that the law of Moses has been abolished, though he does have difficulty spelling out precisely how Christians should use it, as, of course, did Paul himself.

The third example is in the *Kerygma Petri*, which was probably written in the first half of the second century.[10] Alas, all we have from this treatise are a handful of fascinating quotations in later writers, especially Clement of Alexandria. Three times Christ is himself called "the Law." Christians worship God neither in the manner of the Greeks nor the Jews. "We worship God through Christ in a new way." "For we have found in the Scriptures, how the Lord says: 'Behold, I make with you a new covenant, not as I made (one) with your fathers in Mt Horeb.' A new one he made with us. For what has reference to the Greeks and Jews is old. But we are Christians, who as a third race worship him in a new way."[11]

What is the relationship of these passages to Paul's intriguing phrase in Gal 6:2, "the law of Christ"? Justin does not refer explicitly to Paul or to his letters, but he does know at least some of them well. In their references to Christ as "the new Law," Justin and the *Kerygma Petri* have in effect offered a profoundly christological interpretation of Paul's phrase: the "law of Christ" is Christ himself. Matthew's view is similar, though the evangelist's knowledge of Paul's letters (whether direct or indirect knowledge) must be left as an open question. I do not think that Paul himself would have been unhappy with the notion that "the law of Christ" is Christ himself, for he too linked Christology and ethics together closely.

THE LAW OF CHRIST AS THE NORM OR PRINCIPLE OF LOVE

The final paragraphs in the preceding section confirm that for several early Christian writers "the law of Christ" is about Christology as well as ethics. This important point is taken much further in another interpretation of Gal 6:2. Here the word "law" is taken to refer to a principle or norm, rather than "law" in the usual sense. In support, appeal is made to Paul's occasional use of *nomos* in a more general sense, perhaps most clearly at Rom 3:27, "the 'law' of faith" and Rom 8:2, "the 'law' of the Spirit of life in Christ Jesus."

Interpreters who defend this general approach always link Gal 6:2 closely to Gal 5:14: "For the whole law is summed up in a single commandment, 'You shall love your neighbour as yourself.'" The admonition in 6:2 to "bear one another's burdens" is then taken as an exposition of the "love commandment" of 5:14.

The strength of this interpretation is twofold. Its strong insistence that "the law of Christ" in Gal 6:2 must be understood in the context of Gal 5:14 is quite correct and very important. This reading of Gal 6:2 underlines firmly the relationship between Christology and ethics, for "the norm of love" is not only "love of neighbour" and "bearing one another's burdens," but it is shown supremely in "the Son of God who loved me and gave himself for me" (Gal 2:20).

This interpretation of Gal 6:2 has also influenced the ongoing Christian tradition strongly. In his first commentary on Galatians (1519) Luther wrote several powerful and perceptive paragraphs on Gal 6:2, which he describes as "a very beautiful and thoroughly golden maxim." "Love is the law of Christ," he wrote. This led him to expound the meaning of love in a memorable way, even though he loses sight of the phrase "the law of Christ." "To love means to wish from the heart what is good for the other person, or to seek the other person's advantage . . . . Love is not even able to exist if there are none who err and sin, who, as the philosophers say, are the proper and adequate "object of love" or the "material of love."

Luther then offers an eloquent and profoundly theological interpretation of Gal 6:2, even though he fails to mention Gal 5:14 explicitly![12] He notes that those who want their own burdens to be borne are "the kind who disdain having the uneducated, the useless, the hot-tempered, the foolish, the troublesome, and the surly as companions in life but look for people who are cultured, pleasant, kindly, quiet and saintly. That is, they want to live, not on earth but in Paradise, not among sinners but among angels, not in the world but in heaven."

In his 1535 commentary on Gal 6:2 Luther goes even further. "The Law of Christ is the law of love" he writes three times over. "After redeeming and regenerating us and constituting us as His church, Christ did not give us any new law except the law of mutual love (John 13:34-5)." "To love does not mean, as the sophists imagine, to wish someone else well, but to bear someone else's burdens, that is, to bear what is burdensome to you and what you would rather not bear."

Two centuries after Luther, J. A. Bengel echoed Luther's interpretation in a typically pithy statement in his influential *Gnomon Novi Testamenti* (1742): *Lex Christi, lex amoris*, "the law of Christ is the law of love." The same interpretation is set out much more fully in V. P. Furnish's standard textbook (*The Love Command in the New Testament*, London: SCM, 1968, pp. 59-65) and supported by many other writers. It is probably the consensus interpretation at present.

Who would want to deny the importance of love in Paul's ethical thinking? In Gal 5:14 love is said to sum up the whole law. Love heads the list of the fruits of the Spirit in Gal 5:22, a list which ends with the ironic comment, "there is no law against such things." Nonetheless, I am not convinced that this interpretation does full justice to Paul's intention in Gal 6:2.

WHAT IS THE LAW OF CHRIST?

So far we have considered two very different interpretations of "the law of Christ," both of which have influenced the Christian ethical tradition strongly. If we take the phrase to refer to Christ's "new" law which complements or fills out the law of Moses, i.e., the teaching of Jesus, we are doing more justice to the evangelist Matthew than to the apostle Paul. If we take "the law of Christ" to be the principle or norm of love, the love commandment which sums up the whole law of Moses, we miss the full significance of both "law" and "Christ" in Paul's phrase.

As J. L. Martyn notes, Gal 6:2 is the thirty-first of Paul's references in Galatians to *nomos*, law. "In all the other significant instances the reference is to *the* Law," i.e., the law of Moses.[13] So it is most unlikely that without alerting his listeners Paul changes tack and refers to the teaching of Jesus as "law," or to "showing love for others" (i.e., bearing the burdens of others) as "law."

In Gal 6:2 Paul speaks about the law positively, but not quite for the first time in this explosive letter. It is no exaggeration to claim that from 2:16 to 4:21a Paul's portrait of the law is consistently negative: in every case he has the law of Moses in mind. Ever since 2:16 "law" has been pounding relentlessly in the Galatians' ears with a negative beat. However in 4:21b, 5:14 and 6:2 Paul's tone changes dramatically: *nomos* is clearly used in a positive sense in all three verses.

In the first clause of 4:21 Paul speaks with heavy irony: "Tell me, you who desire to be under the law." Here "under the law" is used in what has become a very familiar way to Paul's hearers. But in 4:21b Paul alters tack: he urges his hearers to listen to what the law really says. The law suddenly and unexpectedly does have positive things to say. Paul does not speak about a different "non-Mosaic" law in 4:21b, or a principle or norm: as in all the earlier uses of *nomos* in Galatians, it is the law of Moses to which reference is made.

Paul had partially prepared his readers for this important positive role for the law of Moses in 3:8. There "Scripture," foreseeing that God would justify the Gentiles through faith, had declared the gospel to Abraham beforehand. In 4:21b it is not "Scripture" but "*the law*," heard aright, which bears witness to the gospel in the allegory of Hagar and Sarah which follows.

In the light of this understanding of 4:21b, the reference in 5:14 to fulfilling the law in loving one's neighbour, is not "the most unexpected development of Paul's thought in this letter,"[14] but an appropriate development of the earlier verse. There is an important distinction between 5:3, "keeping the entire law," and 5:14, "fulfilling the whole law": quite different verbs are used. It is the verb "fulfill" in 5:14 which would have caused Paul's listeners to prick up their ears. For this verb is not used with "law" in the LXX or in Greek Jewish literature.[15] What does "fulfilling the law" mean? John Barclay's exposition is apt. He notes that in 5:14 Paul uses the verb "to describe the total realization of God's will in line with the eschatological fullness of time in the coming of Christ."[16]

As many exegetes have observed, 6:2 with its reference to the law of Christ is closely related to 5:14: verbs from the same root are used. Although "Christ" and "law" have regularly stood in stark contrast earlier the letter, in 6:2 they are brought together in a striking and memorable phrase. Since "fulfilling the law" in 5:14 clearly refers to the law of Moses, the use of the similar verb in 6:2 strongly suggests that "law" here also refers to the law of Moses, and not to a norm or principle. As we noted above, those who claim that Paul uses the term *nomos* in a more general sense in Gal 6:2 have to appeal to Rom 3:27 and 8:2. But it is rarely wise to interpret Galatians with the help of Romans!

The careful reader of Galatians can hardly fail to miss Paul's insistence that Christ himself "bore the burdens of others." Paul's expansions of his opening "grace and peace" formula in his letters are always important. Like the thanksgivings which usually follow, they foreshadow several of the letters' main theological themes. This is certainly the case in Galatians. In 1:4 Paul notes that Christ "gave himself for our sins." Christ's self-giving love forms the climax of what is probably the richest section of the letter, Gal 2:15-20: "the Son of God loved me and gave himself for me." Christ has fulfilled the law himself in his self-giving in love for others.

At last we are in a position to offer a provisional answer to our question, What is the law of Christ? *In Gal 6:2 it is the law of Moses redefined by Christ, with the "love commandment" and "carrying the burdens of others" as its essence; it is fulfilled by Christ in his own self-giving love.*[17]

Several further comments are in order. First, Gal 4:21b, 5:14, and 6:2 stand in counterpoise to Paul's other references to the law of Moses in Galatians. These verses confirm that in spite of the numerous negative comments on the law elsewhere in this letter, Paul did not repudiate the law of Moses, as some of his later followers (most notably Marcion) and some of his opponents (see Acts 21:28) wrongly supposed.

Second, the immediate context emphasizes that those who live by the Spirit are not free to gratify the desires of the flesh (5:16). However Paul does not spell out the precise ways in which the law of Moses is to be retained now that believers in Christ have been set free from the present evil age (Gal 1:4). No one will be right-wised by God on the basis of carrying out the law of Moses (2:16), but the law is not to be ignored or discarded, for it is not opposed to the promises of God (3:21).

Perhaps Paul continued to mull over this antinomy. The apostle takes a further step in Romans 13:8-10. "Love is the fulfilling of the law" to be sure, but this axiom does not mean that the commandments concerning adultery, murder, theft, and covetousness may be ignored. This passage seems to have encouraged the later strong Christian conviction that the ten commandments are the core of the Mosaic law; they (and for some, they alone) have abiding significance for Christians. A further step was taken in the middle of the second century in Ptolemy's *Letter to Flora*: the moral and the ritual law are differentiated, a step Paul himself did not take.

Third, I noted above that it was the encouragement to bear one another's burdens which caught Luther's eye. H. D. Betz sees this as a commonplace maxim "in the Socratic tradition and the Greek doctrines about 'friendship.'" If this is the case, and the case seems to be strong, a well-known maxim is transposed by Paul into a new key.

We should welcome Paul's appropriation of the conventional ethical teaching of his day at several points in Gal 5 and 6, and especially in the lists of virtues and vices in Gal 5:19-23. For in so doing Paul has given us an example to follow. Why should we not appropriate some of the insights of the moral philosophers of our day and set them in a firmly drawn theological framework, as Paul himself does?

I have insisted that "the law of Christ" in Gal 6:2 is not a reference to the teaching of Jesus, even though that understanding of the phrase has been dominant throughout the Christian tradition. I have also suggested that to interpret the phrase as "the law or principle of love" does less than justice to Paul's intentions. In Gal 6:2 "the law of Christ" is the law of Moses redefined with the "love commandment" and "carrying the burdens of others" as its essence; it is fulfilled by Christ in his own self-giving love.

However, if we are forging a Biblical ethic for our own day which takes the whole canon of Scripture seriously, then of course we need not confine ourselves to Gal 6:2 in expressing what "the law of Christ" is for us today. We may well wish to complement Paul's understanding with Matthew's presentation of the teaching of Jesus as "the law of Christ." We will want to hold together Christology and ethics, as both Matthew and Paul did in their different ways. And we may find that Justin Martyr's comments enrich our theological reflection, for as we have seen, he insisted explicitly that Christ himself is both "the new law" and the "new lawgiver."

NOTES

1. See especially C. D. Marshall, *Beyond Retribution. A New Testament Vision for Justice, Crime, and Punishment* (Grand Rapids: Eerdmans, 2001).

2. I owe the phrase to the General Introduction to *The Oxford Bible Commentary* (eds. John Barton and John Muddiman; Oxford: Oxford University Press, 2001), 1. I have been using the principles they have in mind for some time, but not their helpful term.

3. See, for example, the excellent commentaries by Ulrich Luz on Matthew (so far only volumes 1 and 2 are available in English, Augsburg/Fortress, 1989 and 2001), Anthony C. Thiselton on 1 Corinthians (Grand Rapids: Eerdmans, 2000), Markus Bockmuehl on Philippians (Peabody, Mass.: Hendrickson, 1998).

4. For a fuller discussion, see G. N. Stanton, "Jesus Traditions and Gospels in Justin Martyr and Irenaeus" in *The Biblical Canons* (eds. J.-M. Auwers and H. J. de Jonge; Leuven: Peeters, forthcoming 2002).

5. John Barclay, *Obeying the Truth* (Edinburgh: T&T Clark, 1988), 129 n.70, astutely notes that in 1935 Dodd had denied that Gal 6:2 could mean the "Torah of Jesus," but had changed his position by 1951 in his *Gospel and Law* (Cambridge: Cambridge University Press), 64-83. See also Dodd's important article "Ennomos Christou," reprinted in his *More New Testament Studies* (Manchester: Manchester University Press, 1968), 134-138.

6. In his *Paul and Rabbinic Judaism* (London: SPCK, 1948), 144, Davies went somewhat further than Dodd in claiming that there was rabbinic evidence (albeit somewhat limited) to suggest that in the new age there would be a new "law of the Messiah." See especially W. D. Davies, *The Setting of the Sermon on the Mount* (Cambridge: Cambridge University Press, 1963), 109-190. H. Schlier also insisted that the "law of Christ" is "die Tora des Messias Jesus" (*Die Brief an die Galater*, 12th ed.; Göttingen: Vandenhoeck & Ruprecht, 1961, 272). As there are major problems over the dating and interpretation of the handful of rabbinic passages Davies and Schlier cite, their case has won little scholarly support. See especially R. J. Banks, *Jesus and the Law in the Synoptic Tradition* (Cambridge: Cambridge University Press, 1975), 65-81.

7. See especially R. N. Longenecker's Word commentary on Galatians (Dallas: Word, 1990, 275-276).

8. For a recent cautious assessment, see D. C. Allison, "The Pauline Epistles and the Synoptic Gospels: the Pattern of the Parallels," *NTS* 28 (1982): 1-32.

9. The most accessible translation of the *Dialogue* is by A. Lukyn Williams, *Justin Martyr, the Dialogue with Trypho*: Translation, Introduction, Notes (London: SPCK, 1930).

10. As O. Skarsaune suggests (*The Proof from Prophecy*, Leiden: Brill, 1987, 72-73) Justin may well be dependent on the *Kerygma Petri*.

11. For the texts and bibliography, see J. K. Elliott, *The Apocryphal New Testament* (Oxford: Clarendon Press, 1993), 20-23; more fully, W. Schneemelcher (ed.) *New Testament Apocrypha* (Cambridge: Clarke, and Louisville: Westminster/John Knox, 1992), 2.34-41.

12. Luther is clearly aware of the relationship between 5:14 and 6:2, for he insists that "all laws are summed up in love."

13. J. L. Martyn, *Galatians* (Anchor Bible Commentary; New York: Doubleday, 1997), 555.

14. Graham Shaw, *The Cost of Authority* (London: SCM, 1983), 50. I owe this reference to J. Barclay, *Obeying the Truth*, 126.

15. See Barclay, 138.

16. Barclay, 140.

17. Cf. Barclay's explanation (p.134): the law of Christ is "the law as redefined and fulfilled by Christ in love"; and also Martyn's comment on the phrase: "the law as it has fallen into the hands of Christ."

CREATION, COMMUNITY, DISCIPLESHIP: REMEMBERING WHY WE CARE ABOUT SEX

SONDRA WHEELER

I suspect that many ethicists cringe a little when they read the statements put forth by their various denominations regarding controversial moral issues. There is in them a tendency to speak in platitudes with which no one really disagrees and to avoid offense by remaining at a level of generality that cannot offer anyone actual guidance. However, there are exceptions. I am a United Methodist, and amid all the convulsions that have wracked the so-called mainline Protestant churches over standards of sexual behavior, at least we Methodists have a straightforward position. In a Book of Discipline notable for its sponginess on many questions, we find a statement about standards of sexual conduct which is admirably clear. It says we think Christians are committed to fidelity in marriage and celibacy in singleness. The trouble is, many of us are not sure we really do think that, or perhaps are even sure we do not. Moreover, even many of us who do think that these are the rules governing sex in Christian life are not quite sure *why* we think so.

Put to it, we find it hard to answer questions about why we even care who sleeps with whom, and questions like those from our youth group members about what is wrong with a little fooling around in the back seat leave us tongue-tied. Of course, we could always reply that the Bible forbids fornication, which would at least offer a clear rule to that minority who know what fornication is. But even a toddler knows enough to follow up an answer like "The Bible forbids it" with the question "Why?" and then we are stumped.

I do not mean we cannot think of any reasons at all to constrain sexual activity: there are always teenage pregnancy and sexually transmitted diseases, the specter of AIDS and the devastation to families caused by broken marriage vows. What I mean is that we cannot think of any distinctively *Christian* reasons for the standards of behavior the church has traditionally commended. We can give no particular reasons why Christians as such should care about how we use the unique powers and intimacies of sexuality. Our ethics about sex have been disconnected from our confession of faith, and that is the same as saying that they are disconnected from our identity. When that happens, our moral conversation stops being persuasive, even to us, and it entirely stops making sense to the rest of the world. Left without a rationale for the genuinely restrictive norms of what Christians used to call chastity, the world at large concludes that we are either pleasure-hating prudes who think sex is dirty, or hypocrites who say one thing and do another. Thus it can cheerfully ignore us as either neurotics or liars.

Rather than enter into the current debates about whether the traditional rules ought to be revised in one way or another, I want to begin by reviewing in broad outline just what it is our biblical tradition teaches about sexual conduct, and especially what broader understandings of sexuality underlie that teaching. I want to pursue the more fundamental question of why the matter of sex comes up for discussion at all, a reading of why we regard sex as a matter of particularly theological concern. Finally, I will spend just a little time on a question deeper and more vexed even than that of the rules about sex by which we should seek to live: the question of how we become the kind of people who can live and flourish within the moral standards we do adopt. Whether we seek to preserve or to revise moral norms about sex, neither of these tasks can proceed without understanding what commitments those norms express, what goods they are thought to protect, and what positive stake we as a contemporary community have in seeking to order sexual life. So I shall begin with, "What the Bible Says about Sex," beginning with the OT.

WHAT THE OLD TESTAMENT SAYS ABOUT SEX

A summary of the Old Testament's rules about sex can be provided in fairly short order if one is not concerned to review all the details of the codes of covenant law that concern purity and defilement. These include regulations regarding what degrees of relation prohibit marriage and the rules of ritual purification that surround sex. They specify what forms of sexual activity make one unfit for participation in worship or violate the norms of sexual practice that serve to separate the people Israel from their pagan neighbors, and they detail the remedies or punishments for such breaches. Now, before we conclude that all these rules signal some vast and central significance given to sexual conduct in the law, it is worth pointing out that there are similarly detailed commandments and prohibitions concerning food: they cover what may be eaten and with what and when and from what kinds of utensils cleaned in what way and how the grain must be grown or the meat must be slaughtered . . . and so on. There is also a large body of texts concerning the care of the sick and the handling of the dead and detailed instructions for washing just about everything you can think of. In fact, all of the basic functions and activities of human life come under scrutiny and governance in the holiness code, and every aspect is comprehensively ordered toward the distinctive pattern of the covenant community.

Anthropologists and theologians have explored at some length the shape and significance of these regulations, and for those who have an interest in them I can recommend some fascinating books. Most of us, however, regard these regulations with merely historical interest, since as Gentiles we are not seeking to order our lives according to the provisions of Leviticus. We make distinctions between the covenant code under which Israel lived and generally binding moral law, expressed pre-eminently, although not solely, in the Decalogue and the moral teaching of the Prophets, which we take still to inform our lives. Following this pattern, what basic moral teachings about sex do we find within the OT canon?

We might say simply that sexual intercourse in the OT is divided into married sex, fornication, and adultery, with the first being approved and the latter two prohibited. That is true as far as it goes, but a little clarification is needed. First, the Hebrew Bible assumes at least in some places that married sex may include sex with multiple spouses if you are male, and there are lots of narrative examples of sex with non-wives (concubines, maids, etc.) which are not expressly condemned. Thus, Sarah gives her servant Hagar to her husband to provide him with a child (Gen 16:1-4), and while the course of the narrative suggests that this strategy is badly advised, no one objects that it is adulterous. To understand this, you have to remember that adultery had to do with the violation of a husband's exclusive sexual claim on his wife, but no reciprocal claim of wives on their husbands was thought to exist in this polygamous society. (Before anyone becomes either relieved or indignant about that distinction, let me pause to say that this assumption is explicitly reversed in the NT, where the same obligations of monogamy and fidelity are applied to both spouses.)

The seriousness with which adultery was regarded is clear not only from its inclusion in the prohibitions of the Decalogue, but from other provisions of the law. If a man forces sex on a woman who is married or engaged, the covenant code makes this a capital offense (Deut 22:25). If the intercourse is judged to be consensual, both the man and woman are to be executed (Lev 20:10; Deut 22:22-24). The judgments on sex outside of marriage are not quite as severe, but are still quite serious. If a man has sex with a woman who is not married or betrothed to anyone, he is required to marry the woman and never permitted to divorce her, or if her father refuses to give her to him as a wife, he must pay what amounts to a large fine in compensation (Exod 22:16-17; Deut 22:28-29). And clandestine sex outside of marriage is also rejected, at least for women; a woman who is found at marriage to have been sexually active in secret while single is also to be condemned as having "played the harlot" in her father's house, and thus having violated her own future marriage (Deut 22:21).

Despite this apparent concern for restricting sex to the stability and protection of marriage, the picture offered by the Law is not unmixed. Based purely on readings of the Law, many critics have concluded that the strictures against adultery had more to do with guaranteeing paternity and protecting inheritance claims than it had to do with ideals of personal fidelity. Deuteronomy gives procedures by which men could divorce their wives for what was interpreted as any reason that suited them, undermining the idea that sex had its place in relationships of mutual responsibility and commitment (Deut 24:1-3). (By Jesus' time there was a lively dispute going, into which Jesus is drawn, about what reasons were really sufficient, a matter we will return to later.) On the other hand, various prophetic texts, most notably Mal 2:14-16, condemn divorce as faithless and hateful to God. So how does all this fit together?

Part of the problem of trying to discover the unity in the OT moral norms about sex is that much, indeed most, of its teaching does not take the form of regulations about sexual acts. To use the most obvious example, the entire book of the Song of Solomon is devoted to an intense dialogue of desire and fulfilment between lovers. The poem's silence concerning God has led to uncounted attempts to account for its presence in the Hebrew canon, but whatever we make of it we cannot miss its delighted affirmation of sexual passion and erotic love. Therefore, it is not enough to look at the rules about who can sleep with whom or at what the consequences are for those who break them. We have to look as well at the stories, the poetry, the metaphors, and the attitudes displayed toward sexuality across the whole range of different kinds of texts. What do the writers think sex is about? Where does it come from? Whom does it concern? What does God have to do with it? Only when we have cast a net more widely will we be able to judge what makes sense of the OT teaching about sex and what we should carry away from it. From "what does the OT say?" we must move on to consider, "why does it say it?"

WHY THE OLD TESTAMENT SAYS WHAT IT DOES ABOUT SEX

The first and most fundamental word about sex given in Scripture, indeed the one that overarches all others, is that it is God's invention. And because the whole delightful and dangerous and perplexing business has its origin in God's good design, God moves immediately to bless, to command, and to claim it for God's own purposes. Human beings barely make it on the scene in Gen 1 before sexual difference and the fruitfulness it makes possible are expressly linked to the divine intention and command. "'Let us make humans in our image.' So God made the human in his image, male and female . . . and God blessed them . . . And commanded them, 'Be fruitful and multiply'" (1:27-28). And all this is very good (1:31).

This is such familiar stuff that it is difficult for us to hear, but it is impossible to overestimate how massive and revolutionary the claim that sex is a good part of God's intention would have been in the ancient world. Perhaps we can come close to understanding if we think seriously about what difference it would make in our own jaded world if we really believed it today. I do not mean the cheap and easy modern version that goes something like this: "Sex is good, so we should have good sex, so it must be good to do whatever ensures my sexual satisfaction." That is not to affirm sex as God made it; instead it is to affirm sex as whatever *we* wish to make of it, and oftener than not we will, in our readiness to make it a god, turn it into a demon. I mean the real and serious affirmation of sex as something intrinsic to the embodied existence in which God confronts and calls and woos and claims us. I mean prizing genderedness and neediness and the comical and clumsy concreteness of loving ourselves and each other in the bodies, at once beautiful and absurd, that God gives us. I mean believing that human sexuality is not a mistake or an embarrassment but a holy gift, inseparable from the human mind and spirit and an occasion for knowing and glorifying God Almighty. And that is a much deeper and more serious thing, a thing that could call us to grand passion or to great renunciation for the sake of sexual love, but could never be mistaken for mere self-indulgence. *So our first and greatest theological stake in sexuality is the doctrine of creation, which makes sex holy in the biblical sense that a vessel or a sacrifice or a life is holy: it belongs to God.*

Again and again the rationale for a given commandment about sexual conduct is given in the same form as commandments regarding compassion, personal integrity and social justice: "For I the Lord am a holy God, so you must be holy." The idea that particular forms of sexual life might actually be holy, somehow expressive of or in accord with the divine character, is taken up and given concreteness in the covenant codes of Leviticus and Deuteronomy which we already sketched. Conversely, God commands, "Do not do these things (chiefly temple prostitution and child sacrifice) for they are an abomination to me." But the same idea, that the ideal of sexual life is rooted in and expresses something of the divine character, is found everywhere in prophetic and narrative texts as well.

Isaiah and Jeremiah continually use the language of marriage to depict the relation between God and God's people, alternating scenes of God's tender courtship and Israel's faithful response with God's rage and grief at Israel's infidelities. Much of the book of Hosea is an enacted metaphor in which Hosea extends to his unfaithful wife the repeated offers of forgiveness and restoration that have characterized God's would-be love affair with Israel. And all three of the great prophets use a vision of a marriage restored to mutual fidelity and peace as their image of the perfected covenant.

Of course, the weight of these extended metaphors is on the theological side rather than the ethical one: it is the covenant they seek to illuminate, not the nature of marriage. Nonetheless, in the nature of the case metaphors cut both ways. As we learn from forgiving spouses the extraordinary character of God's passion for his people, we learn as well the power and depth and resilience of faithful love which can overcome even unfaithfulness, and we learn something of what it means to call marriage not a contract but a covenant. Faithful marriage stands in the world as an image and a sign of God's strong and enduring love which overcomes unfaithfulness, a love within which union is nurtured and from which God's people is brought forth. And the unending love of God is the standard by which human fidelity to this covenant is measured.

It is crucial to understand that the demand for holiness in sexual life is not addressed to individuals, but to the entire covenant community, and it is upon the community as a whole that responsibility rests for ordering Israel's life according to the provisions of the Law. Because God is the Lord of Israel as a people, the blessings of fidelity and the weight of infidelity fall on the nation. Thus when holiness is commended, or wrongdoing condemned, the address is always in the plural, and it is always the well-being of the community that is at stake. The rationale for the punishment of wrongdoers in the Hebrew Bible is always the same: "thus shall the evil be purged from among you." But the sense of a common interest in sexual conduct is not merely a sign of the communal character of the covenant. It is also a recognition of a basic truth that we have all but forgotten, which is that human life and human flourishing is social at its very heart. It is part of the nature of human beings, recognized from the outset in the divine declaration that it is not good for the human being to be alone, that our deepest and most necessary joys are found in relation with other persons as well as with God. Counter to the individualist cast of American society, the Bible assumes that we cannot live well or be well all by ourselves. The goods we all need most profoundly are not the goods that fill our retail shelves and clutter our garages, but the goods of relationship: of families and neighborhoods, of shared commitments and shared lives. And through all these goods runs deeply the current of our sexuality with its unrivaled power both to form and to sever human community.

Out of sexual life springs the most elemental form of community, the bond between parents and their children, which is not only the foundation of Israel's tribal organization but the last linchpin of our own fragmented and transient society. And out of sexual life as well spring a thousand, thousand stories of exploitation and rejection and betrayal, of abandonment and the shattering of lives. It does not require the judgment of psychologists to tell us the relational costs of sex-as-entertainment, sex-as-self-gratification, sex-as-athletic-competition, or sex-as-refuge from real intimacy. Despite our countless betrayals and disappointments, we know that the capacity to form and sustain trusting relationships is as basic to the functioning of human society as the capacity for language. Nor do we need the studies of sociologists to tell us that we will all bear the costs of children traumatized or embittered, abandoned or simply overlooked in our pursuit of sexual self-fulfillment. These are soon-to-be adults. If we do not care for them now, we will surely have reason to fear them later.

Thus, nothing would have seemed stranger or more ludicrous within a biblical world view than the contemporary assumption that sex is a private realm immune from public assessment or public accountability. Israel knew what we as a society have forgotten or ignored, which is that the capacity of a people to live as a people rests upon the practices by which they cherish and order the power of sexuality. *So, the second theological stake Christians have in the character and shape of sexual life is community: the support of the shared life for which human beings were made.*

Both of these fundamental commitments about the theological significance of sex are carried forward into the NT, along with most of the norms about the form of sexual life that arose out of them. At the same time, they are subtly transformed by being placed in a new moral framework, both peculiar and central to Christian moral life. But now we are getting ahead of ourselves; it is time to shift our focus to the content of the New Testament's teaching about sex.

WHAT THE NEW TESTAMENT SAYS ABOUT SEX

There are not many innovations in the rules about sexual conduct in the pages of the NT. In fact, there are relatively few passages which address specific norms of sexual behavior at all. The basic division of sexual intercourse into married sex, immorality, and adultery is assumed rather than argued for, as are most of the actual moral norms which are drawn from Jewish Scripture and tradition. Both Jesus and Paul, when seeking to summarize the way to the kingdom or the concrete requirements of neighbor-love, summarize by quoting the second table of the Decalogue, including the prohibition of adultery (Mark 10:19; Rom 13:9). However, though neither Jesus nor Paul undertake general or systematic teachings about sexual conduct, both of them do respond to specific inquiries and situations in illuminating ways. I will begin with Jesus' own teaching, since it is this that Paul is trying to interpret and apply in his churches. Perhaps the most famous and the least popular of Jesus' sayings about sex is his declaration that a man who looks at a woman to lust after her has already committed adultery in his heart (Matt 5:27). You remember this one: it comes in Matthew 5, just before his announcement that divorce and remarriage for any reason short of infidelity is also equivalent to adultery (5:31-32). (It could be worse, of course; the versions of this saying in Mark 10:11-12 and Luke 16:18 provide for no exceptions at all.)

As serious and flat footed as these sayings are, it is important to understand them in their place, as part of Jesus' exposition of the cost of discipleship. Matthew's text about looking with lust comes in the Sermon on the Mount, where it is framed as part of a series of contrasts between the standard interpretation of the Law and Jesus' own teaching about the inward righteousness to which his disciples are called. The parallel texts in Mark and Luke are similar, part of sustained units of teaching on the costs and demands of following Jesus. The sayings are meant not to add new provisions to the Law, but to restore the fullness and depth of its existing provisions. Later in Matthew (19:3-9) when Jesus repeats his rejection of divorce in response to a question about the grounds the Law allows for divorce, his teaching is not interpreted by him as a new commandment. Instead it is a return to the way it was "from the beginning" (v. 8), when God gave the couple to one another to forge a union in flesh. Thus, the demand for fidelity in marriage in all its radicality and inwardness is placed squarely within the demands of following Jesus. And it is understood as rooted in the divine intention that the marriage covenant reflect and imitate the unreserved and permanent attachment of God to his people.

But it would be misleading to mention only the way in which the requirement of fidelity in marriage is placed within the call to discipleship. There is another side to the reframing of sexual life in relation to the gospel. In this same passage in Matthew Jesus concludes with a somewhat mysterious saying about those "who have made themselves eunuchs for the sake of the kingdom" (19:12). This receives no elaboration, but he seems to be speaking of those who forego sexual life for the sake of devotion to God. It is difficult for us, who are raised with at least the idea if not the practice of celibate clergy, to see how remarkable a thing this was for a Jew to say. The commission to be fruitful and multiply had always been, and in Judaism still is, taken as a commandment. Marriage and sex and the procreation of children are for Jews religious obligations which only impossibility can remove, part of the duty to raise up children who will take on the obligations of the covenant. To say that such duties could be subordinated to loyalty to the kingdom, to say even (as Jesus will say repeatedly in Matthew, Mark and Luke) that obligations to existing family members must take second place to one's loyalty to Jesus himself, is to make an astonishing claim. Not only the form but even the possibility of sexual and familial relationships are to be determined in light of one's allegiance to Jesus, which trumps all other duties. In the context in which Jesus spoke, it verges on a claim of divinity.

To return to our summary of the NT, both the demand for marital fidelity and the surprising subordination of marriage and family life to the work of the kingdom appear as well in Paul's teaching about sexual conduct, along with the underlying inheritance of Jewish norms reserving sex to marriage. All of these can be seen in 1 Corinthians. Paul directs the congregation to discipline a member sleeping with his stepmother (5:1-5), a capital offense in the holiness code, and he repeats as from the Lord the charge not to desert a spouse, or at least to remain single if reconciliation is impossible (7:10-11). But Paul cannot just repeat the tradition to this Gentile congregation: his role as pastor forces him to make judgments concerning Christian spouses deserted by unbelieving partners (implicitly because of their conversion). In such a case, he concludes the believer "is not bound," being thus free to remarry (7:12-15).

However, Paul has also absorbed Jesus' teaching about the priority of the kingdom. Asked by the Corinthians whether Christians should forego marriage, or even give up sex within marriage, Paul offers a carefully balanced judgment. On the one hand, Christian marriage partners owe one another sexual availability, out of consideration and to avoid the temptations to immorality which Paul takes for granted would arise (7:3-6). This obligation is utterly mutual and reciprocal on Paul's account, for the body of each belongs to the partner. And those whose passions are strong, in his phrase, should certainly marry and not fear it is sinful (7:9). On the other hand, those who are not married and do not find themselves greatly troubled by sexual desire ought to remain unmarried so as to focus undivided attention on pleasing the Lord. Now many have noted that "It is better to marry than to burn" seems a rather qualified endorsement of marriage, but it is important to note that Paul's reservation about marriage has nothing whatever to do with sex. Sexual desire in Paul's view is a reason for marriage, not a reason against it. He is concerned with distraction, not sensuality, and the moral danger of "worldly concerns" he has in view has more to do with avarice than with lust.

Despite the popularity and historical importance of misreadings of this text, Paul is not a secret ascetic with some positive stake in virginity. He is just a matter-of-fact Jewish boy giving good practical advice. It is easier to be utterly free for the demands of the gospel, particularly under the "distress" of persecution and opposition, if one does not have the practical responsibilities of satisfying and providing for a family. Paul's judgment may be unromantic, but it is not puritanical.

WHY THE NEW TESTAMENT SAYS WHAT IT DOES ABOUT SEX

I have already said the actual rules applied to sexual behavior in the NT are for the most part drawn quite directly from the OT. However, they are given a new and added significance by their placement within the framework of life transformed by the advent of the reign of God in Jesus Christ. The commitments to sex as created and intended by God and to the well-being of the community as undergirding sexual morality are still very much in evidence. It is to God's intention at creation that Jesus appeals in his recasting of the demand of fidelity in marriage, as it is to the well-being of the congregation that Paul refers in his demand that the sexual offender be cast out in hope of reform. But in all these things the over-riding question and concern is, "What form of life, what pattern of conduct, what character of sexual behavior, frees one to follow and imitate and bear witness in the world to the one Lord who calls and claims your life?" *Thus, the third theological stake Christians have in sexuality is discipleship, the coherence of forms of sexual life with uncompromising testimony to Jesus Christ.*

So at last we are in a position to return to our original question, Why should Christians in particular care about sex? For three fundamental reasons: because it is the creation of God, who in making and blessing it has claimed it for God's own purposes; because we recognize that human flourishing is deeply communal, a matter of relationship with God and neighbor, and sex is a powerful force either to forge or to destroy those relationships; and finally because sexual life like all of life is claimed by the one we call Lord, brought into the service of God's redemptive purposes for the world.

Since redemption is not the annulment of creation but its fulfillment, and since the whole point and purpose of Christian community is to declare and embody the truth of the gospel, these three rationales for why sex matters can be expected to converge much more often than they diverge. Still, there may be tensions. We have seen already that a sexual ethic rooted in creation and in a community constituted primarily through kinship will have a different take on the centrality of procreation and family life than an ethic centered in discipleship.

Certainly for those whose highest loyalty is the reign of God, the satisfactions of sexual love cannot be presupposed as an entitlement. They might be preempted by the requirements of one's more fundamental vocation to bear witness to the gospel or forfeited as part of the price exacted by faithfulness.

Perhaps this is the place to give an example of what difference all this would make. How would our sexual lives and our judgments about them be distinct from those of our surrounding society if we really were formed by this tradition and its core concerns? Since our space is limited, let me be blunt and say that we would have to begin by recovering Christian marriage as a distinctive theological vocation. To do this we would have to embrace marriage as a practice which embodies by imitation the unswerving loyalty and long-suffering love of God, a practice marked by fidelity in which divorce is a rare and desperate measure.

This would require that we repudiate the concept of marriage borrowed from our secular culture as a personal relationship aimed primarily at the happiness of the couple, and reasonably to be dissolved when it fails to fulfill that aim. We would have to ground it once again in the primal intention of God to join human lives and to make them fruitful. Most radical of all, we would have to abandon our understanding of marriage as a realm of private success or failure and return to the practices of a moral community with both the privilege and the duty of supporting and holding one another accountable. That would mean entering into real discernment with one another about what we might do to sustain marriage through all of its difficulties, and how we might recognize a cause grave enough to warrant even the drastic remedy of divorce. And finally, for all this to make sense we would have to renew our commitment to the priority of the kingdom. We would have to let its priority extend even to this area of deepest intimacy where we seek comforts and satisfactions so basic to our sense of ourselves that we have long since assumed that we had a right to them and could do whatever we needed to secure them. Only then can we begin to imagine making and keeping promises as deep and serious as those we undertake before God and the community when we promise to love faithfully, for better or worse, for as long as we live.

There is no use denying that embracing such a practice would be difficult and costly, an occasion of suffering as well as of blessing. This is just the particular expression of a more general feature of Christian ethics, which is its unflinching commitment to the priority of the reign of God over and above every other good, however rightly we prize it. The Sermon on the Mount is famous for terrifying sayings, so much so that we have all learned to take them with a grain of salt: "If your eye causes you to sin, pluck it out and throw it away; it is better to enter life with one eye than with both to be cast into the eternal fire" (5:29). "Well," we tell each other, "he does not really mean for us to pluck out an eye." And that, of course, is true, especially since it is never the eye that causes one to sin, but always the heart! But we mistake not only the Sermon but the NT canon as a whole if we forget that running through the canon like a scarlet thread is the expectation that faithfulness to the gospel might well cost one not less than everything.

Now it may well be that we are not prepared for any such reading of the gospel, not interested in being the kind of community where we would seriously count on the support of our brothers and sisters and seriously expect to tell and be told the truth about moral life. We may not be sufficiently committed to discipleship that we are willing to have it order even how we live out our sexual lives. In that case, I honestly think the church should get out of the business of performing wedding ceremonies. Let people go to the state, which will test them for diseases and register and license them and give them the right to sue one another in civil court, none of which is any particular business of ours. And let us acknowledge that we have given up a basic form of evangelical witness, the testimony on earth to the long-suffering love of God which overcomes evil with good. But whatever conclusions we reach as we wrestle with questions about the forms of sexual life that are becoming to the gospel whose bearers we are, we must remember that to make discipleship the testing point for proposals about sexuality is not to place it under special burdens. We must not single out sex as if by being bodily and non-rational and pleasurable it must require extra justification. Despite what you may have heard, Christians are not committed to the belief that sex is way too much fun to be okay with God. To make the demands of discipleship central to judgments about sex is just to recover something that our modern preoccupations have obscured, which is that sexuality like every other aspect of human life is affirmed and prized and blessed and welcomed—but it cannot be made sovereign. It is a good gift of God, but it will remain good only so long as it is servant and not master, a means by which we honor creation and celebrate communion, and not the point of human existence. Sex is like everything else human: a dimension of life which is brought under the sway of God and into the service of the Lord who calls us.

SEX AND CHARACTER: FORMING A LIFE WORTHY OF THE GOSPEL

And this brings me around finally to a more general point about the morality of sexual life, which is that it is nothing special. What I mean is that moral goodness in the realm of sex is not a separate thing all its own, a certain kind of capacity unrelated to others, like having perfect pitch or a photographic memory. Just as sex is simply one more arena to be brought under the Lordship of Christ, sexual morality is simply bringing to bear in our choices about sex the same convictions and commitments, the same thoughtfulness and care that we need to bring to other areas of life.

All the ordinary questions—questions about truth-telling and fairness and respect, matters of justice and responsibility and promise-keeping, the duties of friendship and of care for those who depend upon us—all these are still relevant. And all the ordinary commitments out of which we live as Christians—reverence for God's will and care for the body of which we are part and the steadfast refusal to let anything stand between us and God whom we love—all these order and inform our judgments about sex as about anything else.

And what we do about them is going to depend on very basic things about us, like what we care about and what we believe in and what we want, and ultimately it will depend on what we love. The claims and commitments which we are called to live out in our sexual lives are not suspended by passion or loneliness or need, but all those things will often tempt us to ignore claims that we would otherwise acknowledge. Good and evil in sexual life may be the same as they are in any other realm, but nowhere is it easier to deceive ourselves than here, easier to behave for a while at least as if we could act in a vacuum and no one would get hurt. As appealing a picture as this can be, it is an illusion, and trying to live there is like trying to satisfy your thirst at a mirage.

To ask that we refocus our consideration of the norms of Christian sexual conduct on the basic commitments that underlie those particular norms is to call upon the church to recognize the extent to which both moral judgment and conduct are determined by moral vision. And we know that moral vision, the capacity to see truthfully, is cultivated over a lifetime. It is inseparable from heart and spirit, shaped by work and worship and study and prayer and attention, a dimension of the character that is both expressed in our actions and shaped by them. But that character is not created in an hour or a day or a week. It is nurtured by hearing the word and receiving the sacraments, by offering and receiving care and counsel, in the daily round of perfectly ordinary Christian activities through which it has pleased God to be present and powerful in the lives of God's people. It is shaped slowly and patiently over time in a community of those molded by the steady and disciplined practices of the faith into disciples of Jesus Christ who have learned to glorify God in their bodies.

RESPONSE TO WHEELER

BRUCE FIELDS

Issues centering on human sexuality have been with us from the beginning. The pervasiveness of this issue is ever before us today, for it is manifested in every aspect of our day-to-day existence from familial relationships in the home to magazine articles and movies absorbed in the public arena. The depictions often offered are indeed troublesome, for apart from divine guidance both in the understanding and in the resulting expression of human sexuality, a poisonous form of dehumanization actually occurs. The church in a very real way is a part of this public arena. The faith of the redeemed community is not experienced in seclusion, in some sociocultural vacuum. As such the church has an opportunity to witness, either negatively as an example of a group inappropriately dominated by the social milieu, or positively as a group demonstrating the reality of transformed lives, able to stand as a beacon of light against the darkness of a ubiquitous confusion on the matter of sexuality. How the church understands human sexuality and acts in accordance with that understanding will testify for or against its focus on love for God, ourselves, and our community. The ancient yet relevant voice of Augustine speaks today to remind us of this need to love God, ourselves, our neighbor, and our bodies *(Christian Doctrine* 1.23.22).

Dr. Wheeler has performed a real labor of love in calling the church to a credible manifestation of love in the matter of sex. This is a love forged in the biblical furnace of God's work in creation, the construction of a unique community, and the call to a costly discipleship. I would like to engage her reflections through three lenses emerging from her paper. The first focuses on the nature and significance of the church's identity. The second facilitates comment on the matter of the church's witness to the "rest of the world." The third lens brings to clarity two issues that I do not intend as criticisms. They are rather points that stem from the richness of biblical scrutiny and the communal emphasis of Dr. Wheeler's work and thus are intended to encourage further reflection and response.

Scripture is full of metaphors that inform the nature and mission of the church. Foundational to all of them is the reality of the church belonging to God. The church, in the name of being holy "because I am holy" (1 Pet 1:16; Lev 19:2), should be governed by God's perspective on all matters, including sexuality. Dr. Wheeler's three theological summaries, which explain the Christian rationale for appropriate understanding and behavior in the realm of sexuality, comprise an invaluable contribution. The contribution of this grid is made not only in its accurate categorizations but also in its facilitation of placing the issue of sexuality in a larger biblical, theological framework.

The theological foundation from the doctrine of creation (that sex is holy because it belongs to God) provides a determinative perspective that should affect both the church's self-identity and practice. We must be a people committed to a congruence of confession and ethic, having, in the words of Dr. Wheeler, "a distinctive pattern of the covenant community." The second theological foundation for the concern for correct expressions of sexuality is the life of the community. Nothing here needs to be added further than Dr. Wheeler's statement:

> The goods we all need most profoundly are not the goods that fill our retail shelves and clutter our garages, but the goods of relationship: of families and neighborhoods, of shared commitments and shared lives. And through all these goods runs deeply the current of our sexuality, *with its unrivaled power both to form and sever human community* [emphasis mine].

The third theological foundation, admittedly, can involve us in excruciating realizations as we consider what it means to follow Jesus Christ and to allow his way to mold every aspect of our lives, including our sexuality. Dr. Wheeler rightly points out that it is a means by which we can witness to the world of the one Lord who calls and claims us for himself.

The concern for witness provides a transition to the next lens, namely, the witness to this sex-dominated culture. I applaud Dr. Wheeler's burden for this "fragmented and transient society." There is a practical witness already to the problems of autonomous human expressions in sexuality as in the cases of "teenage pregnancy and sexually transmitted diseases, the specter of AIDS and the devastation to families caused by broken marriage vows." I will address a proposal as to the content of the church's needed witness to this society at the end of this response.

The third lens focuses on some considerations for further reflection and response. I cannot respond to all matters that I believe are important and that are worthy of response in Dr. Wheeler's work. For example, the issue of the meaning of Deuteronomy 24:1-4 with its seeming liberal policy for the dismissal of a displeasing wife, as compared to the Lord's expressed hatred of divorce in Mal 2:14-16, would be an important exercise in biblical theology touching the areas of sexuality and marriage. The use of the language of marriage to inform on the relationship between God and his people deserves much more expansion. This is true of much of Dr. Wheeler's prophetic presentation. I must engage in a much more modest endeavor. I want first to raise the point of the need for grace in the realm of sexual conduct as an element of discipleship. Second, I will return to the matter of the church's witness to the surrounding society through its sexual consciousness and behavior.

I again consult Augustine who sheds light on the need for the grace of God in every aspect of life, a principle certainly applicable to the realm of sexuality. He wrote in his *Confessions*: "Strengthen me too, that I may be capable; give what you command, and then command whatever you will" (*Conf.* 10.31.45). Paul in Holy Scripture testifies to this foundational need for enabling grace: "But by the grace of God I am what I am, and his grace to me was not without effect. No, I worked harder than all of them—yet not I, *but the grace of God that was with me*" (1 Cor 15:10, NIV; italics mine). Sexuality is an essential characteristic of what it is to be human, as Dr. Wheeler succinctly identifies: ". . . human sexuality is not a mistake or an embarrassment but a holy gift, inseparable from the human mind and spirit . . . ." Against something so powerful, so potentially all consuming, so prone to lead us to all kinds of self-deception, I am convinced that the soul-searching disciple needs to be reminded that God commands, but also gives grace, i.e., that which strengthens to stand. Apart from such strengthening, who can stand the internal fires of human sexual expression that are then fed in many ways by our surrounding sociocultural setting? Many texts in Scripture call believers to walk in the Spirit for in the Spirit there is the fruit that sustains believers and contributes to the building of community (Gal 5:22-23).

I wholeheartedly concur with Dr. Wheeler's call for the church to be credible witnesses to our society that is consciously, and unconsciously, in the throes of a post-modern fragmentation of any possibility of adopting communal morals and values on a cross-community scale. I believe that there is still a power of persuasion simply in the realm of credibility. On this point, I affirm the need for consistency between our theology of sexuality and its expression in covenant-based marriages. Dr. Wheeler is right to connect fidelity in marriage with the call to Christian discipleship, which certainly inculcates a relinquishing of personal rights between the married parties. We will be ineffective witnesses if we do not show our discipleship at the determinative level of marriage.

There was so much of a profound nature that was discussed in this paper. My lenses did not do justice to its substance. They were just tools for engagement. Though I was struck by many observations, as a parent I was drawn to one particular statement:

> Nor do we need the studies of sociologists to tell us that we will all bear the costs of children traumatized or embittered, abandoned or simply overlooked in our pursuit of sexual self-fulfillment.These are soon-to-be adults. If we do not care for them now, we will surely have reason to fear them later.

I am grateful for theological frameworks, specific commands, and the call to discipleship as they all interface on the matter of human sexuality. I am particularly thankful for the reminder of parental responsibility regarding the precious stewardship of my children.

SEEKING THE VIRTUES AMONG THE PROPHETS: THE BOOK OF AMOS AS A TEST CASE

M. DANIEL CARROLL R.

THE NEED FOR A DIFFERENT APPROACH TO THE ETHICS OF THE PROPHETS

I begin this paper with an autobiographical tale. I suspect that for many a conviction regarding the centrality of social ethics for the Christian faith was born out of personal experiences and is not simply an intellectual addendum to one's set of "necessary beliefs." This account will explain how I came to have a passion for OT ethics in general and how I began to see the need for virtue ethics in particular. The two succeeding major parts of this essay provide a summary introduction to virtue ethics and a reading of the book of Amos from that perspective.

My interest in OT ethics was born and has been nurtured over the years in large measure out of a fascination with the OT prophets. That interest was first sparked while I was at seminary. At that time (the late 1970s), the passion for my Latin American heritage (I am half-Guatemalan) was being rekindled after lying dormant for a while. Part of what sparked that renewed awareness was the challenge to traditional theology that was being championed by Liberation Theology. Here was a way of doing theology—a theology demanding a flesh and blood commitment to social ethics—that claimed to be speaking on behalf of that continent's millions of poor and to be reclaiming a central focus of the biblical message that had long been ignored (even suppressed) by theologians and church bodies. Not to heed the cries of the oppressed meant to ignore inexcusably God's option for the poor and to perpetuate the suffering of the masses of the Two-Thirds World.

The lives and message of the OT prophets always were a fundamental component of Liberation Theology's argument. It appealed to the prophetic literature, broadly speaking, in two ways.[1] On the one hand, there was the call to individual believers and to the Christian church as an institution to speak out with *a prophetic voice*. To fulfill this commission required denouncing unjust socioeconomic structures, raising the poor's awareness of their plight, and announcing the possibility of a different future for Latin America.[2] This was to be a future of peace and equality for all, within a different, more just socio-political system in the form of a compassionate and contextualized socialism. Of course, the Sandinista regime in Nicaragua (1979-1990) was Liberation Theology's supreme experiment, its most tangible historical project, attempting to turn this hope into an actual concrete reality.

On the other hand, liberationist exegetes and theologians turned to *specific prophetic texts* to support their point of view. Interestingly, these scholars utilized a variety of critical approaches to highlight what they believed to be the moral core of the prophets' words.[3] For example, José Porfirio Miranda appealed to source and tradition criticism to reconstruct what he felt to be the original prophetic message of an uncompromising demand for social justice. Elsa Tamez analyzed several Hebrew roots related to oppression and explored the nuances of each in a variety of passages, and J. Severino Croatto utilized recent literary theory to advocate new readings of the canonical texts (*relecturas*) that would open up their "reservoir of meaning" for Latin America today.[4]

A prophetic book that always had a high profile in liberationist biblical studies was that of the eighth-century prophet Amos. Its critique of oppression is unwavering and harsh. Moreover, Amos, the man, appears as a profile in courage. He denounces the economic and social elites of his day and refuses to be intimidated by either the high priest or the king, when he delivers his divine message at the national sanctuary at Bethel (7:10-17). Because of its lessons for justice and because of a desire to work out an evangelical biblical approach that could serve as an alternative (both critical and appreciative, yet distinct) to Liberation Theology, I began to concentrate much of my own research on Amos. So, this prophetic text took hold of me years ago and since then has served as my "workshop," so to speak, for serious ethical reflection.

Liberation Theology and the scale of poverty and violence in Latin America, therefore, drove me to wrestle with OT ethics, particularly as it pertained to the prophetic commitment to social justice. What I found surprising as I began to investigate prominent studies in OT ethics written by evangelical scholars was that the profound ethical message of the prophets often is not given its due. Instead, much more attention is given to the Law.[5] Walter Kaiser's *Toward Old Testament Ethics* states bluntly, "The heart of Old Testament ethics is to be placed squarely on the explicit commands found mainly in the Pentateuch, but also to a lesser degree in the Prophets and Wisdom books."[6] His book is a detailed analysis of the major blocks of laws in the Pentateuch (the Decalogue, the Book of the Covenant [Exod 20:22-23:23], the Holiness Code [Lev 18-20] and Deuteronomy). His hermeneutical discussions deal with how it might be possible to apply those particular laws to our situation today.[7] Passages from the prophets are cited primarily to demonstrate how they echo the theology and legislation of the Pentateuch. Christopher Wright's work also highlights the Law. He does offer shorter sections on the prophetic insistence on social justice and acceptable worship, but Wright uses the prophets above all as part of his threefold scheme to visualize the abiding applicability of the Law's ethical themes.[8] The prophetic hope of a messianic community and ultimately of an entirely new creation at the end of time serve to link the OT to the church and to all of humanity. His model is very helpful and illuminating, as is Kaiser's, but it too can mute the singular contribution of the prophets' message.

The central feature that Liberation Theology stressed from the prophets' condemnation of the poverty within ancient Israel was their biting unmasking of the nation's oppressive socioeconomic and political structures. For many of these liberationists, to contextualize this message into Latin America required acquiring power to effect the necessary, parallel sort of social changes that the prophets seemed to be calling for—hence, their involvement in a variety of social protest or revolutionary movements and the efforts of some within the Sandinista regime. What became evident over time across the entire continent, however, is that even dramatic structural change was not enough to create *a different moral climate*, even if the formal, official social configuration appeared to be more equitable. In the past decade or so a series of negotiated peace settlements have brought an end to armed conflict (with the important exceptions of Columbia and of Chiapas in southern Mexico), and several countries have made significant, howbeit stumbling, strides toward greater democracy and economic reform. Still, a general malaise and disenchantment casts a dark shadow over Latin America.[9] Corruption and violence continue; cynicism grows, while hope for enduring change fades. What is increasingly clear is that something beyond—perhaps one should say deeper than—mere external change is lacking. In the jargon of philosophical ethics, I would suggest that what is missing in this context of so much death and despair is the nurturing of *a culture of virtue*, especially of the specific virtues of justice and peaceableness. Accordingly my quest within the field of OT social ethics became an attempt to discover whether, and how, virtue ethics had been utilized in the study of the ethics of the prophets.

Once again, I met with frustration. Scholarly interest in prophetic ethics, with a few exceptions that we will mention below, usually has been directed elsewhere than toward the virtues. For instance, many have tried to discover the specific theological tradition that informed the prophets' social concern and which shaped the literary expression of those convictions. One candidate for this theological basis is the wisdom teachings of the extended family and clan. The most common option has been to ground the social ethics of the prophets in the Pentateuch or in a certain set of laws within the Pentateuch that some might consider early enough to have been taken into consideration by the eighth-century prophets. This position is often connected to the notion of covenant. This concentration on the Law also is evident in more systematic treatments. Oliver O'Donovan has recently published a masterful, comprehensive political theology entitled *The Desire of the Nations*.[10] O'Donovan envisions the task of the OT prophet to be that of the guardian and the "contextualizer" of the moral tradition found in the Law, principally before the king in order to remind him of the demands and limits on the monarchy under God's sovereign rule. Some scholars turn less to specific theological roots and instead point to broader cultural backgrounds. They would compare the prophetic message with the ethical ideals of the Ancient Near East and posit that the source of its norms is to be found in a common moral perspective shared across the Fertile Crescent and Asia Minor.

While this set of approaches has looked for the theological underpinning of prophetic ethics, another group of scholars has tried to define the social message of the prophets with the help of the social sciences. For example, each prophet is positioned vis-à-vis his sociological and ideological orientation to the hub of royal, religious, and economic power and is labeled either a "central" or "peripheral" prophet. A central prophet would be more supportive of the status quo and generally would accept the present order of things as divinely established and sanctioned; on the other hand, a peripheral prophet stands on the margins of those circles of influence and is more critical of the way that the society operates. Another type of sociological study proposes that the prophetic ethic has its roots in the tribal ideals of Israel's distant nomadic past and vehemently opposes the urban and power-driven values of the monarchies of Canaan, Egypt, Assyria, and therefore of Israel as well. One final type of sociological perspective turns its attention to the socioeconomic target of the prophets' condemning words. One suggestion has been that the eighth-century prophets attacked a system called "rent capitalism," in which the oppressive owners of the farmland live in urban areas, while the peasants inevitably fall into debt in a losing struggle to meet the demands of their patrons and do not have enough left over for their own family needs.

Each of these quite different approaches illuminates in valuable ways important dimensions of the ethical message of the prophetic books. At the same time, what is missing in these studies is an investigation into the formation and testing of *the moral character* of the nation, which is the focus of virtue ethics. The level of moral character will determine in large measure the ethical makeup of the people, how the social structures operate, and the treatment of the outcast and the poor. Studies on character in the OT have tended to be drawn more to the narratives (Genesis, Judges, Samuel-Kings) and to the Wisdom literature, especially the book of Proverbs.[11] Nevertheless, there have been a few scholars who have probed issues related to virtues in the prophets.

Benjamin Farley dedicates an entire chapter to the prophets and argues that their messages attempted to push the nation to live out the virtues that are embedded in the Ten Commandments.[12] He suggests that the two tables of the Decalogue can be summarized (as can the virtues) by the love of God and neighbor. The Decalogue begins by turning the people's attention to Yahweh, because a right view of God is the basis for the proper treatment of others in the covenant community and of humanity in general. The second table of the Decalogue (Exod 20:12-17; Deut 5:16-21) in its list of prohibitions would encourage the virtues of gratitude, respect, faithfulness, truthfulness, and contentment.

In Part One of his work on OT ethics, *Let Justice Roll Down*, Bruce Birch stresses the importance of character and explains how the biblical text can serve to address and shape the moral life of the church today.[13] In his chapter on the preexilic prophets, he points out that one of the purposes of announcing a hope beyond the judgment was to communicate a vision of the kind of community that the people of God could one day become. Another scholar, Waldemar Janzen, champions the ethical power and relevance of OT narratives, which present an array of persons of character who can function as models of behavior. He presents an ethics built around what he calls the "familial paradigm" of life, land, and hospitality.[14] The prophets, he believes, called the nation as a whole, and individuals in positions of influence in particular, back to these ideals. In time the prophets themselves, as they struggled to fulfill their calling in the midst of suffering and loss, became a paradigm of obedience for the rest of the nation.

These few studies have begun to point the way toward looking at the prophets through the lens of virtue ethics.[15] Our reading of the book of Amos from a virtue ethics perspective is an initial, exploratory attempt to try to broaden the application of virtue ethics to the OT. My hope is that others with more expertise might take this lead and carry it further for the benefit of the social life of the Christian church. Before turning to Amos, we offer a brief introduction to virtue ethics.

A BRIEF INTRODUCTION TO VIRTUE ETHICS

In very general terms, the three classical "schools" of philosophical ethics are deontology, teleology, and the virtues.[16] The first two are primarily concerned that the ethical subject make the correct decision in a given situation. The deontology approach (from the Greek *dei*, "it is necessary" or "it is right") evaluates the rightness or wrongness of an act on the basis of established or revealed (in the case of the church, within the Scriptures) principles and rules. A major challenge then is to choose the correct norm for that situation. Teleology (from the Greek *telos*, "the end") would carefully weigh the consequences (both possible and probable)[17] of an action and make a decision according to which course of action might best promote the greatest good for the majority.

Virtue ethics received its classical expression in Aristotle's *The Nicomachean Ethics* in the fourth century B.C.E. It has been experiencing a revival of sorts in the last two or three decades, especially through the work of philosopher-ethicist Alisdair MacIntyre.[18] From an expressly Christian perspective the efforts of ethicists such as Josef Pieper, Stanley Hauerwas, and Gilbert Meilander stand out. We have already mentioned above some OT scholars who have appropriated this perspective. Virtue ethics does not ignore the moral quandaries of those difficult moments of decision so important to deontology and teleology. Nevertheless, it directs its primary focus to the character of the person who will make that decision. The goal is to shape the character—that is, the habitual behavior, attitudes, and intentions—in order that this person might be able properly to discern and live out what might be the best choice of action in that circumstance. It is more a question of becoming the right kind of human being, one who can mature toward an ethical lifestyle that is marked by integrity, sensitivity, and consistency.

There are several basic components of a virtue ethics approach. First, it is crucial to define the "*good*" to which all ethical reflection is to be directed. The "good" is that supreme end that ideally should orient and define all of our existence. It is in achieving this good that we best fulfill our purpose as human beings. This transcendent "good" to which all other more finite goals ultimately should point cannot be limited to some quantifiable material gain or emotional satisfaction. It has absolute value in and of itself and is to be sought for its own sake. For Aristotle the highest good for humans was "happiness" (Greek *eudaimonia*, by which he meant more than simply the feelings associated with being glad).[19] The Westminster Confession of Faith declares (although not in a context of a discussion of ethics) that the supreme good of the Christian is "to glorify God and to enjoy him forever." Farley's comments on the Decalogue would echo this classic statement of the central purpose of the life of the Christian believer.

The second term requiring a definition is "*virtue*." The virtues are those dispositions that one must possess in order to approximate and to embody the "good." The virtues usually are grouped into two fundamental categories: the four cardinal virtues (prudence, justice, courage, and temperance) and the three theological virtues (faith, hope, and charity—or love). These last three were added to Aristotle's list and expounded by early Christian theologians (the key figure here is Thomas Aquinas).[20] To possess these virtues is to acquire the requisite *skills of moral reasoning* and to exhibit *habits of behavior* commensurate with the good. All of this demands *a life-long process* of training in the virtues, moral reasoning (*phronēsis*), the transformation of the self, and continued ethical practice within a specific community.

For the purposes of this paper, the virtue to which we wish to draw particular attention is justice. The conventional definition of this virtue is *suum cuique*, "to each his due."[21] The virtue of justice is that conscious and consistent endeavor to grant to each person what is rightfully his or hers. What is minimally owed each person is a share in the basic provisions for existence (such as food and protection) and the special benefits of the life of the community (such as celebration in worship). At one level, this virtue is visible through external criteria, such as by pursuing acts of justice and respecting the community's laws; but to be just is also to have some definite internal attitudes that inspire a person to do what is right for others, irrespective of the social demands or strictures. In other words, it is not enough simply to do the right thing; interest in the virtue will probe more deeply.[22] Moreover, a commitment to justice carries with it what James Gilman calls "empathetic emotions," "those emotional attachments that are crucial to the practice of Christian virtue."[23] Indignant anger is one emotion appropriate to the virtue of justice. As he explains, this is not a destructive passion for revenge and retribution. A righteous anger moves beyond those feelings to a firm hope in the final vindication of those who have been wronged; it empowers the defender of justice to speak out and care for the victims of injustice and to work responsibly for a better world. Another suitable emotion for justice is gratitude toward God for the mercy one has received; this remembering of God's grace must then lead to showing mercy toward others.

The third component is the *community*. Every community establishes for itself what the "good" is for its members and tries to mold them in accordance with it. The formation of the character of its members is grounded in a particular set of traditions (in both oral and written narratives) and in its own explanations of the nature of human society and the meaning of life, all of which point to the desirability, advantages, and utility of that good. The good also is modeled in certain exemplars—that is, in those individuals who best exemplify the virtues in their day-to-day lives.

In the OT, of course, the key community is the people of God, Israel, who were brought into existence through the election of Abraham. The foundational narratives of Israel are the accounts of the patriarchs, the giving of the Law at Sinai, and the miracle of liberation at the Exodus. These narratives serve, among other things, to provide the motivation for the ethics of God's people. In their families and in multiple public ceremonies they are to remember these stories that explain from whence they came and that highlight the gracious acts of Yahweh on their behalf. These stories serve to provide Israel with a distinct perspective on reality and moral responsibility, different from the competing narratives and the social models of the cultures all around them. God himself is the greatest exemplar for Israel's moral life. This is fitting, if a proper understanding of his person is the foundation of the moral life. Throughout their history he also raises up certain persons, who in their own way epitomize what he requires of the nation as a whole. Unlike Yahweh, these individuals are not perfect, but nevertheless they are the ones who strive in the power of God to be obedient to his demands and to be faithful to the nation's calling.

This issue of traditions and depictions of reality leads us to a fourth (and, for us, final) component of virtue ethics. For the people of God, these distinctive pictures of what life is really like beyond human pretense and sin and how it should be fleshed out are found in the *biblical text*, the revealed narrative of Yahweh's dealings with the world and especially with those who are called by his name. In other words, the Bible has an important part to play in inculcating the virtues in the Christian church.[24] This sacred canon has the power to mold the moral imagination of believers, and it does this by portraying an ancient world that is at once both historically true and realistic. It is this aspect of being a realistic depiction of human existence that allows its representations of life to resonate with readers today, even though they are separated by millennia from the Israel found in its pages.

In the Bible readers recognize themselves, their pressing personal and social issues, types of people similar to the ones they know, and situations they experience. They acquire from the Bible a very candid and trustworthy vision of human life and about God, and they can become skilled at differentiating this newfound perception from the self-deceptive and false illusions of the broader society within which they live. Individual Christians and the Church as a whole can begin to appreciate the biblical text as an "identity document" that defines who they are, why they are here, and how they are unique yet still connected to the world around them. The text thus authorizes the formation and the particular form of Christian communities. In turn, as believers and churches live out this vision, they in some sense, in reciprocal fashion, authenticate the power and relevance of the Bible.

This moral information and dynamic shaping is communicated to some degree through the direct commands and exhortations within the Old and New Testaments, and these are the parts of the Bible that many ethicists rightly have emphasized. This process also occurs, however, by paying attention to the presentation of the characters within the Bible. It is by looking at these complex characters in an assortment of compelling scenes that we can see others who believe in God wrestling with moral dilemmas and demands, as they strive to embody faithfully—virtuously, as it were—the "good". From their limitations, their reflections, their failures, and their triumphs we can learn about the kind of people that we should be today. In sum, the Bible offers its readers a rich course in the virtues. The task before us now is to see whether and how this kind of approach to the book of Amos might help us to glean new insights into its moral imperatives with which we are so familiar.

A VIRTUE ETHICS APPROACH APPLIED TO THE BOOK OF AMOS

Our reading of Amos will concentrate on three interrelated topics: defining the "good" that Israel is to follow, probing the book's observations on the virtue of justice, and demonstrating the kind of moral model Yahweh is for his people.

The meaning of the "good." If a virtue ethics is founded on the notion of the good, then this is where we start our investigation of Amos. Coincidentally, two verses utilize the term "good" (ṭôb; 5:14a, 15a). These two lines are not only parallel in some degree in content (that is, both contain a command concerning the good), but they also are interconnected by an inverse parallelism (or, chiasm) of this command: "seek good and hate evil . . . hate evil and love good." Several literary devices emphasize the importance of this exhortation to pursue the good. The most obvious, of course, is this artistic repetition of the same command in adjacent lines; this, in other words, is not a casual mandate. Note, too, in the lines that describe the consequences of heeding the command (5:14b, 15b), the repetition of the extended divine name "LORD[25] [Yahweh] God of Hosts" (*YHWH ʾĕlōhê ṣĕbāʾôt*), which combines his covenantal name (LORD) with a title that underscores his mighty, sovereign power. This call to seek after the good, therefore, is given a divine seriousness. This name had already appeared in 3:13 and 4:13 in ominous contexts of impending doom and will so again later (6:8, 14; cf. 5:27). These occurrences and the wording in these two verses point to the gravity of the option before the people. Only by seeking the "good" can the nation ("perhaps"! v. 15b) hope for any sort of future after the horrific destruction that now looms on the horizon.

What, then, is that "good" that Yahweh so emphatically demands?[26] To begin with, the double juxtaposition of "good" with "evil" in 5:14-15 strongly suggests that here the term, at least in part, will be defined by its opposite. In the immediate context, the meaning of "evil" is implied in 5:10-13, where the forthright are intimidated in the city gate, the ancient venue for the administration of justice, the powerless are taken advantage of through unfair taxation, and the legal process is perverted through bribery. The specification of the "good" in the second colon of 5:15a ("establish justice in the gate") fits well with the legal emphasis of the evil the prophet has just described. At one level, therefore, the good has a very tangible, day-to-day component, yet one that is crucial for the well-being—even the survival—of the less fortunate. The good requires, as the classical definition suggests, giving each his due or share in the basic provisions for life with fairness and dignity. At the same time, since the good is inseparable from the legal and economic system within Israel, the text reveals that the good also is communal. It cannot be reduced just to the personal, as here the personal makes no sense apart from the social structures and processes that impact the daily existence of each individual.

Within a broader context, the "good" is related to the tradition of the ancient covenant at Sinai.[27] To do good before Yahweh means to obey the covenant regulations and to fulfill its obligations of social solidarity and so enjoy the fullness of God's bounty and protection; to disobey is to bring the covenant curses (Hos 8:1-3; Mic 6:8; cf. Deut 4:39f.; 6:17-19; 12:28). The transgressions of

Israel are not sins of omission. Nor do the prophet's words in 3:10, "They do not know how to do 'right'" (that is, "upright conduct"; *nĕkōḥāh*), mean that the ignoring of the good is due to ignorance (cf. Jer 4:22; in contrast to Deut 1:39; Isa 7:15f.; Jonah 4:11). Their actions and attitudes reflect a willful turning away from covenantal ethical requirements. This internal dimension of doing the good is made manifest by the prophet's decision to use words of emotion: "hate evil, love good" (5:15a). To seek the good is a disposition, a conscious choice that arises from the depths of the individual and communal soul. The "good" that Amos preaches then is the equitable provision of life's necessities within the context of that moral, covenant community, which Israel was called to be.

But, the significance of the "good" stretches beyond that horizontal plane. Some scholars have proposed that "good" in 5:14-15 actually is an epithet or title for Yahweh and that in similar fashion "evil" is a reference to another deity. The clauses would then be translated: "Seek the Good (One) and not the Evil (One) . . . Hate the Evil (One) and love the Good (One)." Whatever the merits of this interpretation, the connection with Yahweh is made abundantly clear when these two verses are set within the larger chiasm that embraces all of 5:1-17. In this literary structure the pericope corresponding to 5:14-15 is verses four through six. There we find the verb "seek" repeated twice, but now its object is God himself. This connection reveals that ultimately the "good" that Israel is to pursue is the person of Yahweh. We will return to this point in more detail in the third part of this section. But at this juncture we can make the observation that the prophets consistently teach that it is Yahweh who brings the full blessings of the "good" to his people as they seek him and who sends curses for their choice of evil.[28] In summary, the "good" is more than a picture of an ideal human community linked by history and religion (and, to some extent, ethnicity). Yahweh is the greatest good, and without him this vision of social harmony is an impossibility.

The virtue of justice. I would hazard the guess that Amos is most known for being the champion of social justice and the defender of the poor. The most recognizable verse of the book is 5:24. What is lost in the English translations is that in the Hebrew text this line has a chiastic structure. The verse literally reads, "and let roll down like water justice, and righteousness like an ever-flowing stream." This kind of structure is designed to focus attention on its center; thus the juxtaposition of the two key terms "justice" and "righteousness" underscores their importance to Yahweh. He would rather have social justice than loud and busy cultic celebrations devoid of any ethical demand (5:21-23). The imagery is vivid as well. In a part of the world where the wadis, or ravines, remain dry most of the year, what is expressed is the desire for justice to be always present, like an ever full and flowing riverbed!

These two terms, "justice" and "righteousness," also appear together in two similar verses, 5:7 and 6:12. Here, too, the imagery is powerful. In this case, though, instead of stating Yahweh's will, the prophet describes the nation's forceful rejection of justice. Once again, the reader encounters chiastic structures: "Those who turn to wormwood justice, and righteousness to the ground throw" (5:7); and "For they turn to poison justice, and the fruit of righteousness" (6:12b). Justice and righteousness are now at the center of what Israel disregards and abuses. Rather than allowing the legal system to flourish as a constructive benefit so that all receive their due, the nation and its leaders pervert it and change it into a bitter herb; they toss it to the ground as something of little importance, as something to take advantage of and trample on—even as they trample upon the needy. These verses reveal that the pursuit and maintenance of justice is not simply an abstract ideal. Justice requires a certain attitude, an active inner interest in fairness and lawfulness.

A related virtue is peaceableness. This virtue, as was the case in our discussion of the good, surfaces by examining its opposite. The world pictured in the text is full of violence. On the one hand, the violence is associated with warfare. The opening oracles against the nations (1:3-2:3) speak of gross cruelty, the buying and selling of populations into exile, the destruction of fortresses, and the violation of the dead in the international conflicts of the region. In the coming invasion Israel will experience the tearing down of its fortresses (3:11; 4:3) and of the homes of the well-to-do and commoner alike (3:15; 5:9, 11; 6:11), defeat in battle and terrible loss of life (2:14-16; 3:12; 5:1-3, 16-17; 6:9-10; 8:3, 10; 9:1, 10), the razing of its sanctuaries (3:14; 7:9; 9:1), and deportation into exile (4:2; 5:27; 6:7; 7:17; 9:9). The book in many ways delegitimizes the military pretenses of the nation.[29] Israel's armies will be no match for the enemy, which will be the instrument of judgment of the LORD of Hosts, and they will be helpless before the onslaught (2:14-16; 3:11; 6:13-14).

On the other hand, there is the internal violence of oppression. The prophet uses striking terminology to describe the lack of compassion exhibited toward the poor: they are bought and sold as commodities because of their debts (2:6; 8:6); their heads are trampled in the dust (2:7); they are crushed (4:1); and they are treaded upon and despised (5:10-11). Those in power hoard violence like so much stock in a warehouse (3:10). In a striking reversal, the book of Amos closes with a vision of a peaceful reconstruction after the war (9:11-15). In that day all will participate in the extraordinary abundance; the violence from without and within will be no more. The violence of the present, however, finds its roots in the lack of justice. The violence from without comes as Yahweh's chastisement for Israel's injustice; the internal violence is that of the injustice committed at the expense of the defenseless. Neither justice nor injustice occurs in a vacuum. Humans are the recipients of each—either for their well-being or for their misery. There can be no political peace, nor a peaceable people, without justice, both an external justice evidenced in legal arrangements and an internal one in the community's soul.

Two more observations will conclude our investigation of the virtue of justice in Amos. First, we had said earlier that for justice to flourish there must be the remembrance of God's gracious acts on one's behalf in the past. These memories should become a strong motivation for acting justly toward others. In Yahweh's opening indictment of Israel he does remind them of his miraculous deeds of liberation (2:9-10) and how he raised up models of moral rectitude (the Nazarites) and spokespersons (prophets) to be his representatives (2:11). But Israel tried to compromise the Nazarites' vows and to silence those who were to speak for God (2:12). The nation has forgotten its roots, and this sinful loss of those redemptive traditions led Yahweh to turn those memories on their head. The election of Israel now is the very reason for singling them out for judgment (3:2). The Exodus is described as a paradigm of Yahweh's involvement with other nations and not as solely Israel's special experience (9:7). In addition, Yahweh reminds them not of blessings but of multiple disasters, and the five-fold refrain "but you have not returned to me" confirms the people's obstinate rebellion (4:6-11). Memory's potential for justice is no more. Memory has now become a dangerous tool in God's hands for proclaiming the guilt of his people and for carrying out his own justice. Israel must now drink the cup of wormwood to its dregs.

Second, the demand for justice should be accompanied by righteous indignation. What we find in the book's descriptions is anything but this emotion toward the reigning injustice in the land. Wealthy women call for wine with complete disregard for the cries of the oppressed (4:1); the celebrants of the *marzeaḥ* feast ignore the suffering (the "ruin") of those without the means to satiate themselves (6:3-6);[30] the national leadership is defiant in its support of Israel's corrupt regime (6:13; 7:10-13); and the nation as a whole cannot envision anything but victory from the hand of God (5:18-20; 9:10). It is clear that Israel does not and cannot possess the virtue of justice.

Yahweh, the supreme exemplar. The person of Yahweh is the very focal point of the book of Amos, a theological fact that many scholars argue is substantiated by literary means. They suggest that the entire book is a chiasm, whose center point is found at 5:8, "the LORD is his name." The primacy of

Yahweh in the prophet's message is evident too by the three doxologies (4:13; 5:8-9; 9:5-6) and the repetition and combinations of the various titles for God throughout the book. What all of this communicates is the incomparable power of Yahweh, his sovereignty over the nations of the earth, and his particular involvement in the social life and history of his people Israel. He is revealed as a God who is uncompromisingly just and who demands the highest standards of justice within Israel (as well as the other nations). He exercises his might to judge injustice at every level.

Earlier we stated that Yahweh is Israel's good (5:14-15 with 5:4-6). He is the "good" in that he is in some sense the epitome of the virtues. For the reader, he alone can serve as the most excellent moral exemplar. The person of Amos is not fully developed. He is mentioned only in the superscription (1:1) and in an enigmatic reference to his occupation when he assumed his prophet's mantle (7:14-15; perhaps also at 3:7-8); there is simply not enough biographical information at hand to propose him as a model to emulate (in contrast to other prophets, such as Jeremiah).[31] The other possible candidates for exemplars, the Nazarites and the prophets, are discarded by the people themselves and remain invisible to the reader (2:11-12).[32] Of course, the leadership—whether the king, priests, elders, military heads, and merchants—are disqualified by their sins and complicity in the injustices. Only Yahweh remains. Of course, as deity, he is not ultimately imitatible in any comprehensive sense, but the text explains that he has exemplified mercy to the nation with his own acts of grace, stipulated how they are to live with his covenant laws, sent them other kinds of models of behavior and faith, warned them of the consequences of continuing in the ways of their social construction of reality and of their individual lifestyles, and briefly painted for them what a life of plenty and peace in his presence might look like. He truly is the source and paragon of their moral good.[33]

The conviction that Yahweh is Israel's good puts the prophet's diatribes against the cult in a different light. It helps us understand why Yahweh cannot separate ethics from worship (5:21-25). To ignore that dimension of his person in the cult is to misconstrue his very essence. No amount of activity, no quantity of fine sacrifices, and no quality of song can bring the community closer to God if there is no call for profound and continuous justice in everyday affairs.

The extent of the failure of Israel's worship is also emphasized in Yahweh's mocking of the priestly call to worship at the historic sanctuaries in 4:4-5: "Go to Bethel and sin; go to Gilgal and sin yet more." What follows these words is a list of celebratory activities, but no offerings for sin are mentioned. But how can Israel be thanking Yahweh for his blessings, when what he has sent is a stream of disasters to bring them to repentance (4:6-11)! The clue lies in 4:5b: "For this is what you love to do." This honest appraisal of Israel's worship exposes its refusal truly to seek Yahweh, with all of the socio-ethical implications that such a quest would entail, and explains the resulting blindness as to the actual condition of the nation. Yahweh's call for a face-to-face meeting now turns out to be not a setting of joyous fellowship but rather an announcement of death in judgment (4:12-5:3; cf. 3:3-6, 12). They have deluded themselves into believing that he is a God of national blessing and that his coming would bring victory and benefits for Israel, but his coming will be a day of darkness and mourning (5:14-20). A religious system that sees the temple as the sanctuary of Israel's monarchy, as the symbol of the divine endorsement of Jeroboam and his policies, will see the end of the royal dynasty and the tortuous exile of its chief religious functionary (7:9-17). Self-deception has brought on self-destruction.

The profound and widespread lack of a proper understanding of God is hinted at in another way as well in several passages that could be allusions to some sort of syncretistic practices. Is the "house of their god(s)" in 2:8 a reference to a sanctuary of Yahweh or of other deities? If it is a reference to Yahweh, then the activity described there would be a perversion of his ideals. An allusion to the adoration of astral deities may appear in 5:26. Also, the *marzeaḥ* feast of 6:3-6 apparently was in part a religious ceremony involving the veneration of the dead, and 8:14 refers either to local Yahweh cults, each of which would have had its own peculiar conceptions of him, or to worship and pilgrimage centers of other gods.

It comes as no surprise then to read that Yahweh has singled out Israel's most important sanctuary at Bethel for special destruction (3:14; 9:1). It cannot stand as a symbol of national security and a center for celebration; it will come down because the Yahweh worshipped there is a creation of the human imagination. That god is a god without justice, a deity without scruples, a Yahweh of national glory and the protector of the status quo. The Yahweh of the prophet, the true God, must destroy this mockery; he must tear down this destructive religious system, beginning with that temple that justifies the society's oppressive structures in his name. Is it any wonder that the beatific vision of the closing verses of the book, which foretells national reconstruction, does not mention the rebuilding of the temple at Bethel (9:11-15)? Is the reader to be shocked that the lion roars from Zion, that other sanctuary in Jerusalem, the city of David (1:1; 9:11a)? Yahweh, Israel's good, demands justice. He will not be mocked nor manipulated. Without ethics, without the virtues, there can be no acceptable worship—or a viable social life.

CONCLUSION

The socio-economic and political cauldron that is Latin America drove me to recognize that social ethics must be an integral part of the Christian faith and the worship of God. Theological currents there pointed me to the OT prophets. I quickly learned that the prophetic literature can serve to provide a lens for seeing our context and ourselves truly and truthfully. Once we do allow the prophets a hearing, their invectives against oppressive social structures can begin to shape our ethical perspectives. Their message is a complex one, however, and its contribution to ethics is multifaceted. I have tried to argue that one dimension that deserves careful attention is the concern for the moral character of Israel. The prophetic scrutiny and condemnation of the lack of virtues in that ancient people of God stands as a challenge across the ages to those of us who claim to follow Yahweh today. He said through another prophet, who years later was witnessing the downfall of Judah:

> "He did what was right and just, so all went well with him.
> He defended the cause of the poor and needy, and so all went well. Is that not what it means to know me?" declares the LORD. (Jer 22:15b-16)

May we seek the virtues among the prophets and in so doing find our God in a new and fresh way.

NOTES

1. In this description of Liberation Theology I use verbs in the past tense. Although for a host of reasons it no longer has the profile it once did (especially from the early 1970s to the mid-1990s), Liberation Theology's lasting influence has been to make the Latin American (both Roman Catholic and Protestant) church—even the worldwide church—more aware of the social responsibilities of the Christian faith. Interestingly, the most recent annual meeting of the American Academy of Religion and the Society of Biblical Literature (Denver, Nov. 17-20, 2001) had a session on "Liberation Theology and the Twenty-First Century: Celebrating Past, Present, and Future." The panel, which had several of the most prominent pioneers of various liberation theologies, argued that Liberation Theology was still very much a relevant perspective, even though its concerns and themes have undergone reformulation and new articulations.

2. Note, e.g., Néstor O. Míguez, "Profecía y proyecto histórico," and Rafael Ávila P., "La profecía en América Latina" in Pedro Negre Rigol et al, *Misión profética de la Iglesia* (Buenos Aires: Tierra Nueva, 1981), 69-83 and 87-103, respectively; J. Severino Croatto, "The Prophet: 'Conscientizer' of Alienated Humanity" in idem, *Exodus: A Hermeneutics of Freedom* (Maryknoll: Orbis, 1981), 39-47.

3. I say "interestingly," because this theology, which claimed to champion readings of the common people, utilized textual and hermeneutical approaches that are foreign to lay people, especially poor lay people in Latin America who may hardly be able to read! Of course, something must be said for academic scholars putting their expertise at the service of the poor.

4. For the bibliographic data on these scholars' works, as well as more detailed surveys of their approaches and those of other authors, see M. Daniel Carroll R., *Contexts for Amos: Prophetic Poetics in Latin American Perspective* (JSOTSup, 132; Sheffield: Sheffield Academic Press, 1992), 312-319; and idem, "Liberation Theology: Latin America" in John Rogerson (ed.), *The Oxford Illustrated History of the Bible* (Oxford: Oxford University Press, 2000), 316-329.

5. It might be interesting to explore what aspects of the socio-historical and theological backgrounds and experiences of evangelicalism might explain the reasons for ignoring much of the prophetic literature, to which those of more liberal persuasions traditionally have appealed. Recently, Gordon Wenham has argued that an ethics of law is not adequate by itself and endeavors to demonstrate the contributions of a narrative approach (*Story as Torah: Reading the Old Testament Ethically* [Old Testament Studies Series; Edinburgh: T. & T. Clark, 2000]). Note especially 79-87.

6. Walter C. Kaiser, Jr., *Toward Old Testament Ethics* (Grand Rapids: Zondervan, 1983), 42.

7. Ibid., 42-78.

8. Christopher J. H. Wright, *An Eye for an Eye: The Place of Old Testament Ethics Today* (Downers Grove: InterVarsity, 1983), 88-102; *God's People in God's Land: Family, Land, and Property in the Old Testament* (Grand Rapids: Eerdmans; Exeter: Paternoster, 1990), xvii-xviii, 174-80. For the discussion of the prophets and social justice and worship, see *An Eye for an Eye*, 145-147, 206-208.

9. It is interesting to observe the disenchantment of the Left after the electoral defeat of the Sandinista government in 1990, the collapse of the former Soviet Union, and the debacle in Cuba in its aftermath. Note the insightful discussions in Jorge G. Castañeda, *La utopía desarmada: Intrigas, dilemas y promesa de la izquierda en América Latina* (Mexico: Joaquín Mortiz, 1993); José Renique, "The Latin American Left: Epitaph or New Beginning?" *Latin American Research* Review 30 (1995): 177-194. Mario Roberto Morales recently has recounted his experiences and profound disillusionment within a faction of the Guatemalan guerrilla movement in *Los que se fueron por la libre* (Mexico: Editorial Praxis, 1998). Some of the icons of the Left have also come under critical scrutiny. David Stoll recounts his surprise at uncovering the falsehoods and pretenses of the Guatemalan Mayan activist and Nobel Peace Prize winner Rigoberta Menchú in his *Rigoberta Menchú and the Story of All Poor Guatemalans* (Boulder, Colo.: Westview, 1999).

10. Oliver O'Donovan, *The Desire of the Nations: Rediscovering the Roots of Political Theology* (Cambridge: Cambridge University Press, 1996). For the OT prophets, see 62-65, 76-81, 187f. A symposium on his work was convened June 2001 in Cheltenham, England. Zondervan will publish the papers on O'Donovan's position, along with his responses, under the (tentative) title, *A Royal Priesthood: The Use of the Bible Ethically and Politically*, in the Scripture and Hermeneutics Series.

11. For Genesis and Judges, see Wenham, *Story as Torah*, 87-107. William P. Brown provides a good introduction to virtue ethics before moving on to an exposition of the biblical text itself in *Character in Crisis: A Fresh Approach to the Wisdom Literature of the Old Testament* (Grand Rapids: Eerdmans, 1996).

12. Benjamin W. Farley, *In Praise of Virtue: An Exploration of the Biblical Virtues in a Christian Context* (Grand Rapids: Eerdmans, 1995). He dedicates two paragraphs to the book of Amos (pp. 83f.).

13. Bruce C. Birch, *Let Justice Roll Down: The Old Testament, Ethics, and Christian Life* (Louisville: Westminster/John Knox, 1991). For Part One, see pp. 29-68; for the preexilic prophets, see pp. 240-279.

14. Waldemar Janzen, *Old Testament Ethics: A Paradigmatic Approach* (Louisville: Westminster/John Knox, 1994). For the explanation of his approach, see pp. 1-54; for the prophets, see pp. 154-178.

15. Another work that speaks of a prophetic vision for contemporary North American society and of the need to nurture a set of constructive virtues (such as compassion, justice, and courage), but which does not come from the pen of a biblical scholar, is Jim Wallis's *The Soul of Politics: A Practical and Prophetic Vision for Change* (New York: The New Press; Maryknoll: Orbis, 1994).

16. I stress the phrase "in very general terms." The landscape of philosophical ethics obviously is much more complex than is presented here. For instance, deontology and teleology each can be subdivided into several subcategories. These three schools are not mutually exclusive and do reflect some aspects of the others in their own view; it is more a question of emphasis. Some, for instance, would classify virtue ethics as a kind of teleology. For a detailed survey of deontology and teleology, see Ian C. M. Fairweather and James I. H. McDonald, *The Quest for Christian Ethics: An Inquiry into Ethics and Christian Ethics* (Edinburgh: The Handel Press, 1984), 3-64.

17. For this reason, this manner of reasoning is also called "consequentialism."

18. Alisdair MacIntyre, *After Virtue: A Study in Moral Theory* (2d ed.; Notre Dame: University of Notre Dame Press, 1985); *Whose Justice? Whose Rationality?* (Notre Dame: University of Notre Dame Press, 1988). MacIntytre's goal is to chronicle the historical developments that have led to the moral incoherence of modern Western societies and to champion the value of the Aristotelian moral tradition.

19. It has been difficult to find adequate English equivalents for some of Aristotle's technical Greek terms. MacIntyre gives several examples of this problem in *Whose Justice? Whose Rationality?* chs. 6-7.

20. There are more than seven virtues; these are considered by many to be the most preeminent. Aristotle's list of virtues was actually quite long. Note *The Ethics of Aristotle: The Nicomachean Ethics* (trans. J. A. K. Thomson; rev. ed. London: Penguin, 1976), 104. Aristotle also divided the virtues into two categories, the intellectual and the moral. The virtues were to be understood according to the doctrine of the mean—that is, in the negotiation of conduct and attitudes between opposite extremes (e.g., courage vs. recklessness and cowardice). Interestingly, some virtues that would be foundational to a Christian ethic do not appear in Aristotle's list (e.g., humility, charity). Cf. MacIntyre, *Whose Justice? Which Rationality?* 162f., passim.

21. Traditionally, justice has been catalogued into three basic forms: the *reciprocal justice* between individuals; *distributive justice* by which the society acts in a proper manner toward individuals; and *legal justice* to which all individuals ideally adhere. It is important to point out that the content of each of these concepts and of what is due in general will depend in large measure on the particular community and tradition under discussion.

22. Note MacIntyre's discussion in *Whose Justice? Whose Rationality?* 111f. At this juncture his discussion of "practices" becomes relevant. Ethical practices, as he understands the term, are concerned with the goods internal to activities that seek moral excellence and are not limited simply to seeking their external consequences or to complying with communal expectations.

23. James E. Gilman, *Fidelity of Heart: An Ethic of Christian Virtue* (Oxford: Oxford University Press, 2001), 112. For his discussion of justice, see pp. 102-131. For a fuller account of the role of emotions in ethical reasoning and practice, see Martha C. Nussbaum, *Upheavals of Thought: The Intelligence of Emotions* (Cambridge: Cambridge University Press, 2001).

24. Those of a virtue ethics persuasion commonly discuss the role of the biblical text in the cultivation of the moral imagination. Note especially Stephen E. Fowl and L. Gregory Jones, *Reading in Communion: Scripture & Ethics in Christian Life* (Grand Rapids: Eerdmans, 1991). For the OT, in addition to those scholars already mentioned (Wenham, Birch, Brown, Farley, and Janzen), see John Barton, *Ethics and the Old Testament* (Harrisburg, Pa.: Trinity Press International, 1998). Several of the works of Walter Brueggemann would also be appropriate to mention here, such as his recent *Texts under Negotiation: The Bible and the Postmodern Imagination* (Minneapolis: Fortress, 1993). For my own theoretical discussion regarding how to appropriate virtue ethics with its connection to narrative approaches for reading Amos, see *Contexts for Amos*, 76-91. The role of literature in shaping the moral imagination is also championed outside expressly Christian circles. See, e.g., Wayne C. Booth, *The Company We Keep: An Ethics of Fiction* (Berkeley: University of California Press, 1988); Martha C. Nussbaum, *Poetic Justice: The Literary Imagination and Public Life* (Boston: Beacon Press, 1995). Cf. MacIntyre, *Whose Justice? Which Rationality?* 382-384.

25. "LORD" is the rendering of Yahweh used by several modern translations, such as the NIV.

26. The term *ṭôb* and other related words from the root *twb* appear over 700 times in the OT. It has a variety of nuances, but here we highlight its ethical connotations. For fuller discussions, see I. Höver-Johag, "*ṭôb*" in *TDOT* 5: 296-318, and R. P. Gordon, "*ṭôb*" in *NIDOTTE* 2: 353-357.

27. Along with several other terms (such as *ḥesed*), *ṭôb* is related to the notion of covenant. Some scholars protest that Amos does not allude to a covenant relationship, because the term "covenant" (*bĕrît*) does not appear in the book. We would answer that, irrespective of the absence of the term, the repeated reference to the nation's election, the obvious echo of the covenant curses of Lev 26 and Deut 28 in 4:6-11 and elsewhere, and the citing of legal violations found in covenant legislation demonstrate the importance of the covenant to the theology and ethics of the book. Neither are we of the persuasion that the concept of covenant is necessarily late (i.e., that it was not crystallized until the eighth century or later).

28. This play on the word "good" appears in a number of texts, especially in Jeremiah. Note, e.g., Jer. 8:15; 21:10; and 44:27. It bears mentioning, too, that the OT (especially in the Psalms) teaches that Yahweh "is good," because of who he is and what he has done for his people (e.g., Ps. 106:1; 107:1; 118:1-4, 29).

29. For more details and for an attempt to contextualize this thought into modern Latin America, see M. D. Carroll R., "Reflecting on War and Utopia in the Book of Amos: The Relevance of a Literary Reading of the Prophetic Text for Central America," in M. D. Carroll R., D. J. A. Clines, and P. R. Davies (eds.), *The Bible in Human Society: Essays in Honour of John*

Rogerson (JSOTSup, 200; Sheffield: Sheffield Academic Press, 1995), 105-121; "The Prophetic Text and the Literature of Dissent in Latin America: Amos, García Márquez, and Cabrera Infante Dismantle Militarism," *BibInt* 4 (1996): 76-100; "Living between the Lines: Reading Amos 9:11-15 in Post-War Guatemala," *R & T* 6 (1999): 50-64.

30. For a helpful description of the *marzeaḥ* feast, see P. J. King, *Amos, Hosea, Micah: An Archaeological Commentary* (Philadelphia: Westminster, 1988), 137-161. Scholars debate the existence or the extent of a religious component to this feast.

31. The prophet, however, does offer intercession for his people (7:1-6), and this can serve as an exemplary activity.

32. In his formal response to this paper, Stephen Hall suggested that it might be helpful to consider the poor/righteous as moral examplars. I believe, however, that this observation is helpful only to a point. In one sense, the poor are innocent victims and are looked upon favorably by the text; on the other hand, the populace in general is condemned for participating in the cult that displeases Yahweh. In the end, no one is guiltless (except perhaps Amos, the Nazarites, and the prophets). In addition, the character of the poor is not developed as exemplars for ethical living.

33. The discussion in this paragraph naturally would lead to the broader issue of the imitation of God in moral life, a topic beyond the purview of this paper but very central to OT ethics (Cf. Wenham, *Story as Torah*, 104-107). For some, however, the character of Yahweh in the book of Amos is problematic. David J. A. Clines, for example, is uncomfortable with the picture of a deity who brings war ("Metacommentating Amos," in *Of Prophets' Visions and the Wisdom of Sages* [R.N. Whybray Festschrift], ed. H. A. McKay and D. J. A. Clines (JSOTSup, 162. Sheffield: Sheffield Academic Press, 1993), 143-160. In his response, Stephen Hall also pointed to 3:6 (Yahweh does an evil) as an observation to be taken into consideration to nuance further what is said about Yahweh in this paragraph. This observation does require that the reader recognize the complexity of the characterization of Yahweh in the book. For further treatments of this issue, see the sources in n. 29.

SCRIPTURE AND STEM CELLS: SEEKING BIBLICAL GUIDANCE WHEN THERE IS NO OBVIOUS BIBLICAL WORD

MARION L. SOARDS

> Those were still more in the wrong who in ancient times allowed that criminals, whatever kind of death they were condemned to, should be cut up alive by the doctors, so that they might see our inner parts in their natural state and thereby establish more certainty in their art.[1]
>
> In short, it is difficult to bring down divine things to our scale without their suffering loss.[2]

Until the events of September 11, 2001, few contemporary subjects had challenged the citizens of the United States to engage in significant ethical reflection as has the matter of human pluripotent cell research or, in more restricted, recognizable terms, human embryonic stem-cell research (hereafter abbreviated HES-CR; a key word here is "embryonic," indicating only stem-cell research involving human embryos). People from all walks of life have thought and commented on this controversial topic and spoken in a wide variety of ways both to advocate and to discourage (or denounce) such medical research. A quick check of the Internet during December 2001 found that there were approximately 463,000 web pages that included some form of information about stem cells. Examination of the range of opinions that people have registered finds that, in nearly every group taking up the questions associated with stem cells and their use in medical science, one can observe self-identified Christians attempting to think and to speak responsibly, indeed faithfully, about what is right and what is wrong regarding research on human embryonic stem cells.

In the mix of materials contributed to this charged conversation, one finds much thought-provoking scientific data, pertinent legal opinions, striking ethical observations, and various kinds of theological reflections. From time to time in the course of exploring the contributions to this discussion of embryonic stem-cell research, one finds biblical materials—in the form of citations, references, and allusions—offered as factors for guiding further reflection in an attempt to draw conclusions about the appropriateness or inappropriateness of these medical studies. At a glance, among the 463,000 web pages treating stem cells, approximately 13,100 pages made some mention or use of the Bible in the course of offering the information that was being communicated. With so many voices, Christians who are concerned with the teachings and the authority of Scripture are right to ask, What are we to think? and How are we to understand and use the Bible at this particular time?

THE POTENTIAL ROLES OF THE BIBLE IN ETHICAL DECISION MAKING

To begin, it is helpful to ask, *What* might be the contribution of the Bible to the consideration of this vital and controversial subject? Then, with some sense of the potential influence of the Bible for ethical reflection one may ask, *How* may we go about reasoning and reflecting in relation to Scripture? The answers to these particular questions may serve to introduce a discussion of the use of the Bible for thinking about almost any topic of contemporary interest. As an apparently generic preliminary consideration, such an introduction may seem superfluous. Yet, the practice of moving immediately to the Bible in seeking guidance, without considering exactly how the Bible may inform one's thought on contemporary issues, often produces sufficiently questionable results. So, it is necessary to ask about our assumptions and expectations of the use of the Bible for guidance in life.

What is the nature of the biblical word? Some persons attempting to make ethical decisions about controversial contemporary issues approach the Bible looking for *a commanding word.* For such people, if the Bible speaks in a clear way about the matter at hand, the biblical word is either to be accepted or rejected. Other persons, however, consult the Bible and expect it to offer *an informative word* that can contribute to the process of decision making. Still other people anticipate that the Bible only offers *an irrelevant word,* something from the past, at best of antiquarian interest, but with no real relevance or significance for the present world and today's problems. In some instances, for any or all of these kinds of persons, the Bible may prove not to speak at all, offering no word, about particular matters of current interest. Attitudes, expectations, and assumptions not only effect, but also may determine the way the Bible does or does not influence ethical decision making. Conversation between persons holding different understandings and expectations of the way the Bible may contribute to the process of ethical decision making will not get far as long as these differences go unrecognized and unaddressed. Thus, a first step in a conversation concerning the contributions of Scripture to the process of ethical reflection is to identify agreements and disagreements between the parties in the discussion regarding the significance and role of the Bible in the process. Frank recognition of agreement and disagreement about assumptions and expectations of scriptural materials is necessary both to foster understanding and to prevent further misunderstanding.

How does the Bible speak its words? Only persons with a will to listen for a biblical word will find that Scripture has importance for weighing options available in determining solutions for difficult ethical questions, since the assumption of the irrelevance of biblical materials to contemporary life renders the perspectives of Scripture useless for ethical reflection. Yet, those who are willing to attempt to think responsibly in relation to the Bible or from a biblical point of view still find themselves in pursuit of a goal that is sometimes simple, sometimes difficult, and sometimes seemingly impossible to achieve. For even assuming that one desires to hear the biblical word, one confronts the reality that when the Bible does speak to an issue of ethical importance, it may speak in a variety of ways. Listening to the word of Scripture requires careful, comprehensive, consistent attention to all pertinent biblical texts, precisely because—as honest exploration of the Bible shows—all biblical texts may not speak in the same manner or even with the same voice. A conscious awareness of *how* the Bible speaks or may speak in relation to various topics clarifies not only how the Bible itself speaks, but also how one attempting to listen to a biblical word is to hear what Scripture is saying. A brief overview of the potential range of ways the Bible may speak also shows us how one trying to hear the word of the text (or words of the texts) may be inclined to listen.

At times the Bible speaks *directly*, *indirectly*, or *not at all* about matters of ethical significance. Direct and indirect statements in Scripture invite readers to grasp and to comprehend what the biblical text articulates. In turn, when the Bible speaks either directly or indirectly, at times the sense of either kind of statement may be *plain*, with all readers in agreement about the substance of the biblical remark. With a secure understanding of the plain sense of a text, readers may accept, reject, or challenge (and then accept or reject) what the scriptural material has to say. For example, Exod 20:13 states, "You shall not kill." Interpreters uniformly understand this text to prohibit murderous homicide. Those who accept this text absolutely advocate pacifism and pledge themselves to a nonviolent manner of life in all circumstances. Yet, some persons who understand the straightforward sense of this proscription of killing argue that the commandment does not forbid acts of self-defense that may necessitate taking the life of another person. Still others, who may regard the biblical assertion as an ideal, reject the plain sense of the text for purposes of self-defense, execution of certain criminals, and necessary acts of aggression in justifiable warfare.

At other times both direct and indirect biblical statements may be *opaque*, with readers understanding the sense of the statements in different ways. Having arrived at an understanding of the biblical text that is recognized to be debatable (no matter how sure a particular reader may be that one specific understanding is correct and that others are wrong), once again the reader may accept, reject, or challenge (and then accept or reject) what he or she understands the scriptural material to say. For example, a few well-known biblical texts—including Lev 18:22; 20:13; Rom 1:26-27; 1 Cor 6:9-11; 1 Tim 1:10; Jude 7—speak in a way that seems to condemn homosexual activity. Various readers, however, understand these passages in different ways. Some readers take the statements to be clear repudiations of all homosexual activity. From such an understanding one group insists that homosexual activity is simply unethical, while another group rejects the validity of the biblical statements that disallow homosexual behavior. Other readers insist that these same texts are not referring to all homosexual behaviors, merely to abusive or exploitative sexual practices and to pederasty. Reading the texts in this fashion, these people accept the limited condemnation of inappropriate sexual activities that they understand the Bible to assert. Yet, still other persons who hold the same understanding of the biblical statements as declaring a limited condemnation of particular homosexual activity contend that the scriptural statements are simply irrelevant to contemporary cultural situations. Thus, ethical reflections done in relation to scriptural materials engage biblical statements that seem somehow to be pertinent to the reflection by working with the biblical materials in a predictable range of sensible ways. Because of these diverse ways of reading and reacting to the Bible, anyone attempting to make ethical decisions while engaging biblical materials is obliged (a) to articulate an understanding of the scriptural statement, (b) to recognize the relative degree of certainty that one may have about the basic sense of the biblical text (are there other opinions and, if so, what are they), and (c) to state how one understands that the biblical material does or does not have an impact on the process of ethical reflection.

THE LACK OF A DIRECT BIBLICAL WORD

Since it was in November 1998 that the world learned scientific researchers had successfully cultivated stem cells from human embryos in cell culture, one should not be surprised to find that the Bible has absolutely nothing to say directly about the subject of HES-CR. For some persons, the absence of an explicit biblical treatment of the topic is significant and means that anyone attempting to consider the ethical parameters and ramifications of such scientific, medical studies are necessarily required to turn to other recognized sources of authority for insights and guidance in ethical reflection and decision making. This disinterest in scriptural materials is problematic and produces questionable results, as may be demonstrated.

Ethical reasoning about HES-CR that is independent of biblical materials takes many forms. Even quite similar lines of reasoning have subtle elements and permutations, so that it is probably impossible to compile a full list of all ethical observations that have been made in this area. Nevertheless, for the purpose of simply recognizing the basic character of the non-biblical ethical deliberations that are currently available, three broad categories provide adequate descriptions. First, some ethical reflections make a primary appeal to *religious teaching or tradition* other than biblical materials in order to draw conclusions about HES-CR. Religious tradition provides the starting point and the touchstone for the ethical thinking and decision making and appears prominently in ethical statements that are issued by a number of religious groups—notably, on both sides of this issue.[3] Frequently, given the understanding of the human embryo (whether in a laboratory cell culture or in a human womb) that is derived from tradition, persons reckoning in this manner refer to the moral status of the embryo. This line of reasoning either claims that there is or is not a distinction between the identity of the human embryo (as a human or not) and the identity of other indisputably recognized humans. Persons appealing to religious tradition may claim that human embryos have either equal, less, or no moral status in comparison with other humans.[4]

Second, another segment of those attempting to do ethical reflection independent of biblical materials relies upon *reason or philosophy* for attempting to decide about the appropriateness or inappropriateness of HES-CR. Typically, distinctions are made between "possible," "potential," and "actual" humans. As one philosophically inclined bioethicist explained, "While in the dish it is a 'possible' human being, but things must be done and decisions made for it to become a 'potential' human being, where it can develop on its own."[5] In this vein, another philosophically inclined theologian remarked, "The whole idea that the embryo is a person is really a philosophical idea more than a strictly religious one. It's based on an idea that as soon as you have an individual human life you have a person."[6]

Third, another group of those entering the dialogue concerning the ethics of HES-CR approach the matter in terms of *experience*, either individual or collective. Experientially based reflections tend to recognize opinion as a key factor in ethical decision making and are likely to incline toward consideration of "rights"—those of the embryo, the donors whose contributions formed the embryo, those who might benefit from the medical treatments derived from human embryonic stem cells, and even the rights of scientists to pursue research in an unhindered manner. Such thinking lies behind the wording of a report from the Office of the Director of the National Institutes of Health: "Science and scientists need to search for the very best sources of these [stem] cells. When they are identified, regardless of their sources, researchers will use them to pursue the development of new cell therapies."[7] In turn, an article in *Christianity Today* reports that "Pro-life advocacy groups such as the National Right to Life Committee oppose the use of live human embryos in research," and observes that, in part, the resistance of such groups comes because "In the United States, embryos kept alive outside the uterus have no independent legal status . . . legal protection [for human cellular tissue] against being patented begins at 'birth,' which would be precluded for human entities kept alive outside the womb."[8]

THE CHALLENGE OF MAINTAINING A BIBLICAL FOCUS

Is it the case, however, that there is no biblical material available for reflecting on the ethical appropriateness or inappropriateness of HES-CR? One should recognize that the absence of direct biblical treatment of this subject and the explicit tendency of the majority of persons working in this area to focus on tradition, philosophy, or opinion, may combine to discourage one from asking about the possible usefulness of biblical materials. The science of HES-CR is a vast, fascinating field that awes and intrigues anyone who approaches it.[9] The prevalence of ethical arguments formulated from religious teaching, reasoned reflection, and practical experience draws one into such discussions on the basis of the terms in which the arguments are presented.[10] In the face of scientific marvels and carefully honed non-biblical ethical proposals, one may set the Bible aside in order to follow fascinating studies and to join stimulating discussions as they are in progress.

Nevertheless, before abandoning any attempt to bring Scripture to bear on the course of this conversation, one should ask whether the matter of HES-CR is as complex, ambiguous, and unfathomable as it may seem. Or, is there a precise way to consider this subject that exposes the relevance of the Bible for consideration of the ethics of HES-CR? A few lines from the physician, philosopher, cultural critic, and author, Walker Percy, help refocus the issue and create an opening that allows biblical materials to illuminate reflection on HES-

CR. In an essay entitled, "A View of Abortion, With Something to Offend Everybody," Percy makes the following remarks, which seem as pertinent to the matter of HES-CR as to the equally divisive subject of abortion:

> The current con, perpetrated by some jurists, some editorial writers, and some doctors, is that since there is no agreement about the beginning of human life, it is therefore a private religious or philosophical decision and therefore the state and the courts can do nothing about it. This is a con. I will not presume to speculate who is conning whom and for what purpose. But I do submit that religion, philosophy, and private opinion have nothing to do with this issue. I further submit that it is a commonplace of modern biology, known to every high-school student and no doubt to you the reader as well, that the life of every individual organism, human or not, begins when the chromosomes of the sperm fuse with the chromosomes of the ovum to form a new DNA complex that thenceforth directs the ontogenesis of the organism.
>
> Such vexed subjects as the soul, God, and the nature of man are not at issue. What we are talking about and what nobody I know would deny is the clear continuum that exists in the life of every individual from the moment of fertilization of a single cell.
>
> There is a wonderful irony here. It is this: the onset of individual life is not a dogma of the Church but a fact of science . . . . Nowadays it is not some misguided ecclesiastics who are trying to suppress an embarrassing scientific fact. It is the secular juridical-journalistic establishment.
>
> Please indulge the novelist if he thinks in novelistic terms. Picture the scene. A Galileo trial in reverse. The Supreme Court is cross-examining a high-school biology teacher and admonishing him that of course it is only his personal opinion that the fertilized human ovum is an individual human life. He is enjoined not to teach his private beliefs at a public school. Like Galileo he caves in, submits, but in turning away is heard to murmur, "But it's still alive!"[11]

Percy's incisive comments state a crucial, focus-giving fact—it is alive. With this simple fact in mind, one may look beyond the lack of explicit biblical materials dealing with the issue of HES-CR to see whether and how the Bible may have something to contribute to the discussion of the ethics of HES-CR from the vantage point that the primary embryonic material used in HES-CR is alive.

EMPLOYING BIBLICAL TEXTS IN REFLECTING ON HES-CR

The subtle differences in ways that people appeal to and use the Bible in ethical reflection seem nearly endless. Nevertheless, the great variety of uses—ranging from the responsible to the irresponsible—that people make of Scripture in deliberations concerning ethics can be summarized and described under four rubrics: *proof-texts, parallels, principles, and paradigms.*

Proof-texts. Biblical materials are used as proof-texts whenever someone employs a passage, usually in the form of a single sentence or a phrase, with nearly complete disregard for the original context and function of the biblical statement. One cites or refers to a "proving" text in the Bible in an effort to establish an argument, idea, or action, whereas the biblical material has at best a questionable relevance to the matter at hand. Although in some circles such proof-texting is persuasive, in general, such loose appeals to Scripture are beside the point; yet, proof-texts are common in ethical discussions. Consider the following examples.

A United States senator claimed to have consulted "sources of truth" and then read Gen 2:7: "And the Lord God formed man of the dust of the ground, and breathed into his nostrils the breath of life; and man became a living soul." He argued that this verse was an allegory of creation that illustrated a two-step process in God's formation of human life—first flesh, then spirit. The senator continued by identifying cells as "dust of the ground," the basic elements for life, but which without "the breath of life" cannot add up to life. The senator further quoted a NT writer: "The body without the spirit is dead" (James 2:26), apparently to validate his belief that life itself begins in a womb, not in a laboratory.

The senator's use of Scripture intended to provide both an informative and commanding word from the Bible. Nevertheless, neither his creative use of allegory in relation to the text from Genesis nor his construal of the juxtaposition of body and spirit in the letter of James as a model for his own juxtaposition of a human embryo in a lab to a human embryo in a womb shows awareness or respect for the substance and sense of the biblical texts in their own rights.

Another senator argued at a particular Senate subcommittee hearing that use of stem cells in therapies that actually resulted in the growth of tumors was an instance of medical scientists "placing the 'new wine in old skins' parable" before the public. This observation was meant to offer an informative word from the Bible, but, in fact, this mere use of a phrase from Mark 2:22 has nothing to do with Jesus' original words in reference to the nature of his own historical ministry.

As a third example, a theologian cited Matt 25:40 rather loosely to give force to her own ethical concerns about potential uses of therapies resulting from HES-CR, saying, "Whatever you do for the least of these you do for me." She intended to use this biblical phrase to provide information that would provoke awareness of the potentially inequitable employment of treatments derived from HES-CR. Her use of the biblical material in the form of a cultural cliché, however, gave only the most general support to her otherwise sensitive appeal that therapies developed from HES-CR should be made available to people without insurance.

As a fourth example, the CEO of a bio-technological operation cited the Apostle Paul in 1 Cor 13:11: "When I was a child, I spake as a child, I understood as a child, I thought as a child: But when I became a man, I put away childish things." That passage, he argued, spoke to the responsibility of the United States as a leader in biotechnology to pursue a mature and reasonable course of action as it makes advancements in HES-CR. This argument treats the biblical word as a popular maxim meant to motivate advancing the work of HES-CR. This contention falls short of being truly persuasive because it completely ignores the historical situation Paul faced and in no way takes into account that Paul's personal remarks were meant to call the Corinthian Christians to whom he wrote away from a fascination with boastful demonstrations of flamboyant spiritual practices.

By way of summary, of the four examples of proof-texting considered above, the first argument alone came close to considering that the embryos from which embryonic stem cells are derived are alive. The fantastic allegorical character of that employment of biblical material reduced the biblical text to a vehicular framework on which the senator hung his position and attempted to advance his case. The other proof-texting uses of Scripture diminished the biblical materials to clichés or maxims that were meant to underwrite points that did not derive their substance from the actual sense of the biblical material. Rather, the biblical words merely decorated the contentions of those who borrowed lines from the Bible in making their cases.

Parallels. Biblical materials are used as parallels whenever someone employs a passage, usually in the form of a sentence or a story, as an analogy to a similar situation that exists in a context other than that of the original biblical text. In such usage, the biblical text is analyzed in its own right and, then, the substance of the biblical material is applied to the issue being considered, which is treated as an analogy through comparison to the biblical text. At times, people draw very poor analogies between biblical texts and independent issues. Remarkably, false analogies are sometimes offered and received without an apparent awareness that the parallel that is being drawn is inappropriate. Consider the following two proposed parallels that are regularly submitted as people attempt to think about HES-CR in relation to the Bible.

A text mentioned already, Exod 20:13, and a matching declaration, Deut 5:17, both of which read "You shall not kill [or, murder]," are both regularly cited as commanding parallels that bluntly disapprove of the destruction of human embryos for the purposes of HES-CR. Yet, one should note that contemporary translations consistently render these verses of Scripture with the word "murder," not with the word "kill." Careful philological work demonstrates that "murder" is correct and that the more general prohibition communicated through the use of "kill" is inaccurate. In turn, the Bible does not declare explicitly that destruction of embryos is murder. Since the question at the heart of the debates about the ethics of HES-CR is whether or not destruction of embryos is murder, citing these texts as commanding words will not add much to the discussion. No one involved in the discussion of the ethics of HES-CR is explicitly advocating the murder of embryos. Whether or not one personally believes that destruction of embryos is murderous, these particular verses of the Bible will not function effectively in an open process of ethical decision making regarding HES-CR.

Another passage frequently brought into the discussion in order to provide instructive information about the status of human embryos or fetuses occurs in Exod 21:22. There, the text states the penalty for causing the loss of a fetus by provoking a miscarriage: "When people who are fighting injure a pregnant woman so that there is a miscarriage, and yet no further harm follows, the one responsible shall be fined what the woman's husband demands, paying as much as the judges determine."

Particularly in debates about abortion, advocates of "pro-choice" cite this passage to argue that the fetus is not accorded the full status of a human, as one sees in the setting of the penalty for the loss. The biblical text, however, says nothing about intentional abortion. In turn, the attempt to use this text as a parallel in considering the ethics of HES-CR is doubly problematic. Embryos used in HES-CR are neither destroyed as a result of a fight, nor were they ever *in utero*. The inexactness of the comparison between the situation described in the Bible and the situation faced in relation to HES-CR makes this text a dubious parallel for deriving insights for ethical reflection on HES-CR.

These two examples of biblical materials frequently presented as parallels for considering the ethics of HES-CR provide neither a commanding nor an informative word that helps to resolve the controversy of destroying embryos in scientific medical work. The biblical texts do deal with the issues of life and the loss of life, but not in a genuinely parallel fashion to the contemporary issues associated with the practices of HES-CR.

Principles. Biblical texts are used to provide principles whenever someone derives a directive or standard from a passage in order to make ethical decisions in relation to particular situations or general practices. One who uses Scripture as a source of principles may either turn from the situation to the Scripture or from the Scripture to the situation. In the encounter with the biblical materials, however, one who derives principles from Scripture recognizes and articulates an objective standard, which has substance and validity in its own right, independent of both the biblical materials from which it derived and the situation (or situations) to which one applies the principle. One may develop biblically based principles either from single sentences or phrases in the Bible or from the general thrust of a larger passage. Because of their nature, such biblical principles almost never function to provide a commanding word; rather, they inform people of a criterion or benchmark in relation to which one may think or form judgments. The appropriateness, adequacy, and authority of principles from the Bible for assessing the ethics of HES-CR are matters that require consideration before the principles can be used effectively in guiding ethical decision making. Among the standards suggested for assessing the ethics of HES-CR, the following five principles merit recognition.

First, citing Gen 1-2, some persons recognize the principle "God created all." This biblical insight serves to inform both those advocating and those opposing HES-CR. Promoters of HES-CR use this principle to argue that the knowledge that exists and that becomes available through scientific medical studies is God's. Humanity discovers and appropriates such knowledge because God has made it available. This interpretation of the stated principle views HES-CR as pursuit of that which God offers humanity. Opponents of HES-CR argue that the life present in embryos, both in laboratories and in wombs, is God's creation and is to be treated with reverence. Thus, the option to destroy human embryos for medical research is not the prerogative of humanity. These different uses of the same principle show that the principle is so general as to provide no unambiguous guidance for reflection on the ethics of HES-CR.

Second, opponents of HES-CR refer to Gen 1:26-27 as the basis of the principle, "All persons are in the image of God and God does not discriminate between humans." In this argument, God's recognition of the identity of all humanity forms the basis of human dignity. In turn, by applying the principle that all humans are in God's image to all stages of life, from the moment of conception to birth and beyond, these opponents interpret the destruction of embryos as an assault against humans whom God recognizes as having a status equal to all other humans.

Obviously, this use of a biblical principle begs the question by arguing in a circular fashion. The argument simply assumes and never demonstrates from the Scripture that is cited that God regards embryos as fully human. A primary point of contention in all debate concerning the ethics of HES-CR is whether or not embryos have the status of a human, and this principle does not provide unambiguous evidence for answering that divisive question.

Third, from a wide range of biblical texts, opponents of HES-CR observe that God is often depicted in Scripture as being involved with the basic creation and development of unborn human life in the womb. God knows, cares for, and has definite purpose for particular persons before their conception and birth, even as God knows, looks after, and directs persons after they are born. Among the passages cited as demonstrating this understanding of God's recognition and connection to unformed, unborn life are Judg 13:3-5; Job 3:3; and Job 10:8-12, the latter of which reads:

> Your hands fashioned and made me;
> and now you turn and destroy me.
> Remember that you fashioned me like clay;
> and will you turn me to dust again?
> Did you not pour me out like milk
> and curdle me like cheese?
> You clothed me with skin and flesh,
> and knit me together with bones and sinews.
> You have granted me life and steadfast love,
> and your care has preserved my spirit—

Also significant is Ps 51:5 and Ps 139:13-16, the latter of which reads:

> For it was you who formed my inward parts;
> you knit me together in my mother's womb.
> I praise you, for I am fearfully and wonderfully made.
> Wonderful are your works;
> that I know very well.
> My frame was not hidden from you,
> when I was being made in secret,
> intricately woven in the depths of the earth.
> Your eyes beheld my unformed substance.
> In your book were written
> all the days that were formed for me,
> when none of them as yet existed—

Other passages with such thoughts include Isa 44:2, 21, 24; 49:1; Jer 1:5; and Gal 1:15-16, the latter of which reads:

> But when the one who set me apart before my birth (literally, "even from my mother's womb") and called me through his grace was pleased to reveal his son to me, in order that I might proclaim him among the nations, I did not immediately consult with flesh and blood. . . .

Those who cite these passages argue that God recognizes continuity in the identity of persons from prior to their conception, through their time in the womb, and into the course of their post-birth existence. God's recognition of continuity in human identity indicates the continuity of life itself—which is God's own creation—and demonstrates the human status of the human embryo. Moreover, since only God's own mysterious power creates life, it matters little whether an embryo begins life in a laboratory or in the womb.[12]

The application of this third principle to the subject of HES-CR merits serious consideration. Nevertheless, these passages do not provide a simple resolution to the controversy of HES-CR. All of these biblical passages speak poetically, often in the form of metaphors. These artful religious assertions cannot simply be pressed into literal scientific declarations, because all these texts are more properly affirmations of God's sovereignty and providence than statements about biology. None of these reflective and insightful passages speaks directly to the questions raised by HES-CR, although all of these texts provide crucial information as they express bedrock convictions about God and the origins and preservation of human life in relation to God.

Fourth, opponents of HES-CR cite many biblical texts stating God's special concern and care for those who are weak and vulnerable: e.g., widows, orphans, the poor, and those who suffer physically from illness or oppression. Passages that express God's interest in those who are especially defenseless are too numerous to list. Psalm 113:5-9, however, illustrates this principle well as it provides a poignant example of the biblical understanding of God's concern for those who are vulnerable:

> Who is like the Lord our God, who is seated on high,
> who looks far down on the heavens and the earth?
> He raises the poor from the dust, and lifts the needy from the ash heap,
> to make them sit with princes, with the princes of the people.
> He gives the barren woman a home, making her the joyous
> mother of children.
> Praise the Lord!

Opponents of HES-CR argue that since embryos are completely vulnerable, embryos are to be included among those for whom God has special concern. Thus, God's care and the responsibility of those already born to care for the unborn are taken as principles to inform ethical assessments of HES-CR. Nevertheless, the poetic quality of the biblical materials and the absence of an explicit passage dealing with human embryos, especially those in laboratory conditions, raise questions about the applicability of principles derived from biblical texts expressing God's concern for those who are defenseless to consideration of the ethics of HES-CR.

Fifth, advocates of HES-CR maintain that the good to be achieved as results of medical advances made through this scientific work warrant the destruction of embryos in laboratory conditions. Yet, opponents of HES-CR attempt to refute that claim by observing that Scripture informs its readers that God is not a pragmatist. In support of this argument those objecting to HES-CR cite Matt 7:21-23, a passage in which Jesus indicates that all those who act to do good things in his name are not necessarily his true disciples:

> Not everyone who says to me, "Lord, Lord," will enter the kingdom of heaven, but the one doing the will of my Father who is in heaven. Many will say to me on that day, "Lord, Lord, did we not prophesy in your name, and in your name did we not cast out demons, and in your name did we not do many miracles?" And, then, I will confess to them, "I never knew you; depart from me you who create lawlessness."

From this text, opponents of HES-CR develop this principle: Good deeds, when done outside a personal relationship to God (or Christ), are apt to be nothing more than well-intended acts of lawlessness that actually run contrary to God's desires.

Nevertheless, the surprising story line in this biblical text should warn even those who disapprove of HES-CR of the danger of applying the principle derived from this text to anyone other than oneself. The irony in the text is that those who said, "Lord, Lord" were not only wrong, but also unaware of the error of their ways. One might argue that those claiming that the good results of HES-CR justify the destruction of embryos are those who are well-intended workers of lawlessness, but the story is equally applicable to those who strive to end the destruction of embryos for HES-CR. The startling outcome of the biblical text should cause all hearers of Jesus' story to ask, Am I acting in presumptuous ignorance? Anyone assuming that actions done in God's name are a guarantee of divine approval, whether those actions promote or decry HES-CR, is liable to the critique at the heart of this biblical text. Nothing in the biblical material itself guarantees that the warning inherent in the story is applicable only to those advocating HES-CR. Using this particular biblical text to find comfort for oneself or to condemn those with whom one disagrees may indicate that one has not listened with sufficient care to the story that Jesus told.

Many additional texts offer statements that are interpreted as providing principles for reflection on the nature of human life and the ethics of HES-CR. Such texts include: "Do not fear those who kill the body but cannot kill the soul" (Matt 10:28); and "He who loves his life loses it, and he who hates his own life in this world will keep it for eternal life" (John 12:25). The use of these texts in the process of ethical reflection on HES-CR can be informative, but one should note that both those for and against HES-CR consistently use the same verses to argue their positions. The ambiguous relevance of principles derived from such texts means that these passages of Scripture may stimulate conversation, but there is no single norm in the principles that settles the conflict regarding HES-CR.

More than proof-texts and parallels, principles formed and articulated from the perspectives of Scripture can provide insight and guidance for serious ethical reflection. Examination of the five principles presented above shows that those seeking to identify principles in biblical texts for guiding ethical decision making often find suggestive standards in Scripture for thinking about complex situations in life. Biblical principles may, when they are actually relatable to specific ethical controversies, be capable of providing valuable information for decision making. Yet, the significance of biblical principles for ethical reflection on particular issues is always a matter for careful consideration, since many principles can be used to bolster both sides in an ethical debate.

Paradigms. Biblical texts that yield examples or patterns and that may give ethical guidance by being compared to life situations are usually identified as paradigms. Paradigms are different from parallels and principles, but there are similarities between these types of scriptural materials. Some biblical texts give guidance by making statements about particular situations that may be understood as parallels to similar situations. Similarly, paradigmatic passages portray complex situations in which decisions are made that may provide guidance for ethical decision making. Some biblical texts make points that may be summarized as principles drawn from Scripture. Similarly, paradigmatic passages of Scripture present pictures, most often in the form of stories, that can serve as examples or patterns for thinking about ethical issues. Two examples of paradigms that are used in the course of conversations about HES-CR demonstrate the range of possibilities in this area.

First, one supporter of HES-CR focused on Matt 25:14-30, a passage known as the Parable of the Talents. In this story a master gives talents to his servants and then goes away. He returns to see what use the servants made of the talents in his absence. One servant in particular buried the talent and did nothing with what he had been given. The master sharply scolded and condemned this servant. Using this parable, first in a paradigmatic fashion, this particular advocate of HES-CR argued that current medical science had been given a talent in embryonic stem cells. His point obviously was that this grant-in-trust should be used profitably. Yet, he moved beyond the use of the parable as a paradigm to advance his contention as far as possible by reducing the parable to an allegory. The medical community, he argued, had received "two talents of gold"—one is a cell that "can form any cell tissue in the body" and the other is the scientific ability "to return a cell back in time with a tiny time machine of nuclear transfer to make these cells identical to a patient."

The attempt to derive inspiration from the parable for pursuing HES-CR further, treating the parable as a paradigm of responsible use of resources, is problematic because of the non-specific character of the paradigmatic point. An admonition to employ resources responsibly might motivate those seeking to preserve embryos as well as those inclined toward destroying them for research. Such general paradigmatic reasoning does nothing to address the basic controversy of HES-CR. In turn, the further allegorizing of the parable trivializes the entire effort by imposing questionable elements onto the framework of the parable. The effort at allegory places a burden of credibility on the paradigm taken from the parable, so that the entire argument collapses on itself.

Second, several participants in the discussion of the ethics of HES-CR make reference to "The Parable of the Good Samaritan" found in Luke 10:29-37. The biblical paradigm is drawn through several observations. The Samaritan shows that the valuing of life means taking risks and making personal sacrifices in order to alleviate suffering. In the parable the Samaritan broke the historical taboo that separated Jewish and Samaritan people from each other by crossing established ethnic barriers to show mercy to a Jew who was the victim of violence and neglect. This daring show of mercy defied cultural sensibilities to do unprecedented good for one who suffered severely. From these lines of thought some persons advocate HES-CR, arguing that the example of the Samaritan challenges persons to defy cultural norms, to act boldly, to make sacrifices, all for the sake of doing good for another person. This presentation of the paradigm of the Good Samaritan informs advocates of HES-CR of the challenge they face to advance the science of medicine in spite of difficulties and resistance.

On the other side of this debate, however, one might read this biblical story in a very different way. Jesus told this story in reply to lawyer (an authority on the Jewish law) who asked Jesus, "Who is my neighbor?" This question sought to justify the hesitance of the Jewish lawyer to minister to anyone outside his own ethnic group. Jesus' story challenged the lawyer to rethink his attitude by recognizing that the Samaritan was a neighbor to a Jew, and in the same way the Jewish lawyer was to recognize those outside his own kind as neighbors to whom he was to be a neighbor. From this perspective on the parable, it is possible to observe that "to define the [embryo in a laboratory] as a nonperson is to narrow the scope of moral concern, whereas Jesus calls upon us to widen it by showing mercy and actively intervening on behalf of the helpless."[13]

The challenge to become like the Samaritan may strike people in diverse ways and motivate them to remarkably different courses of action. As we have seen in relation to biblical parallels and principles, it is possible for persons on both sides of the controversy related to HES-CR to find a message in biblical materials that will encourage—if not endorse—their efforts. The different paradigmatic understandings of the grand character of this particular parable illustrate the possibility of different uses of this and other biblical paradigms in ethical reflection. But, the common ability of persons with varying points of view to use this story means that all persons concerned with the ethics of HES-CR may engage one another in serious conversation concerning their common concerns while trying to take the guidance of the Bible seriously by focusing on a common Scripture. Thus, the paradigm becomes the arena of an ethical discussion that is shaped and guided by the elements of the biblical text.

Because of the considerable and complex character of the models that are communicated through paradigms, biblical texts of this kind have a great capacity to inspire, inform, and guide efforts to make ethical decisions concerning HES-CR. Nevertheless, even texts that offer paradigms for ethical reflection are open to poor interpretation and trivialization. As is always the case with biblical materials, the best use of Scripture in ethical reflection comes as persons who wish to engage the Bible in ethical deliberation pay attention to both the plain sense of the texts and the place of the texts in their original biblical contexts. Yet, the advantage for persons with different ethical sensibilities taking a common text as the basis for conversation is that in the midst of their differences, the partners in the conversation often find that the biblical text provides a unified focus that fosters further unity in ethical decision making.

SOME FINAL THOUGHTS

What becomes evident through this look at the ways people understand the Bible to speak and how those listening to the biblical texts try to employ the biblical materials in ethical decision making is this: People do not always agree on the nature of the biblical word. For some persons the Bible offers information, while for others it issues commands. Recognizing similarities and dissimilarities in assumptions about the character of biblical material is an important first step toward understanding in a discussion of ethics. In turn, the way(s) that people bring biblical texts to bear on ethical issues may differ. The Bible becomes a source of proof-texts, parallels, principles, and paradigms. Not all of these uses are equally valuable. Yet, even when there is merit to the way that people use particular texts, often persons on both sides of an issue will use the same text in the same basic way, but to completely different ends. People on both sides of a debated ethical issue may take the same biblical material to provide parallels, principles, or paradigms for their ethical decisions. Different understandings of the same texts can inform the same kind of use of the texts—as parallels, principles, or paradigms—in shaping very different solutions to ethical problems. Still, the very use of common texts for ethical reflection by participants on both sides of a discussion can provide a uniting focus for working toward an ethical decision on a controversial issue. The significance of this advantage should not be underestimated, although one must ask whether there is a way beyond the use of similar or the same texts in similar or the same ways to arrive at different conclusions concerning ethical issues.

While there are clear benefits to at least three of the uses of biblical materials that we examined (parallels, principles, and paradigms), each of these ways of employing Scripture for ethical reflection has the liability of drawing on individual passages and not on the canon of Scriptures at once. Thus, what may be needed is to inform ethical reflection in relation to the Bible in a more comprehensive way than is possible from a single parallel, principle, or paradigm—or, even from an extensive set of such treatments of biblical texts. What I would suggest is that one needs to engage the panorama of the Bible, to become sufficiently steeped in the perspectives of Scripture, that one emerges from the study of Scripture not only with parallels, principles, and paradigms, but also with a comprehensive, integrated worldview. I would suggest further that within the framework of such a biblically inspired worldview, those wrestling with vexing ethical issues may employ particular biblical texts as parallels, principles, or paradigms in an even more effective manner than persons using biblical texts independently from the larger canon of Scriptures. This is because the matter of congruence between a biblically formed worldview and the ethical significance understood to derive from appropriate scriptural materials provides a system of checks and balances in order to critique the application and adequacy of particular biblical passages for guiding ethical decision making. In this way, the interpretation of biblical texts as parallels, principles, and paradigms finds confirmation when the particular interpretation of a text or texts is consistent with the biblically formed worldview. Such harmony between the understanding of particular texts and the worldview that is constructed in conversation with the entire canon of biblical writings gives force to the interpretation and use of the specific text or texts in ethical reasoning. Thus, the matter of HES-CR can be viewed in the context of a biblically inspired understanding of reality—of God, of creation, of humanity, and of human life in relation to God and in the context of creation—and, at the same time, particularly pertinent biblical passages may be considered and employed for guiding the development of ethical reasoning.

In constructing a comprehensive biblically based worldview I think we see in the first place that God is the sovereign creator of all that exists. Life itself is God's own creation, a manifestation of God's living power that demonstrates the reality of the life of the living God. Life is God's from a biblical point of view, as vast numbers of biblical statements, poems, and stories communicate with clarity. Life is God's, and humanity lives because God endows us with this mysterious gift. Life does not have its origins in creation itself. Creation manifests God's power of life so that humanity lives as an instance of God's power. As such, life does not belong to humanity, nor does humanity hold the power of life in an absolute fashion. Rather, from a biblically informed perspective God remains forever the Lord of creation. The texts of both Testaments understand and present God as the personal creator, redeemer, and sustainer of all creation. Contemporary theological reflection that casts humanity—even divinely created, redeemed, and sustained humanity—as "partner" or "co-creator" with God finds absolutely no foundation in all of Scripture.[14]

For me, in the context of a biblically formed and informed worldview both life itself and the place of humanity in the experience of the power of life are under the authority of the living God. We humans are embodiments of life and God exhibits life all around us in the created world. Nevertheless, we do not have the God-given authority to control the reality of the power of life, although we embody life and interact with life in the course of living. Our own lives and the power of life in which we are given the privilege to participate are God's alone. Whether or not we comprehend this truth about God and life may determine how we think and live our lives. If understanding God's sovereignty and our own limited creaturely role in relation to the God of life, we are not likely to claim God's own prerogatives for ourselves. Recognizing God as the Lord of all life, especially human life, reminds us that life is not our own creation and that we are not simply free to do with life whatever we judge to be suitable.

With this broad understanding of God, of life, of ourselves, of our relationship to God, and our rightful relationship to life as God's creation, we are able to think more comprehensively about HES-CR than from the simpler perspective of a single passage of Scripture or even a set of scriptural materials. In turn, we are able to examine more critically the biblical "word" that may be spoken by a seemingly pertinent text or texts. As a fitting example, let us consider portions of Paul's second letter to the Corinthians. In that letter we find Paul writing in relation to a controversial matter that has striking similarity to the issues at the heart of the ethical questions of HES-CR, viz., the reality of the power of God in the context of human existence and humanity's right understanding and manner of relating to God's power. This letter can be studied for parallels, principles, and even a paradigm for thinking about the ethics of HES-CR, although in his own remarks, Paul presents his comprehensive understanding—clearly derived from Scripture—about God, God's power, and humanity. Paul's thorough, religious worldview provides a coherent, consistent point of reference for reflecting on our own complex situations in which particular—e.g., HES-CR—ethical problems demand careful consideration.

In Corinth some persons had come among the Christians claiming to have and to be able to employ the power of God. The impression one gets from Paul's letter is that these persons, whom Paul designated as "superapostles," claimed to possess and to control God's power. The superapostles appear to have said that God's power is present and available and that they were capable of making use of it, but there is nothing in Paul's report of their position that suggests that they understand God to be in charge of their manipulation of God's power. Paul took sharp exception to the position of the superapostles, and in order to counter their claims, he informed the Corinthians of his own understanding of the power of God.

Paul writes, "We have this treasure in earthen vessels, so that the surpassing greatness of the power will be of God and not from ourselves" (2 Cor 4:7). With this statement Paul indicates the true source of superhuman power (God) and the actual human role in the experience of that power (humans are vessels or conduits of God's power). Paul does not deny that the superapostles may have done remarkable things, but he denies that it is their legitimate privilege to manipulate God's power as they will. God's power is always God's alone, although God may make that power available to humans. God's power, however, is not simply handed over to humanity to do with that power whatever humanity deems best. Paul understands that God's power can be abused, but he insists that a proper understanding of God, God's power, and the relationship of God and humanity means that humans are called to be faithful agents of God's power, not independent miracle-workers who use God's power for their own purposes (and in the case of the superapostles, for their own self-glorification). Precisely because the power is God's, God's own purposes or intentions are the only legitimate standard for a valid critique of the human use of that power.

Paul informed his readers in Corinth that God's extraordinary power, which is experienced by humans in seemingly miraculous ways in the course of everyday life, extends from God alone and is rightfully displayed in the human context only when that power produces results that are in accordance with God's own purposes. Humanity experiences the reality of God's power in the context of human life, but faithful reception and use of God's power always recognizes that God's own will is to determine the effect of God's power at work in the world. Thus, the real question is never, Can we do these things? Rather, we ask, What is God doing? What is God directing us to do? All this means that the ethics of HES-CR are not ours to determine alone. Only God gives life. Only God is free to do with life as he pleases. Thus, the proper question is not, What is the right thing for us to do? Rather, as Christians we ask, What is God doing and what is God leading us to do?

The application of Paul's teachings in 2 Corinthians to HES-CR is instructive, though comprehending the significance of that teaching requires both careful, disciplined thought and an equally inspired imagination. Paul's understanding in 2 Corinthians and its significance for ethical reflection on HES-CR become apparent only as we bring our lives and our view of the world into an honest encounter with Paul's teachings. In such a meeting we are able to reflect on the consistency or lack of consistency of our potential conclusions and actions with the basic values about God that Paul presents in his writings.

Without an unambiguous mandate from God, humanity is never in a position to destroy human life that comes into existence solely through the power of God—whether that life takes form in a human womb or in a laboratory. God is the Lord of life and humanity is the beneficiary of God's gift of life. A large part of the problem of attempting to think ethically from a biblical point of view about HES-CR is that the issue of destroying embryos often takes place as an aftermath of the controversial, even questionable, activity of humans creating human life in a laboratory in the first place. Yet, as we inherit the reality of thousands of frozen embryos created and kept in fertility clinics around the world, no matter how convenient or economically efficient it may be to kill such simple forms of human life in order to harvest stem cells for medical procedures, God gave life to each human life-form and God alone has the authority to end human life.

The plain fact of a biblically based understanding of humanity's relationship to the reality of God's creation of life is this: We humans are not simply free to do whatever we can do or want to do. We are not even in full possession and charge of our selves, of our lives, for our lives are not our own, but God's. To reiterate an elementary biblical truth and to apply that perspective to the matter of HES-CR: God alone creates life. Humanity receives life as a gift, to live life and to deal with other human creatures under the authority of God. Humanity is not authorized by God to destroy life at will, even in pursuit of laudable causes. God gives life to human beings and God raises up dead humanity to a new life. God's will is the affirmation of life, not the taking of life. From an adequately informed biblical point of view, taking life to extend other life is contrary to God's revealed purposes in the creation and resurrection of humankind.

NOTES

1. Michel de Montaigne, "Of Evil Means Employed to a Good End," *Essays* II:23.

2. "We Should Meddle Soberly with Judging Divine Ordinances," *Essays* I:32.

3. For a statement based on religious tradition that is opposed to HES-CR, see "Address of Pope John Paul II to the President of the United States of America, H. E. George Walker Bush," Monday, July 23, 2001, available through the Web site of the Vatican at http://www.vatican.va/holy_father/john_paulii/speeches/2001/documents/hf_jp-ii_spe_20010723_president-bush_en .html. For a statement based on religious tradition that expresses cautious approval of HES-CR, see "Rooted and Grounded in Love," a paper from the 213th General Assembly (2001) of the Presbyterian Church (USA), available through the Web site of the PC(USA) at http://www.pcusa.org/ga213/business/OVT0150.htm. This latter statement comes from my own denomination and sadly demonstrates the dearth of engagement with biblical materials by contemporary Christian bodies that are attempting to reason in a religiously responsible manner regarding controversial ethical issues. Except for one passing reference to God in this 1,777 word document, which makes the dubious claim that "as people of faith we are called to be partners with God," there is no further reference to God or Scripture. Rather, readers of this denominational proclamation see that this statement "proposes approving a resolution that enunciates ethical guidelines for fetal tissue and stem cell research, building on previous General Assembly policies," with no demonstrable consideration of Scripture. The entire work finds its points of interaction and departure in ethical reasoning by consulting previous denominational statements about other, seemingly pertinent, controversial contemporary ethical issues.

For two broader, general surveys of reactions from religious organizations to the question of HES-CR, see Bill Broadway, "Faith Is a Force On Both Sides of Stem Cell Debate: Religious Communities Split Sharply On Permitting Embryonic Research," *The Washington Post*, August 4, 2001: B9, available at http://www.washingtonpost.com/wp-dyn/metro/religion/A30256-2001Aug3.html; and Gustav Niebuhr, "Religions Ponder the Stem Cell Issue," *The New York Times*, August 27, 2001, available at http://www.nytimes.com/2001/08/27/politics/27RELI.html?searchpv=nytToday.

4. For example, Suzanne Holland, "a professor of ethics at the University of Puget Sound in Tacoma, Wash.," is quoted, "I think a 3-day-old embryo is a human life, but I don't think it has the same moral status as you or me" in *The Courier-Journal*, August 11, 2001: A4. Dónal P. O'Mathúna ("Stem Cell Research and the Moral Status of Human Embryos," American Life League: Fetal Tissue Research, World Wide Web posting: http://www.all.org/issues/dpo001.htm) sketches the issue succinctly in a series of questions: "Is the embryo a person, with all the rights of other human persons? . . . On the other hand, what if embryos are not persons? . . . So what are we to think of these microscopic entities we call human embryos?"

For a succinct presentation of Reform Judaism's "traditional" and "scriptural" reasoning regarding HES-CR, see Rabbi Geoff Dennis, "Potential Healing Powers Make Stem-cell Use a Life Affirmation," *The Dallas Morning News*: Religion, Guest Column, July 28, 2001, available at http://www.dallasnews.com/religion/42957_guest28_28rel.html.

5. Carol Tauer as cited by Rick Weiss (*The Washington Post*), "Changing Conceptions of When Life Begins," in *The Courier-Journal*, July 22, 2001: D4.

6. Lisa Sowle Cahill, according to transcription, "Religion & Ethics Newsweekly: Perspectives—Religious Views on Stem Cell Research," WNET New York, week of August 24, 2001.

7. Office of the Director, "Stem Cells: A Primer, National Institutes of Health, May 2000," see "Summary" paragraphs.

8. Denyse O'Leary, "Embryo Research Contested,"*Christianity Today*, 43 (May 24, 1999): 26.

9. A lengthy report advocating HES-CR is available from the National Institutes of Health; see "Stem Cells: Scientific Progress and Future Research Directions," available at http:www.nih/gov/news/stemcell/scireport.htm. Equally weighty critiques of the NIH position that discourages HES-CR are available from Do No Harm: The Coalition of Americans for Research Ethics; see "On Human Embryos and Stem Cell Research: An Appeal for Legally and Ethically Responsible Science and Public Policy," "NIH Guidelines (Still) Mislead on Stem Cells: NIH Unaware or Indifferent to Adult Stem Cell Research Advances," "Stem Cell News," and in the series, "Stem Cell Report—Series," available http://www.stemcellresearch.org.

10. The National Bioethics Advisory Commission makes available an exemplary collection of papers, illustrating and taking into account a wide range of essentially non-biblical data for formulating ethical arguments related to HES-CR. See NBAC Publications: NBAC "Briefing Book"—reports and commissioned papers, *Ethical and Policy Issues in Research Involving Human Participants*, available at http://bioethics.gov/pubs.html. See especially John C. Fletcher, "Deliberating Incrementally on Human Pluripotential Stem Cell Research," in *Ethical and Policy Issues*, pp. E1-50.

11. Walker Percy, "A View of Abortion, with Something to Offend Everybody" in *Signposts in a Strange Land* (New York: Farrar, Straus and Giroux, 1991), 341-342.

12. For a brief, clear discussion of the matter of "continuity" in life as a principle for thinking about the nature and value of life, see Richard B. Hays, *The Moral Vision of the New Testament: Community, Cross, New Creation; A Contemporary Introduction to New Testament Ethics* (San Francisco: HarperCollins, 1996), 447-448. For a longer, eloquent presentation of this principle articulating "the Christian conception of the value of human life," see Carlo Maria Martini, "Human Life is Part of God's Life" in Umberto Eco and Cardinal Carlo Maria Martini, *Belief or Nonbelief? A Confrontation* (New York: Arcade Publishing, 1997, English Translation, 2000), 45-52.

13. This observation borrows and adapts a statement by Hays (*The Moral Vision of the New Testament*, 451) that originally applied to the use of the parable of the Good Samaritan for considering the ethics of abortion.

14. One often cited passage used to lay claim to such status for humanity is 1 Cor 3:9, which has been badly translated, "for we are God's fellow-workers" (RSV), but which actually reads, "for we are God's servants, working together [one human with another]" (NRSV, bracketed addition mine). Another passage also used to claim extensive authority and freedom for humans who are seeking to do God's work is Matt 16:19, "I will give you the keys of the kingdom of heaven, and whatever you may bind on earth will have been bound in heaven, and whatever you may loose on earth will have been loosed in heaven." Remarkably, the form of the word "you" in this verse is consistently a second person singular that relates specifically to Simon Peter alone, while the references to "binding" and "loosing" are standard metaphors for teaching with authority what is correct and incorrect. In the context of Matthew's Gospel, Jesus' affirmation of Simon Peter comes after Peter's own declaration of the true identity of Jesus ("You are the Christ, the son of the living God" [Matt 16:16]), indicating Peter's privilege and responsibility for protecting and perpetuating the truth concerning the identity and teaching of Jesus. That neither Peter nor any other disciple of Christ is offered an absolute authority in this world is manifestly clear from words spoken by the risen Jesus in the closing lines of Matthew, "To me has been given all authority in heaven and on earth" (Matt 28:18b). Jesus commissions but does not

absolutely hand over authority to the disciples as Matthew's story comes to its ending.

RESPONSE TO SOARDS

SONDRA WHEELER

In his article, Professor Soards does a fine job of sorting out all the different things we may mean when we talk about getting moral guidance from Scripture and all the different judgments which are folded into any concrete "application" of biblical text to contemporary issues. He distinguishes between topics about which the word of Scripture is direct, those about which it offers indirect guidance, and those about which it speaks no word of guidance at all. He lays out the three distinct judgments (about the meaning of the text, the certainty of our understanding, and its relevance for informing our own practice) embedded in any use of Scripture for ethics. After ruling out proof-texting (defined as uses which wholly ignore context and disregard original meaning to derive an illegitimate conclusion about an unrelated matter), he goes on to lay out in absorbing detail the variety of legitimate kinds of appeal to Scripture which are available. These range from divine command to informing framework to parallels, formal general principles, and moral paradigms. All of this is illustrated with biblical texts and with examples from public documents of attempts that have been made to use Scripture to address the contested question of human embryonic stem cell research.

Soards is careful and candid in his judgments about the ways in which these attempts and others like them fail. He begins with the acknowledgment that "the Bible has absolutely nothing to say directly about the subject of [human embryonic stem cell research]." He then goes on to review the other options, repeatedly concluding that the proffered appeals to Scripture, while serious and illuminating in some cases, cannot offer us any decisive guidance on whether this line of scientific endeavor is to be approved or condemned. Of the appeals to the various commands prohibiting murder, Soards observes, "Since the question at the heart of the debates . . . is whether or not the destruction of embryos is murder, citing these commanding words will not add much to the discussion." He provides similar critiques of efforts to draw parallels to accidental miscarriage or to adduce principles regarding the sanctity of human life as grounds for ruling out research which destroys embryos: "This use of a biblical principle begs the question by arguing in a circular fashion. The argument simply assumes and never demonstrates from the Scripture cited that God regards embryos as fully human. A primary point of contention in all debate concerning the ethics of HES-CR is whether or not embryos have the status of a human and this principle does not provide unambiguous evidence for answering that divisive question." Equally nuanced are Dr. Soards's comments about efforts to draw conclusions about HES-CR from prophetic texts about God's care for the vulnerable or from wisdom passages about God's involvement in the lives of his people while yet in the womb. These, he insists, are poetic and metaphorical speech; powerful and important as they are, they "are more properly affirmations of God's sovereignty and providence than statements about biology."

It is important to recognize the value of this basic work, mostly negative in character though it may be. Ruling out misuses of Scripture in moral argument is just as vital as identifying legitimate uses of it, and indeed the two tasks are usually intertwined. At the end of his rich discussion, Soards offers some helpful general comments, including the observation that while the use of specific biblical texts may give Christians a "unifying focus" for their conversation, what is really needed is "to become sufficiently steeped in the perspectives of Scripture . . . so that one emerges with a comprehensive, integrated worldview." He goes on to make some general assertions that he takes to be so grounded: "Both life itself and the place of humanity in the experience of the power of life are under the authority of the living God." A little later, he adds, "God's power, however, is not simply handed over to humanity to do with that power whatever humanity deems best." Near the end of the article this becomes, "The ethics of HES-CR are not ours to determine alone. Only God gives life. Only God is free to do with life as he (sic) pleases." These assertions are not likely to be much debated by Christians, echoing as they do principles already alluded to about God's sole sovereignty over life which grounds the immunity of human beings from murderous assault. But at its conclusion, the argument takes a surprising and decisive turn.

Soards finishes by declaring, "Without an unambiguous mandate from God, I do not see how humanity can ever destroy human life that comes into existence solely through the power of God." Thus, by implication, and only at the last, the impermissibility of HES-CR is asserted. But Professor Soards has done his work too well. It is by now all too clear that the question that has repeatedly been lifted up as central (whether the 5 day embryo at stake in this research is in fact a full human being) has here been leapt over as completely as it was in those efforts to resolve the matter with the prohibition of murder or God's impartial protection of the vulnerable. Anyone who knows biology knows that the entity in question is alive and is a form of human life. The matter at issue is whether this very early stage of development, one which in the natural course of things in the womb more often than not fails to implant and survive, is to be protected as a human being or not. The trouble is that the question in HES-CR is not the one that Walker Percy identifies as, "is it alive?", for this no rational being can doubt. It is, What do we owe this very early form of human life? Many would point out that the question arises long before any of the features of human existence which we normally act to protect are present. What is the moral status of a group of undifferentiated cells which might nevertheless, if development proceeds successfully, become one of us? This is a genuine and difficult question, one to which it is perfectly legitimate to reply, "We owe it the same protection as human life at any other stage." But it is essential to recognize that this is a substantive moral judgement of its own, one for which we cannot turn, as Soards himself has demonstrated so well, to any Bible text or principle or paradigm for a warrant. It must be defended in its own right and not smuggled in at the last minute as if it were entailed by general theological principles about God's sovereignty over life. I have great sympathy for Dr. Soards's normative position; I simply do not find an argument for it here.

And all of this takes on much greater significance if we back away from the currently fashionable debate about embryonic stem cell research that occupies our popular media to consider the actual context in which this issue arises and will be resolved. For the fact is, whether or not we use public funds for research which involves the disaggregation of some number of frozen embryos (the sole matter under present discussion within the government) is the least of our worries. Whatever we decide about that, the research will in any case go on with private funds. All that will happen is that there will be less public oversight if no federal funding is provided: witness the recent announcement by a private Massachusetts bio-tech firm, whose name I will decline to advertise, concerning its (truncated) cloning of a human embryo as a stem cell source.

Moreover, the public debate seems wholly to ignore the fact that the estimated 100,000 frozen embryos presently resting in cryogenic preservation vats are going to continue to exist no matter what we decide about research. The logical options are ignoring them, discarding them, using them for research, or making them available for so called prenatal adoption by women who are willing to have them implanted in hopes of a live birth. This last option has the advantage (alone among the possibilities) of clearly showing regard for their potential as human lives, but it also has a number of practical and moral problems associated with it. For one thing, the likelihood of such embryos actually coming to term if introduced into the womb is presently thought to be only about 8%. It would be hard to justify so many invasive implantation procedures on so many women with a 92% failure rate. Besides that, we have nothing like 100,000 women ready to undergo such a procedure to gestate and give birth to a genetically unrelated child. Finally, it is not entirely clear that it is good social policy so to separate genetic and social parenting.

Even if we resolved all the issues associated with these existing embryos, the present conversation does not reckon at all with the fact of how these embryos came to be, nor with how many, many more of them are presently being formed in the laboratories of the lucrative reproductive technology industry, which remains at this point almost entirely without regulation or public oversight. By the time we are finished with hand-wringing and political grandstanding about what to do with the 100,000 embryos we now have, we will be well on our way to making another 100,000. And all of this takes place against the backdrop of a fractured public consensus regarding the moral status of prenatal life in general, evident in the festering sore we call the abortion debate. In truth, it is now hardly a debate, but more like some toxic public ritual of mutual misunderstanding and mutual recrimination. But these questions will not go away.

We have, in our hurry to give potential parents what they want (and are able to pay for), already largely acceded to a set of practices that render embryos and the children that may be born of them perilously close to one more marketable commodity in a consumer economy. We have done so largely without deep reflection or public consultation, even though what is at stake in the commercialization of reproduction is nothing less than the moral meaning of parenthood. It remains to be seen whether we can muster the deep and serious public conversation, and public accountability, that might enable us to draw back from the precipice we have been edging toward for decades.

THEOLOGY FOR A WAY OF LIFE*

MIROSLAV VOLF

THE CHALLENGE OF "REAL" LIFE

"But what does that have to do with real life?" I have come to expect an occasional question like this in courses on systematic theology. I confess that I am often tempted to snap back, "If you would just abandon your vulgar notions of 'real' life and muster some intellectual curiosity you could spare us your question!" Usually, I overcome the temptation and give a little speech instead. If students complain that theology is too "theoretical," I invite them to consider Kant's argument that nothing is as practical as a good theory.[1] If they object that theologians entertain outdated and therefore irrelevant ideas, I offer them a Kierkegaardian observation that the right kind of non-contemporaneity may be more timely than today's newspaper. I conclude by explaining how ideas that seem detached from everyday concerns may in fact touch the very heart of those concerns.

And yet, when I am done with my disquisition, I have dealt with only half of the worry expressed in my student's skeptical question. We theologians sometimes do teach and write as if we have made a studied effort to avoid contact with the "impurities" of human lives. We do so partly by our choice of topics. The number of pages theologians have devoted to the question of transubstantiation—which does or does not take place during any given Sunday—would, I suspect, far exceed the number of pages we have devoted to the daily work that fills our lives Monday through Saturday. We also take flight from the concerns of the quotidian by how we treat great theological themes such

*This article was originally published in *Practicing Theology: Beliefs and Practices in Christian Life* (eds. Miroslav Volf and Dorothy C. Bass; Grand Rapids and Cambridge: Eerdmans, 2002), 245-263. Gratitude is expressed to both the author and the publisher for permission to reprint it here.

as the Trinity, Christology, and soteriology. As thinkers we rightly focus on conceptual difficulties—"How can God be one and three persons at the same time?" "How can Christ be both God and man?" "How can we owe salvation to nothing but grace and yet be free?"—but in the process we sometimes lose the larger significance of these doctrines. Moreover, as academics we are caught in the movement toward increased specialization. On the one hand, specialization seems a necessary condition for fundamental research. On the other hand, it tends to make us lose sight of the overarching subject of theology. The scholarly interests of theologians then fail to match the realities of the people in the pew and on the street.[2]

There is yet another important reason for a perceived disconnect between theology and so-called "real" life. It lies in the distinction between the theoretical and the practical sciences that goes all the way back to Aristotle and his disciples. According to this distinction, the goal of the theoretical sciences is truth, and the goal of the practical sciences is action. Aristotle considered the theoretical sciences, in which knowledge is pursued for knowledge's sake, a higher wisdom than the practical sciences, which are pursued for their usefulness.[3] It has long been debated how theology fits into this Aristotelian scheme—Thomas Aquinas, for instance, weighed in on the side of theology being a theoretical science,[4] and Duns Scotus argued that it was a practical one.[5] Obviously, if theology is a theoretical science, then it only secondarily has something to do with practices; one has to make separate inquiry into practical implications of knowledge pursued for its own sake. But if theology is a practical science, then practices are from the start included within the purview of its concerns.

Often theologians have done theology as if it were a theoretical science; that, too, has contributed to a sense that theology is unrelated to "real" life. In different ways, the essays in this volume all share the persuasion that theology is more properly described as a practical than as a theoretical science—"science" in the loose sense of critical and methodologically disciplined reflection.[6] In this concluding chapter, I will explore in more general terms how we should understand this claim. I will argue that theology is an (academic) enterprise whose object of study is God and God's relation to the world and whose purpose is not simply to deliver "knowledge," but to serve a way of life. Put slightly differently, my contention is that *at the heart of every good theology lies not simply a plausible intellectual vision but more importantly a compelling account of a way of life, and that theology is therefore best done from within the pursuit of this way of life.* I will begin with a story that revolves around a practice, and then reflect on its implications for the relation between beliefs and practices and therefore also for the relation between systematic theology (as a critical reflection on beliefs) and a way of life (as the sum of Christian practices).

Before I proceed, I should briefly indicate what I mean by "beliefs" and "practices." First, I am using the term "beliefs" in the sense of the "core Christian beliefs." In the life of individuals these are convictions implicit in the basic act of faith through which God constitutes human beings as Christians; they are the ideational side of the most basic act of faith.[7] In the life of Christian communities, core beliefs are convictions that a Christian community "must hold true in order to maintain its own identity."[8] "Beliefs," in my usage here, is equivalent to "authentic doctrines."

Second, I am using the term "practices" in the sense of cooperative and meaningful human endeavors that seek to satisfy fundamental human needs and conditions and that people do together and over time.[9] With this brief statement I could be done with describing my use of practices were it not that a relation between practices and sacraments features prominently in my text. Sacraments can be plausibly construed as practices, but I use "practices" in a narrower sense that does not include sacraments, for no other reason than to keep historically situated and cooperative activities that satisfy fundamental human needs ("practices") conceptually distinct from sacraments. The distinction is especially important to maintain in treatments of the relation between beliefs and practices, because beliefs—I am running a little ahead of myself here—relate to sacraments differently than they do to "practices." Core Christian beliefs are *by definition normatively inscribed in sacraments* but not in "practices." Hence sacraments ritually enact normative patterns for practices.

STRANGERS AND HOSTS

His name I have forgotten, but the image of him at our table is indelible. On the first Sunday of every month he would make his way from the back country to the city of Novi Sad in Yugoslavia, where my father was pastor of a small Pentecostal church. Our guest, the lone Pentecostal in his village, who was surrounded by a sea of hostile non-believers and Orthodox Christians, would come to our church for Holy Communion. After feasting at the Lord's table, he would join our family for the Sunday meal. A rough-hewn figure, both intriguing and slightly menacing, he would sit quietly, a bit hunched, at the table opposite me, a teenage boy. A moustache that put Nietzsche's to shame dominated his face.

I resented his coming, for when he entered our house my memory would always play back a sound from his previous visit. The sound was that of my mother's soup—delicious to the point that whatever preceded and followed it served only to frame its unsurpassable taste—leaping noisily across the gap between his spoon and his mouth through his moustache. And so the climax of the week's menu, as Mary Douglas calls the Sunday lunch,[10] was ruined for me. Though my parents never said anything, I could sense their unease with our visitor's manners. Yet they not only thought it important to invite him repeatedly, but also admired the robustness of his commitment despite the great adversity he suffered on account of his faith.

One could apply a hermeneutic of suspicion to my parents' practice. They wanted to impress parishioners, atone for secret guilt, make payments into a heavenly investment portfolio. In their own minds, however, they were extending the invitation to this stranger because they did not think one should hold the table of the Lord at which my father presided in the morning apart from the table of our home at whose head he was sitting at noon. I am not sure how much they *knew* about the original unity of the Eucharistic celebration and the agape meal, but they clearly *practiced* their inseparability. Had I objected—"But must we invite him every time he comes!?"—they would have responded, "As the Lord gave his body and blood for us sinners, so we ought to be ready to share not only our belongings, but also something of our very selves, with strangers." The circle of our table was opened up by the wounds of Christ, and a stranger was let in. Had I continued to protest, they would have reminded me of that grand eschatological meal whose host will be the Triune God, a meal at which people of every tribe and tongue will be feasting. I had better be ready to sit next to him at *that* meal, they would have insisted.

The relation between the ecclesial and eschatological table and the many tables to which we do or do not invite guests is a case in point of the relation between beliefs—some of them ritually enacted—and practices. The sacrament of the Lord's Supper itself is very much a summary of the whole of Christian life, at whose heart lies the self-giving of God for sinful humanity,[11] and the eschatological Feast is the sum of Christian hopes for communion between the Triune God and God's glorified people. So how do some of the most basic and sacramentally enacted Christian convictions intersect with the practice of hospitality?

BELIEF-SHAPED PRACTICES

At one level, the answer to the question of how Christian beliefs and practices intersect seems plain enough—if my parents' practice offers a window on the way beliefs relate to practices. The celebration of the Lord's Supper, and a whole range of beliefs that are embedded in it and that explain why and how it is undertaken, shaped my parents' practice of hospitality. So Christian beliefs shape

Christian practices. But how, more precisely? One can explore how beliefs shape practices from two angles—by examining the nature of Christian practices and the nature of Christian beliefs.

Let us look first at the issue from the angle of practices. Christian practices have what we may call an "as-so" structure (or correspondence structure): *as* God has received us in Christ, *so* we too are to receive our fellow human beings. True, the way in which Christ's life is exemplary has to be carefully specified. Above all, the important difference between Christ and other human beings should counter both the temptation to supplant Christ and the presumption that human beings can simply "repeat" Christ's work. But in an appropriately qualified way, in relation to the practice of hospitality as well as in relation to all other practices, we must say: "As Christ, so we."[12]

Beliefs about who Christ is and what Christ did, expressed in the form of narratives, ritual actions, or propositions, provide the norm for the Christian practice of hospitality. This practice is Christian only insofar as Christ serves as the model for its practitioners, and Christ is available as a model only through such beliefs. This is not to say that practices of non-Christians cannot be Christomorphic; they often are. But to be a Christian *is* to explicitly believe in Christ and commit oneself to follow his way of life. Thus the internal constitution of a *Christian* practice points to the story of Christ as its external norm. Hospitality as a Christian practice is suffused with particular Christian beliefs that shape it normatively. Put more generally, Christian practices are *by definition* normatively shaped by Christian beliefs.

Our guests have gone home. As we clean the dishes, we muse about whether we have been good hosts. We ask ourselves many different questions, but if we are engaged in Christian hospitality we will examine what we did in the light of the story of Christ, in the light of his words and deeds. We will, for instance, remember the following injunction from the third gospel:

> When you give a luncheon or a dinner, do not invite your friends or your brothers or your relatives or rich neighbors, in case they may invite you in return, and you would be repaid. But when you give a banquet, invite the poor, crippled, the lame, and the blind. And you will be blessed, because they cannot repay you, for you will be repaid at the resurrection of the righteous. (Luke 14:12-14)

From this we may conclude that hospitality at its best should not be part of the economy of exchange among equals or with superiors, but instead be part of an economy of donation to the destitute and weak. So to evaluate whether we were good hosts, we might ask ourselves whether we expected to get as much (or more) out of the invitation as we put in. If we did, we have missed the mark.

There is a second way in which Christian practices are unthinkable without Christian beliefs. The story of Christ, which informs the "as-so" pattern, is itself embedded in the larger story of God with Israel and the nations, and this larger story again is framed by the narratives of God's creation and final consummation. That nexus of stories draws a map of the normative space in which human beings exist as agents of Christian practices. As Charles Taylor has argued in *Sources of the Self*, such a space is essential for moral action because it is within it that "questions arise about what is good or bad, what is worth doing and what is not, what has meaning and importance for you and what is trivial and secondary."[13] Christian beliefs are indispensable for the creation of the Christian moral space in which alone engagement in Christian practices makes sense.

PRACTICE-SHAPING BELIEFS

By attending to the character of Christian practices, we have observed an intimate link between beliefs and practices. We see a similar link when we consider the nature of Christian beliefs. Shaping practices—shaping a way of life—is internal to the very nature of these beliefs.

To determine whether beliefs are essentially practice-shaping, it is particularly important to examine the nature of beliefs about God. These beliefs lie at the heart of the Christian faith, and the tradition has therefore rightly claimed that God and God's relation to the world constitute the proper "object" of theology.[14] Everything theology studies, is studied, as Wolfhart Pannenberg states in *Theology and the Philosophy of Science*, "from the point of view of its relation to God (*sub ratione Dei*)." "It is only this consideration *sub ratione Dei* which distinguishes the treatment of a wide range of topics in theology from their treatment in other disciplines which concern themselves with the same areas but from different points of view."[15] Because beliefs about God shape the whole of theology, the relation of these beliefs to practices is at the heart of the issue we are discussing.

Consider one important feature of beliefs about God. It emerges as soon as one remembers that God is not an object in the world to which human beings may or may not be related in significant ways. Rather, God is the creator, redeemer, and consummator of all that is. Human beings live in a relation of inescapable dependence on God—dependence which grounds human freedom along with all other human good and is in no way incompatible with it[16]—to which gratitude is the appropriate response. Moreover, the identity of human beings and the goal of their lives are bound up with the fact that God created them to image God and live in communion with God. The "as-so" structure, which we noted in how what

Christ did for sinful humanity relates to our practices ("As Christ, so we"), applies more generally to the relation between who God is and who human beings are and therefore how they ought to behave ("As God, so we").

This claim is *already implied* in affirmation of God's existence—which is to say, in the affirmation that a relationship between God and human beings obtains such that human beings owe their existence to God and find their fulfillment in imaging God and living in communion with God. As a consequence, whenever we speak of God, we are always involved; the import of the claims about God for human beings does not need to be brought in subsequently but is already part and parcel of the talk about God. As Gerhard Ebeling puts it in commenting on the way Luther speaks of God, "what is said of God does not have to be applied later to man . . . what is said of God is addressed to man."[17]

What bearing does this claim about the nature of Christian beliefs have on the relation between beliefs and practices? Rightly to espouse the belief that God is "the God of peace" (Romans 15:33), for instance, *is*, among other things, to commit oneself to the pursuit of peace. Similarly, the obligation to ensure that one person does not "go hungry" while "another becomes drunk" is part and parcel of believing rightly about the Lord's Supper (1 Corinthians 11:21). No doubt one can believe and fail to act accordingly; one can believe and expressly intend not to act accordingly.[18] Indeed, as the Old Testament prophets' critique of religious devotion makes manifest, one can profess a belief precisely in order not to act accordingly.[19] But such situations are clearly at odds with the inner dynamics of beliefs themselves—otherwise one could not cover one's wrongdoing with a demonstrative profession of belief. Espousing a belief puts pressure upon the one who believes to act accordingly. Put more generally, basic Christian beliefs *as beliefs* entail practical commitments. These commitments may need to be explicated so as to become clear, or they may need to be connected to specific issues in concrete situations, but they don't need to be *added* to the beliefs; they inhere in the beliefs. Christian beliefs are not simply statements about what was, is, and will be the case; they are statements about what *should* be the case and what human beings should do about that. They provide a normative vision for practices.

To sum up my argument thus far: Christian practices are such that a Christian normative vision is part and parcel of what these practices are; and Christian beliefs are such that informing Christian practices is part and parcel of what these beliefs do. Practices are essentially belief-shaped, and beliefs are essentially practice-shaping.

GRACE, BELIEFS, PRACTICES

The role of beliefs in relation to practices is not only providing a normative vision for practices; from a theological standpoint, this role of beliefs, though immensely important, is secondary. The whole Christian way of life, with all its practices, is supported and shaped by something outside that way of life—by what God has done, is doing, and will do. The Christian faith is not primarily about human doing; the gospel is not reducible to the barebones formal injunction, "Look at Christ and imitate a wholesome way of life," or "Understand God and act accordingly." The Christian faith is not primarily about human *doing* but about human *receiving*. The barebones formal injunction to which the gospel can be reduced is, "Receive yourself and your world as a new creation." More than just normatively guiding practices, Christian beliefs narrate the divine action by which human beings are constituted as agents of practices, by which they are placed into a determinate normative space, and by which they are inspired and charged to imitate God.[21]

Consider once again the Lord's Supper. Eating the bread and drinking the wine, we remember the body broken for God's enemies and the blood spilled to establish a "new covenant" with those who have broken the covenant. In that act of ritual commemoration we dramatize the central elements of a normative vision that should guide our practices. But if that were all we thought we were doing, we would be profoundly misunderstanding the Lord's Supper. Central to the celebration of the Lord's Supper is the truth that the body was broken and the blood spilled "for us" and for the "life of the world." The Lord's Supper is a sacramental representation of the gift of new life through Christ's death and resurrection—new life whose reality underlies every single properly Christian act and therefore all Christian practices. Understandings of how the gift of new life is re-presented in the Lord's Supper differ, but most agree about the primacy of the Eucharistic reference to the divine work for us, rather than our imitation of that work.

Of course, we would also be misunderstanding the Lord's Supper if we thought of it only as a sacrament of God's embrace, of which we are simply the fortunate beneficiaries. Inscribed in the very heart of God's grace is the rule that we can be its recipients only if we do not resist being made into its agents. In a precisely defined way that guards the distinction between God and human beings, human beings themselves are made participants in the divine activity and therefore are inspired, empowered, and obliged to imitate it. Which is where practices come in.[22] Christian practices may be construed as human "resonances," under a variety of circumstances, of the divine engagement with the world through which human beings are sustained and redeemed.

FIRST COME PRACTICES

My argument so far about the relation between beliefs and practices amounts to the claim that Christian beliefs do not express "pure knowledge" but are intended to guide Christian practices by situating the practitioner within the overarching narrative of God's dealings with humanity and by offering an account of his or her constitution as an agent. Seen from within that way of life, beliefs describe the constitution of agents of practices and offer normative direction for that way of life. So beliefs shape practices. But do practices contribute anything to beliefs?

One way to explore this issue is to ask the following question: Do we first accept Christian beliefs and then engage in Christian practices, or the other way around? As attested by the accounts of those who have experienced conversion through reading the Bible without having had previous contact with Christians, one can accept Christian beliefs without previously engaging in Christian practices or even observing Christian practices. A person can start engaging in Christian practices because he or she has found Christian beliefs intellectually compelling. In such cases, Christian beliefs come first and Christian practices follow.

As a rule, however, this is not how things happen. People come to believe either because they find themselves already engaged in Christian practices (say, by being raised in a Christian home) or because they are attracted to them. In most cases, Christian practices come first and Christian beliefs follow—or rather, beliefs are already entailed in practices, so that their explicit espousing becomes a matter of bringing to consciousness what is implicit in the engagement in practices themselves.

Recall my parents' example. Notwithstanding my occasional grumbling at the liberality with which my parents practiced hospitality toward people around whom I felt uneasy, I arguably have embraced the Christian faith along with its core beliefs partly because I saw it embodied in their practices. Moreover, the way they engaged in the practice of hospitality profoundly shaped the way I came to understand basic Christian beliefs (just as the way my saintly nanny treated me as a young boy helped form my image of God). People make Christian beliefs their own and understand them in particular ways partly because of the practices to which they have been introduced—in which their souls and bodies have been trained[24]—in the course of their lives. Put differently, by being attracted to and habituated in a set of practices, they have embraced the set of beliefs that sustain these practices and that are inscribed in them.

The movement from practices to beliefs is, however, not as simple as my account so far suggests. It is not at all clear that I would have *rejected* the

Christian faith had I seen a major discrepancy between my parents' beliefs and practices. What if I had overheard them say to each other the evening after we had entertained our guest, "What a brute! He will never step into our house again," and if from that day on we had invited to our table only those who "behaved"? It does not follow that I would have concluded either that the Lord's Supper was just a religious sham or that—my soul and body not having been trained in the practice of inviting strangers—the Lord's Supper does not contain an imperative to do so. Instead, I might simply have deemed my parents weak, inconsistent, or even hypocritical—and embraced the beliefs they espoused and ritually celebrated with a determination to live a more consistent life (much in the way a person might observe his or her parents' failed marriage and vow not to make a similar mistake).

On the other hand, even the excellence of my parents' Christian practices need not have led to my espousal of Christian beliefs. In fact, at one point in my life, the exact opposite happened. I rejected the faith precisely because my parents were such good practitioners and because their practices had had a claim upon my life. The dissonance between the practices of the peer group with which I identified and my parents' practices, and the clash between what I was taught at school (Marxist indoctrination!) and some basic Christian beliefs, were simply too great. In my teenage years, my parents seemed to me to be duped and dense people who were imposing on me an outdated way of life. When it comes to embracing or rejecting Christian beliefs, practices do influence beliefs, but they do so in complex and not always predictable ways.

The second way in which practices are crucial for beliefs concerns not so much the acceptance of beliefs but their *understanding*. What George Lindbeck says in *The Nature of Doctrine* about proclamation is true of all Christian beliefs: "[it] gains power and meaning insofar as it is embodied in the total gestalt of community life and action."[25] "Right (communal) doing" seems in some sense a precondition for right understanding. The obverse is also true: "wrong doing"—especially if deeply patterned and long lived—leads to twisted understanding. It would be, however, too much to claim that the wrongdoers *cannot* know rightly and that the "right-doers" *cannot* know wrongly. The connection between engaging practices and understanding beliefs is a loose one. Nonetheless, right practices well practiced *are likely* to open persons for insights into beliefs to which they would otherwise be closed.[26] Inversely, wrong practices can "suppress the truth" (Romans 1:18)—that is, have an adverse impact on which beliefs are deemed true and how beliefs that are deemed true are understood.

For theology, the hermeneutical impact of practices is crucial for the simple reason that formulation of Christian beliefs is fundamentally a hermeneutical task. So far I have spoken only of "core beliefs" or "authentic doctrines." But we always hold these core beliefs in situationally rendered forms. Such rendering is done implicitly and explicitly simply as an integral part of living a Christian life,[27] and, whether it occurs in academic or non-academic settings, is an exercise in understanding. Which is where practices come in. Engagement in practices helps open our eyes to how core beliefs are to be understood and re-formulated as Christians live in ever-changing situations.

WHAT GROUNDS WHAT?

Here is a stripped-down sketch of my argument so far: Christian beliefs normatively shape Christian practices, and engaging in practices can lead to acceptance and deeper understanding of these beliefs. The crucial issue that remains to be addressed is this: Do beliefs ground practices, or do practices ultimately ground beliefs? In one sense, this is not quite the right way to put the question. Are not beliefs—core Christian beliefs—an integral part of Christian practices? I have argued that they are. And yet we still have to inquire about the *status* of beliefs precisely as components of practices.

Contemporary academic and popular culture tends to subordinate beliefs to practices to the point of completely functionalizing beliefs. Pierre Hadot's important book *Philosophy as a Way of Life* might serve as an example. In his account, as in a qualified sense in my own, "the choice of a form of life" comes first. Philosophical discourse "gives justifications and theoretical foundations" for that choice.[28] Hadot rightly sees discourse not as an end in itself but in service of a way of life. Notice, however, how he understands the service proper to discourse. The choice of the form of life is "justified *after the fact* by a given systematic construction." Choosing the good is not a consequence of holding a set of true beliefs, but the other way around.[29]

Would Hadot's account of the relation between "the choice of the good" and "philosophical discourse" work in theology as a model for the relation between Christian beliefs and Christian practices, between theology and a way of life? That depends on how one interprets Hadot. One could take him to mean that a set of beliefs will develop from a chronologically prior choice of the good.When such a set of beliefs does develop, it will be a *true* set of beliefs, capable of adequately grounding the choice of the good. The choice of the good would chronologically precede this set of beliefs, but this set of beliefs would logically ground the choice of the good.

Such reading of Hadot's ordering of "beliefs" and "practices" would be analogous to the way in which, according to John Zizioulas, the doctrine of the

Trinity emerged: ecclesial communal practice led the church to claim that communion of three divine persons is ontologically ultimate. But what made possible the emergence of the church and its claims about the ontological ultimacy of communion was, of course, the reality of the divine communion, which can be expressed in the form of true Trinitarian beliefs.[30] Whether or not one agrees with Zizioulas's account of the emergence of the doctrine of the Trinity, the more general understanding of the relation between beliefs and practices which it instantiates is plausible.

It is unlikely, however, that giving chronological priority to a way of life and logical primacy to a set of beliefs would satisfy Hadot. He believes that the one and the same choice of the good can be "justified by extremely diverse philosophical discourses."[31] Depending on changing situations—depending on reigning plausibilities—the set of beliefs will vary, and will do so in order to be able to "justify" a given choice of the good.

Will this do as a model for the relation between Christian beliefs and practices? There are theologians who think so.[32] Whether they are right depends a great deal on how one understands theology's relation to its primary subject matter, God. Practices, I have argued earlier, are Christian insofar as they are "resonances" of God's engagement with the world. But how should we understand "God's engagement with the world"? Above all, does such talk purport to sketch—in human conceptualities and therefore in a broken way—what is truly the case and what is in accord with God's self-revelation in Christ as attested in the Scriptures?

I take it that theology is not simply reflection about how communities of faith use language about God—not "critical talk about talk about God." God, not just human talk about God, is the proper object of theology. If this is so, then Christian beliefs about God are not analogous to Hadot's philosophical discourse. No doubt, one's interest in God may be awakened and one's understanding of God will be deepened through engagement in practices. But we engage in practices for the sake of God; we don't construe a picture of God so as to justify engagement in a particular set of practices. As the highest good, God matters for God's own sake, not for the sake of a preferred way of life. Since we identify who God is through beliefs—primarily through the canonical witness to divine self-revelation—adequate beliefs about God cannot be ultimately grounded in a way of life; a way of life must be grounded in adequate beliefs about God.[33]

If Christian beliefs ultimately ground Christian practices, theology cannot limit itself to explicating the significance of "God" and of what "God has done" for a way of life, but must concern itself with the disputed truth claims about God—and *do so precisely also for the sake of a way of life*. It matters, for instance, a great deal for a way of life whether human beings are God's creatures or God a human creature, a projection of our greatest ideals or an imaginary rectifier of our own impotence. Ludwig Feuerbach, Karl Marx, and Friedrich Nietzsche rightly felt the need to offer alternative accounts of human history and of the cosmos to the one they inherited from the Christian tradition in the light of their persuasion that God is a human creation and not the other way around.

To be concerned with truth claims about God means also to be interested in how beliefs about God and God's relation to the world *fit* among themselves and with other beliefs human beings hold. The fit between Christian beliefs may be very tight (say, such that one can reduce all of them to a single complex belief) or rather loose (say, such that one can situate them in a narrative framework or a set of factually related but logically independent narrative frameworks),[34] but fit they must. If the truth of the Christian faith matters, then the way you understand the Lord's Supper must fit with your account of Christ's death, and this must fit with your doctrine of the Trinity, and all of this must fit with the way you understand the nature and predicament of human beings.

Moreover, since Christian beliefs coexist with a host of other beliefs about the world—from claims about the future of the universe to theories about the kind of work neurons do in human brains—the question of the relationship of Christian beliefs to all these other beliefs must also be posed. Theology must pursue the question of truth and must do so in conjunction with, and not in isolation from, other disciplines. In a word, because Christian beliefs relate to everyday practices as a fitted set of beliefs with a claim to express truth about God and God's relation to the world, theologians must be concerned with more than just how beliefs relate to everyday practices—and must be so concerned precisely *for the sake of* everyday practices.

THE APOSTLE PAUL, THEOLOGY, PRACTICES

The Apostle Paul was arguably the first Christian theologian and certainly the most influential of the early Christian theologians. In conclusion it may be instructive to compare briefly the model I have developed above of theology's relation to a way of life with Paul's way of theologizing. True, contemporary theologians are in some important ways unlike Paul: the risen Lord has appeared to Paul, and his writings have a canonical status to us. This makes beliefs even more critical in our theologizing than they were in Paul's. This said, Paul's and our theological tasks are arguably analogous.

There is a long history of New Testament scholars' making what I think is on the whole a mistaken distinction in Paul's writings between the "indicative" and the "imperative" sections. In this distinction, the indicative sections come first; they are doctrinal (they explicate Christian beliefs) and foundational. The imperative sections come second; they are ethical (they admonish to Christian practices) and are of secondary importance because they are grounded in beliefs. Beliefs can and should be explicated in their own right, without relation to practices; practices can be understood only in relation to beliefs. According to this picture, Paul operated with something analogous to the accepted disciplinary distinctions between "systematic theology" on the one side and ethics and "practical theology" on the other, as well as with the corresponding clear demarcation between "self-standing" beliefs and "derived" practices.

Not everything is wrong with this picture. As the momentous "therefore" in Romans 12:1 attests ("I appeal to you therefore, brothers and sisters, by the mercies of God, to present your bodies as living sacrifice"), beliefs about God and what God has done do serve for Paul to justify ways in which Christians relate among themselves and with outsiders. And yet, to let the matter rest at this is to simplify things to the point of distortion. As Troels Engberg-Pedersen has shown in *Paul and the Stoics*, the parenetic sections in Paul do not simply follow the doctrinal sections; rather, "at the most fundamental level and from one end to the other" his letters are an "exercise in parenesis." "Parenesis has two components," a doctrinal and ethical one, for it consists "in Paul's *reminding* his addressees of what *has* happened and his *appeal* to them to put it into *practice*."[35]

Significantly, the description of what has happened—what God has done and what God will do for Paul and his readers—is "tilted towards what we may call its anthropological side: towards what the 'objective' Christ event set going by God has meant to Paul and his addressees." The "tilting" is present because Paul offers what God has done "as a basis for his appeal to them [his addressees] to put it into practice." So in Paul beliefs *as beliefs* are practice-shaping. And yet, he does not consider beliefs to be justifications *after the fact* of a way of life. As Engberg-Pedersen puts it, "The 'objective' framework remains very solidly in place, of course. It is God who *has* done something in the Christ event and God and Christ who *will* do something in the future."[36]

Paul had a realistic perspective on what God has done for humanity, as Engberg-Pedersen recognizes. At the same time, he suggests that we, Paul's contemporary interpreters, reduce Paul's claims about God and God's relation to the world to "metaphysical 'constructions' whose function is to give ontological substance" to his ethical ideas.[37] Engberg-Pedersen's suggestion on how to appropriate the teaching of Paul is structurally similar to Hadot's recommendation on how to appropriate ancient spiritual exercises: he discards ancient justifying philosophical discourses and keeps the moral vision.

For Christian theology, this will not do. Such account of the status of beliefs would be deeply at odds with the nature of Christian practices themselves. For these are done precisely in response to what God has done for the life of the world, which is what Christian core beliefs seek to express. Like Paul, we should resolutely place theology in the service of practices and precisely for this reason concentrate our reflection on God, for whose sake we live a Christian way of life and therefore, as theologians, engage in explicating Christian beliefs.

Will theology so conceived have sufficiently to do with "real" life? Not nearly as much as the God for whose sake we are theologians, but more than enough, I believe, to satisfy the concerns of those who are justly troubled by theology's seeming irrelevance.

NOTES

1. Immanuel Kant, "On the Common Saying: 'This May be True in Theory, but It Does Not Apply in Practice'," in *Kant: Political Writings*, trans. H. B. Nisbet, ed. Hans Reiss, 2d edition (Cambridge/New York: Cambridge University Press, 1991), p. 61.

2. See Miroslav Volf, "Introduction: A Queen and a Beggar: Challenges and Prospects of Theology," *The Future of Theology: Essays in Honor of Jürgen Moltmann*, ed. Miroslav Volf et al. (Grand Rapids: Eerdmans, 1996), pp. ix-xviii.

3. See Aristotle, *Metaphysics*, 982a 14ff. and 993b 20-21.

4. Thomas Aquinas, *Summa Theologiae* I.1.4.

5. Duns Scotus, *Ordinatio*, prol. pars 5, qq. 1-2.

6. I am leaving aside here the question of whether or to what extent theology is a science in the same sense as other sciences. On this question, see Wolfhart Pannenberg, *Theology and the Philosophy of Science*, trans. F. McDonagh (Philadelphia: The Westminster Press, 1976), pp. 23-224; Philip Clayton, *Explanation from Physics to Theology: An Essay in Rationality and Religion* (New Haven: Yale University Press, 1989), pp. 154-167; Nancey Murphy, *Theology in the Age of Scientific Reasoning* (Ithaca: Cornell University Press, 1990), pp. 174-208; Wentzel van Huyssteen, *The Shaping of Rationality: Toward Interdisciplinarity in Theology and Science* (Grand Rapids: Eerdmans, 1999).

7. My "core beliefs" overlap in significant ways with the notion of "doctrine" that Reinhard Hütter employs in his chapter in this volume. See also Reinhard Hütter's notion of "doctrina evangelii" in *Suffering Divine Things: Theology as Church Practice*, trans. Doug Stott (Grand Rapids: Eerdmans, 2000), pp. 135-145.

8. Bruce D. Marshall, *Trinity and Truth* (Cambridge: Cambridge University Press, 2000), p. 19.

9. See Craig Dykstra and Dorothy C. Bass's definition in this volume, p. 18.

10. Mary Douglas, "Deciphering a Meal," in *Myth, Symbol, and Culture*, ed. Clifford Geertz (New York: W. W. Norton & Co., 1971), p. 67.

11. See the brief reflections on Eucharist as "ordering ritual" in Ingolf U. Dalferth, *Theology and Philosophy* (Oxford: Blackwell, 1988), pp. 222-223.

12. For an extended exemplification of the "as-so" structure of Christian practices, see Miroslav Volf, *Exclusion and Embrace: Theological Reflections on Identity, Otherness, and Reconciliation* (Nashville: Abingdon Press, 1996).

13. Charles Taylor, *Sources of the Self: The Making of the Modern Identity* (Cambridge: Harvard University Press, 1989), p. 28.

14. For different accounts of theological enterprise that are agreed on the basic idea that God is the subject of theology see, for instance, Pannenberg, *Theology and the Philosophy of Science*, and David Kelsey, *To Understand God Truly: What's Theological about a Theological School* (Louisville: Westminster/John Knox Press, 1992).

15. Pannenberg, *Theology and the Philosophy of Science*, p. 298.

16. See Karl Rahner, *Foundations of Christian Faith*, trans. W. Dych (New York: Crossroad, 1978), p. 79; Kathryn Tanner, *Jesus, Humanity, and the Trinity: A Brief Systematic Theology* (Minneapolis: Fortress Press, 2001), pp. 2-4.

17. Gerhard Ebeling, *Luther: An Introduction to His Thought*, trans. R. A. Wilson (Philadelphia: Fortress Press, 1972), p. 248. See also Gerhard Ebeling, "Cognitio Dei et hominis," *Lutherstudien*, vol. 1 (Tübingen: Mohr, 1971), pp. 221-272.

18. For an analysis of disconnects between beliefs and practices see Amy Plantinga Pauw's chapter in this volume.

19. See Miroslav Volf, *Zukunft der Arbeit—Arbeit der Zukunft. Das Marxsche Arbeitsverstaendnis und seine theologische Wertung* (Munich: Kaiser, 1988), p. 106; Hans-Joachim Kraus, *Theologische Religionskritik* (Neukirchen-Vluyn: Neukirchener Verlag, 1982), p. 251.

20. See Jürgen Moltmann, *Theology of Hope: On the Ground and the Implications of a Christian Eschatology*, trans. J. W. Leitch (London: SCM Press, 1967).

21. On the constitution of the Christian subject see Karl Barth, *Church Dogmatics* IV/1, 749.

22. In their essay for this volume, Dorothy Bass and Craig Dykstra have underscored that Christian practices are forms of participation in divine activity.

23. For a theological appropriation of the notion of "resonances," see Michael Welker, *God the Spirit*, trans. John F. Hoffmeyer (Minneapolis: Fortress Press, 1994), pp. 313ff.

24. On the socially informed body, see Pierre Bourdieu, *Outline of a Theory of Practice*, trans. R. Nice (Cambridge: Cambridge University Press, 1977), p. 124.

25. George A. Lindbeck, *The Nature of Doctrine: Religion and Theology in a Postliberal Age* (Philadelphia: Westminster, 1984), p. 36.

26. See the chapter by Dykstra and Bass, p. 17, and the chapter by Sarah Coakley, p. 78.

27. See the chapter by Kathryn Tanner, pp. 228ff.

28. Pierre Hadot, *Philosophy as a Way of Life: Spiritual Exercises from Socrates to Foucault*, ed. Arnold I. Davidson trans. Michael Chase (Oxford: Blackwell, 1995), p. 281.

29. Hadot, *Philosophy as a Way of Life*, pp. 282-283. Commenting on Stoicism and Epicureanism, Hadot notes as mistaken the view that from the theories of Chrysipus or Epicurus "would spring, as if by accident one could say, a morality. But the reverse is true. It is the abstract theories that are intended to justify the existential attitude. One could say, to express it otherwise, that every existential attitude implies a representation of the world that must necessarily be expressed in a discourse. But this discourse alone is not the philosophy, it is only an element of it, for the philosophy is first of all the existential attitude itself, accompanied by inner and outer discourses: the latter have as their role to express the representation of the world that is implied in such and such an existential attitude, and these discourses allow one at the same time to rationally justify the attitude and to communicate it to others" (quoted by Davidson in Hadot, *Philosophy as a Way of Life*, pp. 30-31).

30. John Zizioulas, *Being as Communion: Studies in Personhood and the Church* (Crestwood: St. Vladimir's Seminary Press, 1985).

31. Hadot, *Philosophy as a Way of Life*, p. 212.

32. Consider, for instance, what Marianne Sawicki does with the creedal Christian claim that Jesus Christ is risen. She justifies it pragmatically: "The hungry little ones, always with the church, are the reason why the resurrection of Jesus must be affirmed as bodily, absolutely, for Christian faith." Sawicki, *Seeing the Lord: Resurrection and Early Christian Practices* (Minneapolis: Fortress Press, 1994), p. 275.

33. The way Hadot relates the choice of a way of life and philosophical discourse is analogous to the way in which some liberation theologians relate praxis of social engagement and theological reflection. In his recent book on theological methodology, at the end of a long chapter on his own fruitful and decade-long engagement with various liberation theologies, Jürgen Moltmann asks the following critical question: "If praxis is the [ultimate] criterion of theory, what is the criterion of praxis?" *Experiences in Theology: Ways and Forms of Christian Theology*, trans. M. Kohl (Minneapolis: Fortress Press, 2000), p. 294.

34. In his forthcoming theological anthropology, David Kelsey argues powerfully for reading the Scriptures as containing three factually intertwined but logically independent narratives.

35. Troels Engberg-Pedersen, *Paul and the Stoics* (Louisville: Westminster/John Knox Press, 2000), p. 294.

36. Engberg-Pedersen, *Paul and the Stoics*, p. 295.

37. Engberg-Pedersen, *Paul and the Stoics*, p. 30.

BIBLICAL ETHICS AT THE END OF LIFE

CLARETTA DUPREE

During a former membership at a Christian church, one of our members, a teenager whom I will call Curtis, was undergoing treatment for cancer. Over a protracted period with several relapses, during which time the church body was praying and believing for his healing, Curtis and his father came to accept that he was going to die. However, our pastor said that demonstrated a lack of belief in the Scriptures on healing and insisted that prayers for complete healing continue. Curtis died, and our pastor, still insistent that we (the church body) should stand firm in our belief for healing, took Curtis's father to the morgue of the hospital so that they could speak to Curtis and command him to get up. Well, Curtis did not get up. This event raised several questions.

How can one simultaneously express faith in James 5:14-15 ("Is any one among you sick? He should call in the church elders—the spiritual guides. And they should pray over him, anointing him with oil in the Lord's name. And the prayer [that is] of faith will save him that is sick, and the Lord will restore him; and if he has committed sins, he will be forgiven." Amp.), in 2 Cor 5:8 ("[Yes] we have confident and hopeful courage, and are well-pleased rather to be away from home out of the body and be at home with the Lord." Amp.), and in Ps 116:15 ("Precious [important and no light matter] in the sight of the Lord is the death of His saints—His loving ones." Amp.)? Is any kind of death of a believer precious to the Lord? Exactly what form should expressions of faith take? Praying? Seeking help from health professionals? Denying the presence of illness by stating, "I am healed?" Though attempting to answer these questions may only serve to raise more questions, I hope to show that it is possible to offer biblically-based comfort to those facing doubts at the end of life. There are many books about healing and about dying. Even those that are Christian-based give barely a mention of the place of the church in helping people to manage end-of-life. I will offer some suggestions for approaching conversations with parishioners about dying.

WHY WAS IT NOT TIME FOR CURTIS TO DIE?

There is a notion in some churches that sickness and death should never occur. The idea derives from the belief that sickness occurs due to sin and the sin nature of humans that results from Adam's fall. With salvation through Jesus Christ comes a new human, a person newly created in Christ and freed from sin, sickness, and death (the consequences of Adam's fall). So sickness and death should not occur in those who have accepted Christ. From this thinking follows that because salvation has done away with sickness, tapping into the Power source can heal sickness that occurs anyway. This is done by fasting and praying.

Some teachers/writers encourage believers to use fasting as a way to reverse sickness and avoid death. E. Towns gives instructions for a fast with the purpose of bringing about physical healing:

> Recall that all healing is subject to the will of God. He may have in mind a purpose in this illness that you cannot see. Remember that God controls all of our lives: no one dies prematurely. When God does heal, it is temporary, because "it is 'appointed for men to die' (Heb 9:27). God controls the hands of the clock that determines the death of all people."[1]

Towns reminded readers to submit to God through fasting and trust Him for the consequences. However, Towns gives several reasons that a fast for such a purpose may not work: one may have been disobedient to God by not fasting earlier and thus fasted too late to do any good; the body may already be too damaged by the disease; or the fasting and praying may have been shallow, rather than "wholehearted." Wimber and Springer also wrote that people are not healed due to a lack of wholehearted praying.[2] Though the teaching about the physical and spiritual benefits of fasting and praying is valuable, it lends more confusion than clarity to those trying to make sense of the process of dying. There are contradictions in its presentation as a fundamentalist teaching in that it proposes that by one's actions (fasting and praying) sickness and death can be forestalled. Yet, it also says that the consequences of our actions should be left to God. This teaching also is problematic in that it blames the sufferer for her suffering. If efforts to get well do not work, it is her fault.

In another instance of contradiction, in his teaching on how to fast for health, Towns writes that God may have a purpose in one being ill.[3] If this is the case, should not one try to discover God's purpose in an illness prior to trying to get rid of the illness? Towns proposes that healing is always temporary and that no death is premature, as God has appointed the time for each person's death. I would not suggest Towns's statement that no death is premature be used to offer comfort to anyone![4]

The belief that believers in Christ are promised a minimum of seventy years of life before death was another reason that Curtis's pastor believed that it was not yet time for Curtis to die. This idea stemmed from Ps 90:10a, which reads, "The days of our years are threescore years and ten . . . ." This verse was explained as meaning that those who accept Christ are promised a lifespan of at least seventy years. The explanation precluded the possibility of a God-given appointment to die any earlier in life. In this case, the fact that Curtis had not yet reached seventy years of age seemed to mean that it was inappropriate for him to be ". . . well-pleased rather to be away from home out of the body and be at home with the Lord." Curtis and his father were not allowed by the pastor to emphasize the application of 2 Cor 5:8 to their context. They were restricted in their attempts to express their autonomy by determining for themselves that this was a sickness unto death. The pastor behaved in a quite paternalistic fashion.

THE INTERFERENCE OF AUTONOMY

Current discussion about end-of-life revolves around issues of autonomy. Caregiving in the United States utilizes a model that places emphasis on individual patient self-determination, also called autonomy. The principle of autonomy, or the principle of respect for autonomy, refers to an individual's right to make decisions for self. To a great extent this emphasis has resulted from a pendulum swing away from the paternalism that was the previous dominant model. Individual autonomy was a response to the overuse of beneficence to the extent that it became paternalistic. I visualize this as a pendulum with beneficence (of the professional caregiver) on one end and caregiver paternalism (substitute decision maker based on knowledge possession) on the other end. In the middle is the ideal of individual self-determination that acknowledges and considers the opinions of and the possible effects of decisions on family, friends, and the church body. The model of individual autonomy stresses the rights of patients independently to make decisions regarding their own care. Patients are expected to make decisions independent of opinions of health care professionals, family members, clergy, or other sources of support. This emphasis on individual autonomy has not left faith-based decision making untouched. The emphasis on individual autonomy offers a contradiction, which is evident in the case of Curtis and his pastor.

Emphasis on individual autonomy sometimes has the effect of negating the realities of the physical condition. No matter how sick one is, and no matter how poor the prognosis, there remains a right to insist on healing. In stark contrast to patient self-determination, this insistence came from the pastor in Curtis's case. It must be noted that individual autonomy can be expressed by deciding to relinquish decision making to family, a spiritual leader, or a significant other. In Curtis's case, this happened passively. Curtis was a minor, so his father made decisions on his behalf. However, Curtis's father believed in submission to the authority of the pastor, believing the teaching that a pastor's relationship with church members is to reflect Jesus' relationship with the church. James 5:14-15 offers a different viewpoint. She who is sick expresses autonomy by calling on the elders of the church. She chooses to believe the promise that ". . . the prayer that is of faith will save her that is sick . . ." and chooses to express expectancy of healing by calling on the elders. Then, the emphasis is no longer on the individual. Interdependence is highlighted, wherein the sick one is dependent on the prayers and faith of the elders and the elders are dependent on the hearing and response of the Lord. Demands for healing or thinking that healing is the right of every believer diminishes the inherent interdependence.

The concept of advance care planning arose from the notion of individual autonomy and self-determination. The Patient Self-Determination Act (PSDA), passed as a part of the 1990 Omnibus Budget Reconciliation Act, addressed this with regard to end-of-life decision making. This act stated that patients had the right to direct their end-of-life care prior to the end of their lives. The legislation was passed to insure that individuals had autonomy as expressed by self-determination of end-of-life preferences. The tools used to express such preferences are called advance directives. There are three major types of advance directives. A durable power of attorney for health care is used to appoint a trusted person to make decisions in the event one becomes unable to do so. Living wills give instructions to use no extraordinary life-sustaining procedures. Medical directives give instructions about the care that will be acceptable in specific diagnoses and illness situations. The use of advance directives to express individual autonomy is actually an expression of precedent autonomy, or self-determination regarding a situation prior to such time that the situation may occur.

A problem with precedent autonomy and subsequent advance directive decisions is that one is expected not only to envision a host of possible illness situations but also to know what one will desire at that time. A more helpful alternative is to turn the focus away from precedent autonomy or the rights of the person completing the advance directive and instead to focus on the concerns of the individual. Professionals engaged in addressing ethical issues do more thinking about metaethical issues. For example, the issue of withholding or withdrawing food and fluids is connected to the issue of sanctity of life and is discussed along with the treatment of embryos, abortion, and Dr. Kevorkian. But individual patients who are preparing an advance directive may be more concerned, for example, about dignity issues, or about how their family will cope with an extended illness. On the other hand, the envisioning that is required to complete a medical directive may be judged by fundamentalists as constituting a lack of faith, as faith requires that a constant healthy state be imagined.

WHO IS SUFFERING?

While emphasis on individual autonomy expressed the right of persons to be self-determining, thus emphasizing the importance of individuals, sick and dying individuals are often concerned about being a burden. People who are thinking about how they want the end of their life to take place often express the desire to "not be a burden" on anyone.[5] Individuals who are facing death may be concerned about their caregivers. Though the concern is appropriate, it may have an effect on the decisions that are made about end-of-life care. For example, a person may decide to forego potentially helpful treatments, believing that it will be physically or emotionally burdensome to others to prolong her life. Caregivers do experience suffering. A nurse who was caring for a dying friend explained:

> I needed to be certain that Steve was not in physical, psychological, or spiritual pain. So I double-checked my assessment with every person who came to see him. Their responses confirmed my conclusion. We were suffering, but Steve was really doing okay.[6]

End-of-life decisions should be made considering the impact of the decision on family and friends, but that is not the sole consideration. The likelihood of being in a condition that might be burdensome to others has increased. Technological advances have led to ". . . longer lives and worse health, longer illnesses, and slower deaths, longer aging and increased dementia."[7] These are changes not only to be faced by health care professionals, but by individuals, their families and friends, and their pastors and spiritual advisors. Some people fear the use of life-extending or life-sustaining technologies or feel they are unnecessary. In interviews I conducted on attitudes toward advance directives, some participants said, "If it is your time to go, it doesn't matter what machine they use. You are going anyway." Some felt God could take care of them without the machines. Others expressed belief that machines might give one a chance to recover, offering time for God to work. M. Kelsey wrote, "His (Jesus) healing practices varied, and He made no explicit suggestion that people should learn to get along without physicians. Nor, of course, did he recommend that they do without God's healing and rely entirely on medical practice. Instead Jesus dignified intelligence as a way for humankind to deal with their problems, while increasing their reliance upon God."[8] One of these "problems" that human intelligence cannot adequately—if at all—address is the aspect of death that is unknown.

There exists a fear of death in this culture. Witness the multiple phrases that are used: depart this life, pass away, cross over, expire, go to a better place, home going, give up the ghost. Then there are some phrases that are more crude: kicked the bucket, pushing up daises, bite the dust, etc. These phrases protect humans from having to face the unknown. Fear of death is really fear of the unknown. No one knows what the actual moment of leaving life and being permanently dead (as opposed to a near-death experience) is. Without entering into a philosophical discussion about personhood, I understand humanness to be physical presence that interacts with and reacts to spirit presence, as well as or while interacting with the physical environment/plane. The majority of what is known tends to be on the physical plane, that which can be experienced with the physical senses. Unfortunately for many people, the illness that is leading to the dying process is filled with overwhelming physical "sensations." The fear is that the actual dying process, the movement from alive to dead, will be more of the same. That fear is judged by some as lack of faith. People should be reassured that demonstration of humanness is not the same as lack of faith. That reassurance should be accompanied by being with the one who is dying and accessing palliative care resources to attend to the overwhelming physical "sensations." James 5:15 reads, "The prayer that is of faith shall save the sick."

It has been suggested that death reminds us of our human limitations. Christians do not always accept these limitations because of not fully understanding grace versus works. The Christian patient may feel that because there has been a life of good works, death should not occur. Humanness must be accepted in the same space as the faith. My faith tradition teaches that there is an enemy (the devil) whose job it is, because of his very nature, to kill, steal, and destroy (John 10:10) in any way possible. This means killing, stealing, and destroying material goods, relationships, and time, as well as physical health. The question is, When you pray or once you have prayed, is it demonstrative of a lack of faith to go a physician? I teach that since the devil will kill, steal, and destroy in any way he can, one should seek healing in any godly way. Pray really hard, and go to the physician really fast. What of an illness that is unto death? Pray for peace and physical relief for symptoms, and go to palliative care specialists quickly. Wimber and Springer stated that prayers for healing should not be offered in this instance, as that will cause false hope.[9] False hope will then cause emotional pain and will turn the patient's focus away from the eternal life ahead. The presence of faith does not require that we demand God act in accordance with our prayers but requires acknowledgment of the sovereignty of God. Thus, the consequences can be left to God.

The Committee on Care at the End of Life offered a model for end-of-life care.[10] This committee was formed by the Institute of Medicine, a member of the National Academy of Sciences, to develop strategies to improve care of people who are at the end of life. The model developed by this committee includes a hospice spiritual care coordinator, while omitting the local church. The model includes "spiritual" dimensions of end-of-life care, along with physical, emotional or psychological, and practical. Interestingly, the local church is seen as valuable in the practical dimension by assisting with meals, home repairs, transportation, etc. In the spiritual dimension emphasis is on the ability of health professionals to identify those who may benefit from a discussion of spiritual issues and to make provision for religious rituals. The local church does need to take a major role in this practical dimension, but the local church (as well as the denomination) should also be the leader in the spiritual care of those who are dying.

Sickness, dying, and end-of-life decision making has been addressed at the denominational level of several Christian churches in official statements and policies. These statements from a variety of denominations[11] demonstrated agreement in issues relative to the end of life. The following points summarize these statements.

First, human life is a sacred gift from God, and as such, should be respected and the dignity upheld. The meaning of dignity varies from person to person, culture to culture. The meaning of Ps 116:15 ("Precious [important and no light matter] in the sight of the Lord is the death of His saints—His loving ones." Amp.) is important to issues of dignity. Painful, tormenting, and agonizing deaths with loss of bodily control are an affront to dignity. Psalm 116:15 could be a visionary statement that helps pastoral caregivers in decision making and guides the practice of palliative care specialists. Palliative care includes hospice, but is much broader. Hospice is usually thought of as a service for cancer patients, and hospice services require that death is imminent, usually within six months. Palliative care does not require that death is imminent and is appropriate for a variety of illnesses. Palliative care attends to symptom control and physical, emotional, and spiritual comfort when there is no cure available for the illness. Its goal is neither hastening nor postponing death. Use of palliative care services can ensure that a death occurs with dignity intact.

Second, Christ experienced suffering.[12] Because of that suffering, the sick and dying can be assured of Christ's understanding and can be assured that Christ is present and offers comfort during human suffering. Though not to be desired, suffering, pain, and sickness can bring us closer to God through refinement and redemption. The issue of whether or not sickness can serve a noble purpose causes some confusion. Suffering is not a method of atoning for sin. Only the suffering of Jesus accomplished atonement for human sin. Christian compassion calls for the alleviation of physical and emotional discomfort of the dying person. When it is not possible to totally alleviate the suffering, the dying person is not abandoned but is offered human presence and prayers as comfort.

Third, decisions regarding the end of life are difficult and are best attempted prior to being in the process of dying. Thoughts about our humanness, illness, death, and advance care planning should occur prior to crises. S. Wheeler writes:

> Unlike the prevailing culture, which must deny death at all costs since it shares no account of a good more fundamental than survival, Christian communities live in the belief that life is directed toward and fulfilled in the knowledge and love of God, goods which cannot be thwarted by death. These convictions can enable a kind of courage and even cheerfulness in the face of death that does not depend on the pretense of personal invulnerability. Thus, Christians need not flee from the intimations of our own mortality, which are inevitably borne by the sick and the dying. We will look, therefore, for a greater readiness to be with, and to be truthful with, the sick and those facing death.[13]

Additionally, no single decision or answer can apply to all situations or to all people. Decisions are made in the context of relationship with and help from God, family, the pastor, and the church body. Absolute individualism should be resisted as anathema to the word of God. God's love and grace through the work of the Holy Spirit is available to help with decision making at and for the end of life.

Fourth, excessively burdensome treatments and treatments which will not be beneficial need not be accepted. Excessively burdensome treatments are those that have severe side effects, those that have high risks and high costs, or treatments that will cause a grave inconvenience to family, friends, or community. Non-beneficial treatments are those that will not result in resolution of the disease or of disease complications. Refusal of such treatment is neither passive euthanasia nor suicide. Christian love is both practical and responsible. Such love neither denies faith nor requires accepting extraordinary life-sustaining treatments. J. Kilner argued that one could plan for no life-sustaining treatments as long as death is not the intent of such plans, but is an unavoidable reality.[14] This explains the difference between so-called mercy killing (euthanasia) and the principle of double-effect. Some treatments might decrease consciousness or shorten life. Such treatments are permitted to alleviate suffering, as the goal is not to cause death but to alleviate suffering.

Fifth, euthanasia is never acceptable or appropriate, and as members of society, the people of the church should resist efforts to legalize it. It is no insignificant occurrence that this was expressed across denominations with great effort to explicate suffering and its meaning and to differentiate between easing suffering and willfully hastening death. Support for euthanasia usually stems from those favoring individual autonomy who argue that one has a right to decide to end her suffering and to choose when to die. However, someone else must agree and give the means. So the argument is really self-refuting. and the expression of individual autonomy is illusory. The Holy Spirit indwells believers, so Christians are really never autonomous.

I agree that euthanasia is not to be considered an option. My framework for understanding its unacceptability is based on a respect for the sacredness of human life and more. My framework also includes 2 Tim 1:7 ("For God has not given us the spirit of fear: but of power, and of love, and of a sound mind") and Josh 1:9 ("Have I not commanded thee? Be strong, and of a good courage. Be not afraid, neither be thou dismayed. For the Lord thy God is with thee whithersoever thou goest"). There are two basic fears that may cause one to consider euthanasia. There is a fear of increased suffering, whether that suffering takes the form of pain, immobility, inability to communicate, loss of bodily functioning, or some other form. In interviews I conducted about end-of-life planning, participants described suffering they had experienced or suffering they had witnessed. They expressed the desire not to be in pain, not to experience a loss of bowel and bladder function, not to be immobile, etc. There is also a fear of causing suffering by becoming a burden. Participants described watching other family members suffer with the illness of a loved one and expressed the desire not to inflict that suffering themselves. There was no acknowledgement that family as caregivers take pleasure in the caregiving and benefit from it. The Scriptures command that we not be afraid and assures us that we have feelings, emotions, and fortitude as options.

I have heard the expression by many people, "I am not afraid to die. I am afraid of dying." It is the process that is frightening. Second Corinthians 5:8 may resonate within us, but the fact that we do not know what will make us leave the body causes fear. The church must assist the dying in apprehending the alternatives to fear. Consultation with and use of palliative care specialists to address suffering should be encouraged. Pastors must begin to emphasize the blessing and rewards that can result from caregiving. At the same time, the church must acknowledge the toll on human emotion and physical strength that caregiving takes, and come alongside the caregivers in support.

The denominational statements emphasized that life is created and given by God. It is a gift from God for which we as humans should be thankful. With that thankful attitude, life during the dying process should be maintained with dignity and respect for humans in the image of God. Dying, like living, occurs within the context of relationship with God and relationship with a caring community. Christian compassion demands that we address the needs of the dying.

What should be the content of prayers when it is known that the end of life is present? Prayers for healing can still take place even if someone has been determined to be terminally ill. One must listen to the patient, or to her family in the case of a comatose or non-cognitive patient, to determine if acceptance of a prognosis of death has taken place. Praying for the healing of the terminally ill may bring unnecessary pain and may deflect attention from trusting in God for eternal life. How to pray in that instance might be ascertained in the following type of exchange:

> Pastor: What is your prayer right now?
> Possible answer: That I would be totally healed.
> Pastor: Let's imagine that you will be totally healed, but it will happen two months from now. What is your prayer for that interim?

Prayers may also be offered for peace (Ps 34:14). Praying for something other than healing does not demonstrate lack of belief in James 5:15. It may demonstrate a faith in and reliance on the sovereignty of God. Believers give much import to 2 Cor 5:8. The goal of being eternally present with the Lord is the motivation for the belief. The salvation or restoration of one who is sick may not happen in this body. That does not require one to wish for death to be hastened. Death then could be conceptualized as the ultimate healing. After all, cancer, for example, ceases to grow in a dead body. So what is required is a reframing of the intent of James 5:15. There is no indication in the text that we should understand that praying in faith would banish death forever. In fact, framing James 5:15 with 2 Cor 5:8 will allow one confidently to approach advance planning for the end of life.

Advance planning usually takes the form of discussions with family members and significant others and may include preparation of legal documents, the advance directives. An advance directive is an individual's expression of wishes about future medical treatment or decision making. There are several types of advance directives. A durable power of attorney for health care names another person to make decisions. A living will gives instructions to institute no extraordinary treatment. A medical directive outlines specific conditions under which one would accept or refuse certain treatments. Do-not-resuscitate orders are a very narrow type of advance directive that instructs that resuscitation attempts not be made in the event the lungs and/or heart cease to function. If a patient and/or her family have engaged in advance planning for the end of life, this may indicate more of an openness to accept the dying process. Pastoral counseling may require educating people about advance directives, offering guidance through the decision making that advance planning offers, as well as supporting them through death.

I must offer a caution about advance directives. Current emphasis seems to be on making choices about specific treatments. However, research has shown that people may be more concerned about how they and their families will manage particular kinds of treatments and about the way that they may die. Patients are often offered what amounts to a choice between death now or artificial prolongation of life, rather than a choice between death and progress toward the previous healthy state.[15] Patients are actually offered an illusion of choice as physicians control medications, technology, and the choices associated with their use. In one study physicians admitted to manipulating discussions and presentation of information so as to influence decision making in accord with the physicians' opinions.[16] Efforts to ascertain patient and family values and goals should take precedence over trying to choose from a variety of different treatments in a range of possible illness scenarios.

THE NEW LAITY—POSTMODERNISM

Today, many congregants are not people who grew up in the church, who had to memorize the catechism and/or church discipline, and who know at least one verse of the great hymns of the faith. These congregants are new to any faith tradition and may not have had opportunity to practice or utilize a belief system to face suffering, sickness, or grief. This offers new challenges for pastors whose comfort largely consists of a soothing Scripture and a verse of "Great is Thy Faithfulness." These newly churched people do not know of God's faithfulness, nor do they know how to appropriate that grace into their everyday lives. We as Christians are no less called to be compassionate to these individuals. As J. Phelan stated, they must be gently led to Jesus and to the cross, and the power of the story of the cross need not be denied.[17] To support these congregants facing end-of-life issues, the approach must rely on knowledge of the secular culture with which they are familiar. The pastoral counselor might ask the following open-ended questions: Tell me about another situation that was difficult for you to face—how did you manage it? What has determined what you value in life? What books have you read/movies have you seen that really had an impact on you? What does spirituality mean in your life? A personal loss history (see the appendix) is also helpful in determining how best to approach supporting these congregants.

SUMMARY

Curtis and his father did not get to rejoice in a home-going with fellow believers. Application of a hierarchy to individual Scripture texts resulted in a demand that God act in a certain way in response to Curtis's father acting in a certain "faith-filled" manner. Pastors need to be able to discern the difference between faith and denial. If denial is present, the thoughts that underlie the denial should be examined. Then the underlying thoughts can be individually supported or redirected. It should also be recognized that some individuals might never acknowledge to others their awareness of being in the process of dying. There may never be attainment of the "perfect death." Pastors need not be afraid to pray for those who are terminally ill. The church must take a greater role in developing biblical ethics for the continuing advances in technologies and subsequent prolongation of the dying process.

NOTES

1. E. Towns, *Fasting for Spiritual Breakthrough* (Ventura, Calif.: Regal, 1996), 139 and see 129-141.

2. J. Wimber and K. Springer, *Power Healing* (New York: HarperCollins, 1987), 158.

3. Towns, 135.

4. For information on avoiding "miserable comforter" type remarks, see http://www.atimetogrieve.net/dart_say.html and http://dying.about.com/ library/blsayb.htm.

5. C. Dupree, "The Attitudes of Black Americans Toward Advance Directives," *Journal of Transcultural Nursing*, 11 (2000), 12-18, see pp. 14-15; M. Pfeifer, J. Sidorov, A. Smith, J. Boero, A. Evans, M. Settle, and the EOL Study Group, "The Discussion of End-of-Life Medical Care by Primary Care Patients and Physicians: A Multicenter Study Using Structured Qualitative Interviews," *Journal of General Internal Medicine* 9 (1994): 82-88, see p. 84.

6. R. MacIntrye, "Nursing Loved Ones With AIDS: Knowledge Development for Ethical Practice," in *Caregiving: Readings in Knowledge, Practice, Ethics, and Politics* (ed. S. Gordon, P. Benner, and N. Noddings; Philadelphia: University of Pennsylvania Press, 1996), 141-152, see p. 147.

7. D. Callahan, *The Troubled Dream of Life: In Search of a Peaceful Death* (Washington, D.C: Georgetown University Press, 2000), 47.

8. M. Kelsey, *Healing and Christianity: A Classic Study* (Minneapolis: Augsburg/Fortress, 1995), 78.

9. Wimber and Springer, 163-165.

10. Committee on Care at the End of Life, *Approaching Death: Improving Care at the End-of-Life* (ed. Marilyn J. Field and Christine K. Cassel; Washington, D.C: National Academy Press, 1997), chapter 3. Available on-line at http://books.nap.edu/html/approaching/.

11. See 1998 Overtures to the 210th General Assembly Presbyterian Church (U.S.A.), available at http://www.pcusa.org/pcusa/ga210/ovt/98-50.html; "A Catholic Guide to End-of-Life Decisions: An Explanation of Church Teaching on Advance Directives, Euthanasia, and Physician Assisted Suicide," available at http://www.ncbcenter.org/eol-guide.html; "Life and Death in Relation to God and Others: A Resolution on Assisted Suicide" passed by the Annual Meeting of the Evangelical Covenant Church, June, 1997, available at http://www.covchurch.org/cov/html/suicide.html; Evangelical Lutheran Church in America (1992), "A Message on End-of-Life Decisions," Department for Studies, Division for Church in Society; The General Council of the Assemblies of God (2001), "A Biblical Perspective on Assisted Suicide," available at http://www.ag.org/top/beliefs/position_papers/ 4193_assisted_suicide.cfm; the General Council of The Assemblies of God (2001), "Euthanasia, and Extraordinary Support to Sustain Life," available at http://www.ag.org/top/beliefs/contemporary_issues/issues_18_euthanasia.cfm; "Care of the Sick and Dying," available at http://www.ewtn.com/library/BISHOPS/SICK.HTM; "The Stand of the Orthodox Church on Controversial Issues," available at http://www.goarch.org/acess/Companion_to_Orthodox_Church/ issues.html; "A Statement of Consensus on Care for the Dying," available at http://www.adventist.org/beliefs/main_stat6.html.

12. For a description of the likely physical suffering of Jesus Christ, see W. Edwards, W. Gabel, and F. Hosmer, "On the Physical Death of Jesus Christ," *Journal of the American Medical Association*, (11) (1986) 1455-1463.

13. S. Wheeler, *Stewards of Life: Bioethics and Pastoral Care* (Nashville: Abingdon, 1996), 24.

14. J. Kilner, "Foregoing Treatment," in *Dignity and Dying: A Christian Appraisal* (ed. J. Kilner, A. Miller, and E. Pellegrino; Grand Rapids: Eerdmans, 1996), 68-83.

15. J. Slomka, "The Negotiation of Death: Clinical Decision Making at the End of Life," *Social Science and Medicine*, 35 (1992) 251-259, see p. 258.

16. Pfeifer et al., 86.

17. John Phelan, Jr., "The Future of the Covenant in the Postmodern World," Lecture delivered at the Annual Meeting of the Covenant Ministerium, 1998, Rosemont, Ill.

APPENDIX

PERSONAL LOSS HISTORY

1. The first death I can remember was the death of _____________. I was age_________.

2. The feelings I remember I had at the time were

3. The first funeral (wake or other ritual service) I ever attended was for___________. I was age____.

4. The thing I most remember about that experience is

5. My most recent loss by death was (person, time, circumstances)

6. I am coping with this loss by

7. The most difficult death for me was the death of

8. It was difficult because

9. Of the people in my life who are now living, the most difficult death for me would be the death of ___________, because

10. My primary style of coping with loss is

11. I know my own grief is resolved when

Adapted from: American Association of Colleges of Nursing and City of Hope (2000). Module 7: Grief, Loss, Bereavement. End-Of-Life Nursing Education Consortium (ELNEC) Curriculum.

THE NEW DEADLY SINS
ROMANS 12:1-2

PETER RHEA JONES

Sometimes we as Christians go after Bengal tigers with BB guns. So it seemed to me one day while sitting in a barber shop and thumbing carelessly through an old issue of *Esquire* magazine. My eyes riveted on an article entitled "The New Deadly Sins." I ran my eye down the list still supposing something roughly corresponding to the predictable sins. I expected to find a twist on things like lust, envy, avarice, gluttony, and all that. Rather this updated catalogue of contemporary sins had the audacity to name things like poverty, ugliness, and failure as sins! Here we confront a secular list of unacceptable behaviors. It boggled my mind as I realized how blatantly secular the article was. It was a luminous moment because it dramatized the fierce contrast between our world and the Word. I found myself startled and intrigued as you may be by now.

Sitting stunned and fascinated in the barber shop, but no longer interested in the haircut, my mind raced to the famous sentiments of the apostle in Romans 12. Listen in a new fashion to the impassioned appeal:

> Therefore I call upon you, brothers and sisters, through the agency of the mercies of God to offer your bodies as a living sacrifice, holy, pleasing to God, which is your spiritual worship. And do not model yourself on this era, but on the contrary be transformed by the renewal of your minds in order that you may determine by searching and testing what is the will of God, what is good and pleasing and perfect.

Upon the basis of the indicative of the gospel extraordinarily developed for eleven chapters, the apostle made direct appeal to the imperative of the Christian life, a life in community. Offer now your life, he seems to be saying. A new humanity appears because of the mercies of God. We might then say that the Christian life is a life of gratitude for those very mercies. The new era has broken in.

The conforming now happening needs to stop, the classic text insists unapologetically. In the grand old commentary by Sanday and Headlam we find this restatement of the part of the text about conforming: "Do not adopt the external and fleeting fashion of this world."[1] We are no longer the helpless victims of tyrannizing forces. Do not be assimilated by this epoch. James Dunn insists that fundamental attitudes must be changed, new perspectives taken up.[2] A total break with the past is commended. Rather, the apostle invites us to yield ourselves so our lives here and now more and more clearly exhibit signs and tokens of the coming order of God.

Cranfield demonstrates how the word *metamorphousthe* in verse two denotes a profound transformation, but while this transformation is not of the Christian's own doing but the work of the Holy Spirit, nevertheless the real responsibility remains to let oneself be transformed. And this transformation must continually be repeated.[3] The Spirit gives us a fresh perspective through the renewal of our minds. C. K. Barrett dared to speak of "a radical renewal of human nature begun in conversion and advanced with every Christian decision."[4] Our symposium on biblical ethics as the body of Christ has sought to discern the will of God on controverted moral issues, also dependent on the renewal of the mind. It was Dodd who put it most memorably in a virtual epigram that the Christian "is not the slave of the conventional judgments of society but has a free and independent insight into moral reality."[5] With this pithy insight and the apostle's call for a distinctive Christian lifestyle let us dialogue with "the new deadly sins."

The magazine article listed *poverty* as a sin. Modern society abhors the sin of poverty. The poor are invariably ugly, sooner old. The old dispensation offered the illusion, "Blessed are the poor," but of course we know now "Hopeless are the poor." After all, the poor cannot buy jazzy clothes or take exciting vacations. They do not belong nor expect to belong. A lot of average Americans may strain to balance the budget, have more month left than money, may hanker after products they cannot buy, but they contribute to the prodigious consumption of our economy. The American poor could be migrants without papers, marginal farmers, city slum dwellers, mentally ill euphemistically dubbed "street people." The children of Lazarus linger on our streets. They live in wretched shacks, squalid apartments, dirty tenements. These poor people eke out life in harsh environments. Brutal poverty still exists in our country.

In striking contrast to secular humanity's denigration of the poor stands the NT. On one memorable occasion Jesus said, "Foxes have holes, birds have nests, but the Son of Man has nowhere to lay his head" (Luke 9:58). Jesus himself became a poor person and included in his ministry those marginalized on the fringes of society. Jesus, the grand catalyst, offered his story about the Rich Man and Lazarus. He preached good news to the poor: "Blessed are the poor" (Luke 6:20).

In days of a student pastorate with a painfully meager fund of pastoral experience I was called to a small rural congregation where I found delightful people who enjoyed one another. Many of them had small farms they worked on the weekend after holding down a job in town they called "public work." The fellowship we enjoyed there was especially good, and we could raise the roof singing, "Blessed assurance, Jesus is *mine*."

Early on, a gracious deacon—there were only two!—introduced me to the "church field" by driving me around the community. We came to the end of the paved road, and he began to turn around. The road continued as a dusty gravel road, so out of my inexperience I asked where the lane led. He explained that it was called Long Lane, so I urged him to drive on down which he gladly did. We found house after house where no one went to church. We would get out of his car and casually visit in the yards with the people. One house stood on stilts, and an old hound dog wandered out from its shadowy labyrinths. The children acted glad to see us, some of them bounding around without shoes. Some of the fathers were sleeping it off in a back bedroom. We met with warmth, but in fourteen houses we did not find a single family going to church.

That Sunday evening we gathered back at the church and reported. The church members seemed interested enough, even fascinated, but one sage said in a kindly fashion to this inexperienced parson that the people on Long Lane are "just not the churchgoing types." Who could disagree?

Later in the year the church held its annual series of revival services in August. Being inexperienced I agreed to spend the night at a different house each evening, putting me in the home of the other deacon one night. In the morning the deacon's son Billy and I went out into the hot August sun and played ball. Perspiring and frantic for shade we settled under the shade of an old oak in the front yard. Somehow the moment of closeness seemed appropriate to bring up the idea to Billy about making his own profession of faith. With tears actually welling up in his eyes he made a boyish commitment of faith. We baptized him, and his father was touched, so much so that he began to drive to Long Lane and bring people to church. The church accepted them graciously. Some of the dear denizens of Long Lane were eventually baptized. We had not planned on it, but we began to be the church! Nothing less than a trembling transcendence of ordinary sociology transpired.

Hear the inspired apostle warn about being assimilated to this world but "on the contrary be transformed by the renewal of your minds." After all, a Christian is "not the slave of the conventional judgments of society but has a free and independent insight into moral reality." While still mulling over this "sin of poverty" in the light of your world go again to the magazine and its revised list of deadly sins, be it partly clever and tongue in cheek but ever so reflective of contemporary reality.

The magazine undauntedly asserts that getting old, another of the new sins, means fatness, sickness, wrinkles probably. Old people are just out of it, objects of contempt and indifference. They are left behind by the cool and the young. Since much of our society idealizes youthfulness, senior citizens are made to feel they are not a dynamic part of society, just past their prime and over the hill. Back there somewhere beyond most of our memories lay a time when children were to be seen but not heard. This does not remotely approach the case today, as children are definitely to be delighted in, seen, and heard. But could it be that senior adults should comprehend their place and be seen but not heard? In cosmetic politics where spin and image count, the savvy and depth of experience of senior statespersons are devalued with little disguise. In the context of marriage some "trade her in for a newer model."

In striking contrast stands the biblical revelation. Consider the enchanting figure in the Gospel of Luke, Simeon of Jerusalem. Simeon believed he would live to see the Messiah (Luke 2:26). We imagine this righteous and devout man in the springtime of life, on into the summer of his life, on into the fall looking for the Messiah. Finally in the winter of his days a peasant couple arrived at the temple to dedicate their child. This old man came out of the shadows as it were and, like a grandfather taking his first grandchild into his arms, grasped this baby and blessed this child by the name of Jesus. This gracious old man sensed the presence of the salvation the Messiah would bring.

How did the old man know that this peasant baby, belonging to unprepossessing parents, could possibly be the long awaited Messiah? No heavenly band played "Hail to the Chief." No e-mail arrived from Headquarters. No medieval halo encircled the head of this Christ child. No legion of angels hovered overhead. There was no celestial Western Union telegram from God, no fax from the Father. How did the old man know?

How did this quaint old man know? Simeon seems the kind of individual who so sensitized his spiritual radar that he knew when he was in the presence of God. Through a long and rich life he had practiced the presence of God. He was not deafened by the noise of downtown Jerusalem. This devout old man allowed himself to be led by the Spirit (Luke 2:27). After long years of waiting Simeon broke out in prophetic ecstasy, the moment of the fulfillment of God's word having arrived. He bursts into a song of poetic praise. Simeon's serene expectation is such that "he can entrust himself to death, knowing that life and immortality have been brought to light through the gospel."[6] This presumably elderly man is presented "as a model in faith, hope and piety."[7] "Prevailingly," Frank Stagg generalized at the end of a study, "old age is esteemed in the Bible."[8]

The words of the apostle reverberate: "Do not model yourself on this epoch but on the contrary be transformed by the renewal of your minds." A Christian actually has a free and independent insight into moral reality.

This magazine article on the "new deadly sins" even had the temerity to name ugliness as a sin. Confident that beautiful people are definitely better than ugly people, the magazine plays on the old line that "skin beauty is only skin deep." Skin beauty may only be skin deep, but in our culture it is deep enough to make or break a life! The "curse of ugliness" has blighted lives in a culture that values appearance more than substance, even for news anchors. The movie "Mask" dramatized the isolation of the ugly who are thereby somehow less valuable.

As a boy with the job of delivering newspapers I often tarried in the nearby Post Office so I could gawk and fantasize of adventure while taking in the mug shots of most wanted criminals. My boyish interest centered on apprehending one of these most wanted, becoming a great hero, and receiving a reward. However, even then I began to notice that these wanted men—no women for some reason—often had ugly countenances. Their faces sometimes carried scars. Some had repulsive and scary physical handicaps. One cannot help but wonder if they were taught at an early age that they were second rate because of their physical appearance. Could it be that parents were not proud of their appearance and failed to disguise it, peers rejected them, school teachers located them in the back of the classroom, and ministers may have taken little interest in unpromising people? It does take on the shape of a tragedy when evaluation of a person on the basis of appearance is bootlegged even into the life of the church.

It is telling to look behind the popular versions of Frankenstein. During a rainy summer in 1816 Mary Shelley created her original story of Frankenstein, published in 1818. Her story contained an eccentric doctor who aspired to bring a body to life in his laboratory. He managed to bring a dead man to life, but this horribly ugly man did not desire to kill and hurt but to be loved and accepted. He ventured out into the world and approached a group of children. They threw rocks. He sought out adults, but they shunned him until slowly but surely he was turned into a monster.

Would there be a word from the Lord the Sunday after 9/11? The congregation would not be disappointed. During the pastoral prayer the minister prayed, "Dear God, I know you have had a bad week, watching your children be cruel to one another and listening to your children cry." This minister elected to depart from the lectionary and took as his text Luke 13:1-5. His personally chosen text spoke of a tower that fell, clearing the rubble, and finding eighteen casualties. The narrative in Luke goes on to recount the voice of people asking if these people were worse offenders, receiving the pastoral answer that they were not. However, Jesus seized the moment to say that all will perish if they do not repent. The sermon turned toward repentance. The preacher, a man by the name of Craddock, went on to warn against assumptions of moral superiority. He held TV news itself partially responsible. He observed how news had become show biz, how it virtually neglected significant reporting of the deaths of millions of Congolese people, preferring superficial attention to appearance. Wound up, the preacher declared there is more focus on the belly button of Britney Spears than on the poor and hungry of our world. Craddock conveyed a critical consciousness concerning our celebrity culture that validates people on the shallow basis of their appearance.

In radical contrast to our celebrity culture Jesus related to all kinds of people as persons of worth. First Samuel 16:7 speaks counterculturally: "The Lord sees not as man sees; man looks on the outward appearance, but the Lord looks on the heart" (RSV). The NT, in turn, speaks of the spiritual loveliness of an unfading beauty (1 Pet 3:4) rather than of a fleeting glamour.

A young sixteen year old girl stepped out on the stage with a certain poise. A large crowd of youth at a national retreat had lingered after the worship service for a program of entertaining talent from the youth themselves. Some played instruments, some did dramatizations or told humorous skits, some sang in trios. Now the crowd waited with a certain particular attentiveness as she began to sing with an exceptional soprano voice. Her words rang out: "Everybody's beautiful, everybody's beautiful, everybody's beautiful in their own way." It was as though the Nazarene was there!

The Christian can exercise a free and independent insight into moral reality. Christians need not be assimilated to the celebrity culture, are not required to model their lives on this era, but on the contrary can be transformed by the renewal of their minds. Christians can determine through searching and testing what is the will of God.

Will you and I be assimilated?

NOTES

1. William Sanday and Arthur Headlam, *A Critical and Exegetical Commentary on the Epistle to the Romans* (5th ed.; The International Critical Commentary; Edinburgh: T. & T. Clark, 1902), 353.

2. James D. G. Dunn, *Romans 9-16* (vol. 38b of Word Biblical Commentary; Dallas: Word, 1988), 714.

3. C. E. B. Cranfield, *A Critical and Exegetical Commentary on the Epistle to the Romans IX-XVI* (The International Critical Commentary; Edinburgh: T. & T. Clark, 1979), 607.

4. C. K. Barrett, *The Epistle to the Romans* (Black New Testament Commentary; London: Adam and Charles Black, 1962), 233.

5. C. H. Dodd, *The Epistle of Paul to the Romans* (Moffatt New Testament Commentary; London: Hodder and Stoughton, 1932), 192.

6. I. Howard Marshall, *Commentary on Luke* (The New International Greek Commentary; Grand Rapids: Eerdmans, 1978), 120 (quoting H. Schürmann, I, 124).

7. Frank Stagg, *The Bible Speaks on Aging* (Nashville: Broadman, 1981), 137.

8. Ibid., 181.

ANNOTATED BIBLIOGRAPHY ON BIBLICAL ETHICS*

The Annual of the Society of Christian Ethics. This is the official publication of the Society of Christian Ethics and is a useful resource for papers on ethics and a broad array of related topics.

Baker, Eric. *The Neglected Factor: The Ethical Element in the Gospel*. Nashville: Abingdon, 1963. Arguing that morality is inseparable from religion, this Methodist author sketches out the ideal character as based on the Beatitudes.

Barcley, William B. *"Christ in You": A Study in Paul's Theology and Ethics*. Lanham, Md.: University Press of America, 1999. This study examines Paul's use of the expression "Christ in you/me" to determine how Paul uses this phrase in his letters. After analyzing what place this phrase has in Paul's larger thinking, the author looks at the relationship between Paul's use of "in Christ" and "Christ in you/me" to see if the phrases are interchangeable or not.

Barker, W. S., and W. R. Godfrey, eds. *Theonomy: a Reformed Critique*. Grand Rapids: Zondervan, 1990. This book is a good introduction to the debate within Reformed circles about the role that OT Law should play in Christian life and in society at large.

Barnette, Henlee H. *Introducing Christian Ethics*. Nashville: Broadman, 1961. This introduction to Christian ethics by a Baptist focuses on the biblical basis (both OT and NT) of ethics and the role of the Holy Spirit. Part One looks at basic principles of Christian morality in different parts of the Bible, and Part Two examines ethical issues such as marriage/family and political life. This section is considerably dated, especially the advice on race relations and economic life.

Barth, Karl. *Ethics*. Edited by Dietrich Braun. Translated by Geoffrey W. Bromiley. New York: Seabury, 1981. This volume contains Barth's 1928 lectures on ethics, which later served as the first draft for the ethical section of his *Church Dogmatics*. In this work Barth treats ethics as a theological discipline grounded on dogmatic theology.

________. *The Holy Spirit and The Christian Life*. Translated by R. Birch Hoyle. Louisville: Westminster/John Knox, 1993. This lecture, given by Barth in 1929, outlines his thoughts regarding the Holy Spirit's relation to humans. According to Barth, Christian ethics is not about what we say or do but about God's determinative action on our part through the Spirit. The essay is divided into three sections: (1) The Holy Spirit as Creator; (2) The Holy Spirit as Reconciler; and (3) The Holy Spirit as Redeemer.

*This bibliography is based on suggestions made by the participants of the symposium and was augmented, compiled, and annotated by James Amadon and Rebekah Eklund, to whom appreciation is heartily expressed.

Barton, John. *Ethics and the Old Testament*. Harrisburg, Pa.: Trinity Press International, 1998. Barton approaches the OT not as Scripture but as an ancient text, one that is rooted in a very different cultural context but still contains a unified and relevant set of ethics. The ethical issues of ecology, sexual morality, and property are briefly examined, and the book concludes with OT motivations for being moral.

_______. "Understanding Old Testament Ethics." *JSOT* 9 (1978): 44-64. Barton's helpful essay on the nature of OT ethics argues against a simple comprehensive system of OT ethics and encourages careful study of ethics in the OT.

Biggar, Nigel. *The Hastening That Waits: Karl Barth's Ethics*. Oxford: Clarendon, 1993. This book takes a fresh look at Barth's ethical writings in his *Church Dogmatics* and three recently published lectures with the goal of correcting previous errors of interpretation, offering some fresh insights into his thinking, and relating his thought to contemporary discussions within the field of Christian ethics.

Birch, Bruce C. *Let Justice Roll Down: The Old Testament, Ethics, and Christian Life*. Louisville: Westminster/John Knox, 1991. This fairly scholarly but very readable book attempts to relate the OT to Christian ethics in the modern church. Part One looks at the role of the OT in Christian ethics, and Part Two takes a thorough look at OT story as a moral resource. Basically the book follows the canonical order moving from creation through covenant to exile and return and concluding with the wisdom tradition.

Birch, Bruce C., and Larry L. Rasmussen. *Bible and Ethics in the Christian Life*. Minneapolis: Augsburg, 1989. Aimed at Christians, this book seeks to be a scholarly but nontechnical text that examines Christian ethics and biblical study, addressing key questions about the use and authority of the Bible in Christian ethics. Focus is on community ethics and moral agency. It concludes with a good summary and a challenge to utilize the Bible fully as an ethical resource.

Bloesch, Donald G. *Freedom for Obedience: Evangelical Ethics in Contemporary Times*. San Francisco: Harper & Row, 1987. This book attempts to navigate the "Scylla of legalism and rigorism" and the "Charybdis of antinomianism" by proposing a Christocentric ethics that calls Christians to uphold Christ as Savior and Lord and follow Christ as Teacher and Example.

Braaten, Carl E. *Eschatology and Ethics*. Minneapolis: Augsburg, 1974. Beginning with the understanding that the central content of Jesus' teaching concerned the Kingdom of God, Braaten proposes an eschatological interpretation in theology and ethics. The first half of the book looks at the theology of the Kingdom of God, while the second half looks at its ethics.

Burgess, John. *Why Scripture Matters*. Louisville: Westminster/John Knox, 1998. This accessible book is useful for pastors and in adult education contexts where people want to reflect on how and why Scripture exerts a shaping influence in the church's life. In grappling with contemporary disputes about the moral use of Scripture, it introduces some of the theological and methodological isssues involved in the appropriation of biblical texts without going so deeply into technical debates that it loses its audience.

Cahill, Lisa Sowle, and James F. Childress. *Christian Ethics: Problems and Prospects*. Cleveland: Pilgrim, 1996. This volume contains essays collected in honor of theologian James Gustafson. The twenty-one essays tackle difficult and contested issues in Christian ethics and range from particular issues like medical ethics to different methods and traditions of doing Christian ethics. Two parts compose the book: shaping theological ethics and the moral life.

Carter, Charles W., and R. Duane Thompson. *The Biblical Ethic of Love*. New York: Peter Lang, 1990. This book is intended as a college or seminary text exploring the relevance of divine love to ethical decisions. Special attention is paid to the Ten Commandments, the ethics of the prophets and wisdom literature, NT ethics, and the ethics of John Wesley. Other topics briefly addressed are Christians in relation to society, trends in contemporary Christian ethics, abortion, nuclear war and terrorism, and poverty.

Cave, Sydney. *The Christian Way: A Study of New Testament Ethics in Relation to Present Problems*. New York: Philosophical Library, 1949. This older work seeks to relate the significance of Jesus' teaching to modern situations. Its treatment of some issues (politics, the state of marriage, industry) is somewhat dated. Part I gives interpretations of ethics in specific NT books; Part II examines the methods, scope, and motives of Christian ethics; and Part III looks at life in community. An epilogue looks at the task of the church in the ethical realm.

Chilton, Bruce, and J. I. H. McDonald. *Jesus and the Ethics of the Kingdom*. Grand Rapids: Eerdmans, 1987. This book brings together a biblical scholar and a theologian to assess the meaning and continuing significance of Jesus' preaching of God's Kingdom.

Collins, Raymond F. *Christian Morality: Biblical Foundations*. Notre Dame, Ind.: University of Notre Dame Press, 1986. Written from a Catholic perspective, the book seeks to provide an understanding of ethical themes in Scripture in five parts: the use of Scripture in Christian ethics, the Ten Commandments from a Christian perspective, love in John 13:34 and Paul, human sexuality in the OT and NT, and a look at ethical perspectives in specific NT texts with attention to their historical context.

________. *Sexual Ethics and the New Testament*. New York: Crossroad, 2000. This book is a study of the pertinent NT texts that talk about sexuality. Using the historical-critical method, it seeks to unpack the original meaning of the texts and concludes with insights into how we should appropriate these texts in our understanding of sexual ethics today.

Crenshaw, James L., and John T. Willis, eds. *Essays in Old Testament Ethics*. New York: KTAV Publishing House, 1974. The fourteen essays in this book are fairly technical and only a few specifically treat ethics, most notably M. Burrows' brief comparison of OT and Jesus' ethics and L. Silberman's treatment of ethics in apocalyptic literature.

Curran, Charles E., and Richard A. McCormick, eds. *The Use of Scripture in Moral Theology*. Ramsey, N.J.: Paulist, 1984. This collection of essays, written by scholars spanning the Catholic and Protestant spectrum, offers several different approaches to using the Bible in Christian ethics. The articles are by scholars noted for their discussions of ethics, such as A. Verhey, J. Cone, S. Hauerwas, and J. H. Yoder.

Daly, Robert J. *Christian Biblical Ethics: From Biblical Revelation to Contemporary Christian Praxis: Method and Context*. Ramsey, N. J.: Paulist, 1984. Written in consultation with the Catholic Biblical Association Task Force, this work aims to develop and test methods of doing Christian biblical ethics. It opens with a useful and understandable summary of approaches to the Bible, including definitions of different methods. Attention is given to the relationship between biblical exegesis, systematic theology, and Christian ethics. In the second section of the book, the method is applied to specific NT texts with moral content.

Deidun, T. J. *New Covenant Morality in Paul*. Rome: Biblical Institute, 1981. This study deals with aspects of Christian morality in terms of Paul's understanding of the new covenant. This is done by comparing how the people of the OT and NT understood the concept of being God's people with specific emphasis on how these understandings shaped Paul's morality. The book also looks at Paul's understanding of *agapē* in the light of the new covenant and ends with a discussion concerning the relation between love and law in Christian morality.

Dunn, James D. G. *Jesus, Paul and the Law*. Louisville: Westminster/John Knox, 1990. This collection of essays, written by Dunn over a ten-year period, attempts to compare how Jesus and Paul understood the Law by analyzing sections of Mark and Galatians.

Eenigenburg, Elton M. *Biblical Foundations and a Method for Doing Christian Ethics*. Edited by Susan E. Eenigenburg. Lanham, Md.: University Press of America, 1994. This work aims to provide a text that assists Christians in addressing present-day moral problems from a biblical basis. The author draws out four biblical foundations for Christian ethics, then applies a three step method of solving ethical problems. Specific issues treated are women in the church, truth-telling, homosexuality, capital punishment, and genetic engineering. Three short appendices discuss the relation of Christian ethics to theology, general ethics, and philosophy and the sciences.

Flew, R. Newton. *Jesus and His Way: A Study of the Ethics of the New Testament*. London: Epworth, 1963. The aim of this book is to demonstrate that the ethical teaching in the NT is something completely unique and transcendent, not just one system of morality among others. The author asserts that Christian ethics must be tied to Christian faith and supports his thesis by examining the moral ideas of Jesus, Paul, and other NT writers.

Fowl, Stephen E., and Gregory Jones. *Reading in Communion: Scripture and Ethics in Christian Life*. Grand Rapids: Eerdmans, 1991. The authors reject a context-independent method of doing ethics and focus on ethics within Christian communities committed to embodying Scripture. The book hopes to help show how Christians in community can develop the moral judgment to discern Scripture's application to contemporary life. A middle section analyzes moral disputes in Galatians and Jeremiah, and the final section presents Dietrich Bonhoeffer as a model of embodying Scripture and reading in communion.

Furnish, Victor P. *The Love Command in the New Testament*. Nashville: Abingdon, 1972. By giving attention to each of the NT writers and to other Christian writings of the first two centuries, this book attempts to trace and define the various ways the love command has been received, interpreted, and applied.

________. *The Moral Teaching of Paul: Selected Issues*. 2d ed. Nashville: Abingdon, 1988. Written for lay people, clergy, and students, this book examines the writings of Paul on the ethical issues of marriage and divorce, homosexuality, women in the church, and the way Christians should relate to governing authorities.

________. *Theology and Ethics in Paul*. Nashville: Abingdon, 1968. The objective of this influential book is to gain an understanding of the structure, ground, and guiding convictions of Paul's ethical thinking. This is done by focusing on the theological content of Paul's major epistles. Included in the appendix is a survey of nineteenth and early twentieth-century interpretations of Paul's ethic.

Gerhardsson, Birger. *The Ethos of the Bible*. Translated by Stephen Westerholm. Philadelphia: Fortress, 1981. The author explains the ethos of postexilic Judaism, then examines the ethos of early Christianity according to Matthew, Paul, and John. The final chapter lays out the characteristics of the Bible's ethos as a whole.

Gill, Robin. *The Cambridge Companion to Christian Ethics*. Cambridge: Cambridge University Press, 2001. These eighteen essays by British and American scholars are aimed mainly at upper level undergraduate and graduate students and teachers and are divided into three sections. The first topic is the ground of Christian ethics, or the relationship of Christian ethics to the Bible and to modern biblical study. Next comes a comprehensive survey of different approaches to Christian ethics. Essays in the third section address crucial issues in modern Christian ethics, including war, welfare, ecology, and genetics.

Goldsmith, Dale. *New Testament Ethics*. Elgin, Ill.: Brethren, 1988. This brief introduction to NT ethics looks at several NT writers from the perspective of their particular experience of Christ. Aimed at stimulating thought and conversation for its readers, each chapter begins with an anecdotal glimpse at a modern ethical problem, is followed by close examination of particular NT writings, and concludes with an analysis of the ways in which the NT writer dealt with ethical issues and how contemporary readers might engage with that writer in ethical dialogue.

Grenz, Stanley J. *The Moral Quest: Foundations of Christian Ethics*. Downers Grove, Ill.: InterVarsity, 1997. Grenz's goal is "to develop a foundation for the specifically Christian vision of the moral life," with attention to its relationship with philosophy and contemporary context. Individual chapters look at ethics in the Western philosophical tradition and in ancient Greece, the foundation of a Christian ethic from the Bible and in a postmodern context, and the idea of comprehensive love as the content of a Christian ethic.

Harvey, A. E. *Strenuous Commands: The Ethic of Jesus*. London: SCM, 1990. This book tries to identify what is unique about the ethic of Jesus and how it related to the way other people of his day practiced moral education in order to ask what response Jesus' ethic would have elicited from his hearers.

Hauerwas, Stanley. *The Peaceable Kingdom: A Primer in Christian Ethics*. Notre Dame, Ind.: University of Notre Dame Press, 1983. In a book intended to be a college or adult study text, Hauerwas presents his theology of a Christian ethic centered around nonviolence. The work includes chapters on conceptual tools for doing ethics, a commentary on Christian social ethics, and a look at casuistry/decision-making.

Hays, Richard B. *The Moral Vision of the New Testament*. San Francisco: HarperCollins, 1996. Written with the church in mind, this important work offers a comprehensive view of the moral vision of the NT and how it might inform us today. The book is divided into four sections: (1) analysis of the moral visions of the characters and writers of the NT; (2) an attempt to find coherence among the different voices of the NT with focus on community, cross, and new creation; (3) a hermeneutical discussion of the way we should use the NT in Christian ethics; and (4) application of the previous sections to several contemporary moral issues such as violence in defense of justice, divorce and remarriage, homosexuality, anti-Judaism and ethnic conflict, abortion, and the use of resources. The conclusion also treats the use of possessions.

Hiers, Richard H. *Jesus Ethics: Four Interpretations*. Philadephia: Westminster, 1968. This book outlines the ethical interpretations of Adolf von Harnack, Albert Schweitzer, Rudolf Bultmann, and C. H. Dodd and also provides shorter treatments of other British and American scholars.

Holloway, Joseph O., III. *ΠΕΡΙΠΑΤΕΩ as a Thematic Marker for Pauline Ethics*. San Francisco: Mellen Research University Press, 1992. This book argues that Paul's use of the word περιπατέω ("walk") as a metaphor for the Christian life provides a window by which to view the whole of the apostle's moral teaching. This is done by examining the use of this Greek word in Hebraic, Hellenistic, and early Christian contexts, followed by careful exegesis of Paul's use of the term, and concluding with a presentation of Pauline ethics based on the insight gained by the previous sections.

Houlden, J. L. *Ethics and the New Testament*. Middlesex, England: Penguin, 1973. This book investigates the "shape" of NT ethics. The author takes a historical-critical approach and examines the context of the religious forces at work in the world of the NT. He then analyzes the standpoint of the major NT writers on ethical matters and examines whether or not the NT can function as ethically authoritative for us today.

Janzen, Waldemar. *Old Testament Ethics: A Paradigmatic Approach*. Louisville: Westminster/John Knox, 1994. This book is aimed at the church and seeks to demonstrate the comprehensive ethic of the OT in an overarching "familial paradigm" and subordinate priestly, wisdom, royal, and prophetic paradigms. Janzen shares a similar goal with Birch (*Let Justice Roll Down*). The final chapter relates OT paradigms to the paradigm of Jesus.

Jersild, Paul. *Spirit Ethics: Scripture and the Moral Life*. Minneapolis: Fortress, 2000. Ethics are examined using the three focal points of the Bible, the church, and postmodern society. Jersild sketches out a "spirit ethics" in the context of a church engaging with a pluralist society. Spirit ethics is shown to arise from the content and authority of the Bible and to be empowered by the Spirit in the community of faith. Specific issues covered are euthanasia and assisted suicide, homosexuality, and genetics.

Jones, David Clyde. *Biblical Christian Ethics*. Grand Rapids: Baker, 1994. Jones is a Presbyterian minister who follows the Reformed tradition in ethics. He treats Christian ethics as a subdivision of systematic theology. The book aims to encourage Christians to improve in the practice of the Christian life and addresses the goal, motive, and direction of the Christian life; the practice of Christian love in justice, mercy, and faithfulness; and the resolution of moral conflicts. The end of the book looks specifically at marriage, family, divorce, and remarriage.

Kaiser, Walter C., Jr. *Toward Old Testament Ethics*. Grand Rapids: Zondervan, 1983. This helpful book encompasses a definition of OT ethics, methodologies, the use of the Bible for ethics, and a review of different exegetical principles for OT ethics. Kaiser summarizes four important moral sections (the Decalogue, the Book of the Covenant, the Levitical holiness laws, and the Law of Deuteronomy) and the overall content of OT ethics. He carefully addresses moral difficulties in the OT and concludes with a brief section on NT application.

Kelsey, David. *The Uses of Scripture in Recent Theology*. Philadelphia: Fortress, 1975. This is a classic exposition of the diverse constructive roles played by Scripture in recent theological proposals. It is invaluable for its subtle and insightful look at the various ways in which Scripture functions in contemporary theological thought.

Knox, John. *The Ethic of Jesus in the Teaching of the Church*. Nashville: Abingdon, 1961. This relatively short work takes the ethical commands of the NT seriously and reacts against those who see the ethical vision of the NT as irrational or irrelevant. The author outlines what the distinctively Christian ethic is and then focuses on the problems that this presents to those who are responsible for teaching and preaching. Knox offers solutions to these problems and concludes with an extensive section on how ethical teaching is related to the preaching of the grace of God.

Lillie, William. *Sudies in New Testament Ethics*. Edinburgh: Oliver and Boyd, 1961. This thematic survey of the New Testament's treatment of various ethical issues opens with a look at the OT background of NT ethics. It then focuses on the example of Christ and analyzes, among other things, how the NT addresses topics such as conscience, goodness, law and justice, wealth, marriage and divorce, and the relation between eschatology and ethics.

Lohse, Eduard. *Theological Ethics of the New Testament*. Translated by M. Eugene Boring. Minneapolis: Fortress, 1991. This book is a topical survey of some of the major themes and questions of NT ethics including the christological grounding of early Christian ethics, the kingdom of God, the new creation, and the worldliness of faith.

Longenecker, Richard N. *New Testament Social Ethics for Today*. Grand Rapids: Eerdmans, 1984. In this relatively short work Longenecker sets forth a hermeneutical approach to the NT that allows it to speak to Christian social morality. He then uses this hermeneutic to discuss the three couplets of Gal 3:28 (Jew/Greek, slave/free, male/female) in terms of their historical background and contemporary relevance.

Lovering, Eugene H., Jr., and Jerry L. Sumney, eds. *Theology & Ethics in Paul and His Interpreters*. Nashville: Abingdon, 1996. This collection of essays is divided into three parts: (1) theology and ethics in Paul, focusing on individual Pauline texts and the broader themes of Paul's theological and ethical thought; (2) theology and ethics in Paul's earliest interpreters, both in the NT and in the early church; and (3) Paul in contemporary theology and ethics. The essays are written not just for scholars but also seminarians, pastors, and those with a general interest in the topic.

Marshall, L. H. *The Challenge of New Testament Ethics*. New York: Macmillan, 1947. In this book Marshall systematically goes through the ethics of Jesus and Paul. Written for pastors and the intelligent layperson, it also has an apologetic emphasis.

Marxsen, Willi. *New Testament Foundations for Christian Ethics*. Translated by O. C. Dean, Jr. Minneapolis: Fortress, 1993. The German author of this book attempts to answer the question of what defines authentic Christian ethics by looking at the ethical views, goals, and presentations of Jesus, Paul, and other NT writers. This is done with a particular emphasis on combining historical exegesis with systematic theology.

Matera, Frank J. *New Testament Ethics: The Legacies of Jesus and Paul*. Louisville: Westminster/John Knox, 1996. This book takes a primarily literary and rhetorical approach in analyzing the Gospels and Pauline epistles for their ethical teaching.

Matura, Thaddée. *Gospel Radicalism: The Hard Sayings of Jesus*. Translated by Maggi Despot and Paul Lachance. Maryknoll, N.Y.: Orbis Books, 1984. Written with the concerned layperson in mind, this book takes an exegetical look at the "radical" sayings of Jesus, primarily in the Synoptic Gospels, and seeks to understand what it means to call them "radical."

McDonald, J. I. H. *Biblical Interpretation and Christian Ethics*. New York: Cambridge University Press, 1993. McDonald looks at the tradition of biblical interpretation in the last century in three stages: liberal scholarship responding to Enlightenment perspectives; eschatology and ethics (including existential ethics and Christian social ethics); and the relationship between text and interpretation in post-modernism. The book provides helpful summaries of different scholars' views as well as examples of different hermeneutics and methods of interpretation during the last century.

________. *The Crucible of Christian Morality. Religion in the First Christian Centuries*. London: Routledge, 1998. This book suggests that the interaction between tradition, text, and context and between cosmic vision and life situation was a feature in the formation of Christian morality from the beginning and therefore can be the approach we use today. This is shown by looking at the ethos of the early Christian communities, how they used Scripture and the tradition concerning Jesus, as well as chapters on what a moral person is, what makes a community, and reflections on the notion of virtue or moral excellence found in Christian moral teaching.

McKeating, H. "Sanctions Against Adultery in Ancient Israelite Society, With Some Reflections on Methodology in the Study of Old Testament Ethics." *JSOT* 11 (1979): 57-72. A useful reflection on methods for studying OT ethics, taking biblical texts on adultery as a test case.

McKnight, Scot. *A New Vision for Israel: The Teachings of Jesus in National Context*. Grand Rapids: Eerdmans, 1999. The teachings of Jesus are examined in light of Jesus' mission to the nation of Israel, with focus on Jesus' understanding of God and the kingdom of God now present and yet to come. The ethics section focuses on conversion (faith, repentance) and cost (vocation, possession, self-denial); and a separate section on morality looks at one's relation to God, self, and others.

McQuilkin, Robertson. *An Introduction to Biblical Ethics*. Wheaton, Ill.: Tyndale, 1995. This excellent, easy introduction to biblical ethics clearly stakes out its approach to ethics as "nonconflicting absolutist, transcendental, theological ethics." McQuilkin examines all the biblical texts that deal with several particular ethical questions. The first part introduces the fundamental biblical doctrines of love, law, sin, and virtues. Situation ethics is also critiqued. Part two lays out specific ethical standards grouped roughly under the headings of the Ten Commandments, the Christian and society, advice on how to approach disputed issues, and guidelines for discerning the will of God.

Meeks, Wayne A. *The Moral World of the First Christians*. Philadelphia: Westminster, 1986. This book looks at the social process by which the character of the Christian communities of the first two centuries took form. This is accomplished by examining the broader ethical world in which the first Christian communities found themselves and then focusing on the specific ethical vision of the early Christians within that world.

Merritt, H. Wayne. *In Word and Deed: Moral Integrity in Paul*. New York: Peter Lang, 1993. This book sketches the linguistic history of the phrase "in word and deed" and then examines 2 Cor 10-13, in which the phrase is fundamental to Paul's argument. The author proposes that Paul established his apostolic integrity on the basis of a moral vision grounded in critical autonomy.

Miller, P. D. "The Place of the Decalogue in the Old Testament and its Law." *Interp* 43 (1989): 229-242. Miller provides a detailed analysis of the Decalogue and its wider OT reflections.

Minear, Paul S. *Commands of Christ*. Nashville: Abingdon, 1972. This book seeks a better understanding of the commands of Christ by analysis of twelve representative commands. For each command the author traces its use by early Christian teachers in their own ethical situations and then assesses the implications of each command to gain insight into the basic vocation of Jesus and the ethical stance of his apostles.

Mott, Stephen Charles. *Biblical Ethics and Social Change*. New York: Oxford University Press, 1982. Mott seeks to establish a biblical theological basis for social involvement and change. The first section lays this foundation, and the second evaluates various ways Christians work for social change, including evangelism and political means.

O'Donovan, Oliver. *Resurrection and Moral Order: An Outline for Evangelical Ethics*. Grand Rapids: Eerdmans, 1986. This theoretical and theological work seeks to provide a systematic outline of theological ethics on the foundation of the gospel and centered on Christ's resurrection. Topics covered include objective reality (creation, eschatology, and history), subjective reality (God at work in us, authority, and freedom), and the form of the moral life (love in acts and character).

Piper, John. *"Love Your Enemies."* Cambridge: Cambridge University Press, 1979. An analysis of the history of the tradition of Jesus' command of love for enemies and an interpretation of the way it was understood in the various stages of early Christian tradition within the NT.

Reiser, Marius. *Jesus and Judgment: The Eschatological Proclamation in its Jewish Context*. Translated by Linda M. Maloney. Minneapolis: Fortress, 1997. This book was written out of the observation that relatively little has been recently said or written on Jesus and his understanding of judgment. The author attempts to remedy this by an extensive survey of judgment in the eschatological thought of Second Temple Judaism, followed by a brief look at judgment in the preaching of John the Baptist, and concluding with a lengthy section on judgment in the preaching of Jesus.

Richardson, Peter. *Paul's Ethic of Freedom*. Philadelphia: Westminster, 1979. This book looks at the roots of Paul's view of freedom, some of the specific features of its impact upon his ethics, general ethical principles, and how these views are worked out in the church.

Rogerson, John W., Margaret Davies, and M. Daniel Carroll R. *The Bible in Ethics*. Sheffield: Sheffield Academic Press, 1995. These eighteen essays represent a wide range of viewpoints about ethics and the Bible, including Catholic, Protestant, traditional, and more liberal views. Issues treated include the difficulties of using the Bible for ethics, the poor, slavery, gender ethics, and nationalism in the Hebrew Bible.

Rosner, Brian S., ed. *Understanding Paul's Ethics*. Grand Rapids: Eerdmans, 1995. This collection of essays from twentieth century biblical scholars presents an overview of the major questions and problems in the study of Paul's ethics. The book is divided into seven sections, which look at the origin, context, social dimension, shape, logic, foundations, and relevance of Paul's ethics. This is a good resource for someone looking for an introduction into Paul's ethics, and it also includes some helpful suggestions for further study.

Sampley, J. Paul. *Walking Between the Times: Paul's Moral Reasoning*. Minneapolis: Fortress, 1991. This book aims to give a clear and full picture of Paul's ethical thought world, examine how Paul thought Christians should live in light of his thought world, and understand Paul's moral reasoning process.

Sanders, Jack T. *Ethics in the New Testament: Change and Development*. Philadelphia: Fortress, 1975. This book seeks to answer the question of whether or not the NT provides a general ethic valid for today, with mostly negative conclusions.

Schottroff, Luise, Reginald H. Fuller, Christoph Burchad, and M. Jack Suggs. *Essays on the Love Commandment*. Translated by Reginald H. Fuller and Ilse Fuller. Philadelphia: Fortress, 1978. The four essays in this collection analyze the love command and its place in the Sermon on the Mount, the antitheses, and the theme of the Sermon on the Mount.

Schnackenburg, Rudolf. *The Moral Teaching of the New Testament*. New York: Herder & Herder, 1965. This important work examines in depth the moral views of Jesus, the early church, and prominent NT writers by allowing the biblical text to speak for itself.

Schrage, Wolfgang. *The Ethics of the New Testament*. Translated by David E. Green. Philadelphia: Fortress, 1988. This ambitious book looks at the theological motivation and justification of NT ethics. This is done by discussing the major representatives of NT ethics and allowing their individual voices and ethical visions to be heard.

Siker, Jeffrey S. *Scripture and Ethics: Twentieth-Century Portraits*. New York: Oxford University Press, 1997. This book analyzes the use of the Bible by nine leading twentieth-century theological ethicists: Reinhold Niebuhr, H. Richard Niebuhr, Benard Häring, Paul Ramsey, Stanley Hauerwas, Gustavo Gutiérrez, James Cone, and Rosemary Radford Ruether.

Sleeper, C. Freeman. *The Bible and the Moral Life*. Louisville: Westminster/John Knox, 1992. Freeman's book is designed for adult study courses and contains thought-provoking exercises in each chapter. He treats the Bible as a source of theological and ethical principles and summarizes biblical approaches to moral reflection in law, prophecy, apocalyptic, and wisdom literature. The second part of the book examines how church bodies have used the Bible to formulate social policy, looking specifically at nuclear weapons and abortion.

Spohn, William C. *Go and Do Likewise: Jesus and Ethics*. New York: Continuum, 1999. What does Jesus have to do with ethics? The answers range from "everything" to "not much." This book attempts to find a middle way and makes the proposal that Jesus Christ is the paradigm for the Christian moral life. This is done by examining how Jesus' words and deeds exemplify moral perception, motivation, and Christian identity and by showing how the practice of Christian spirituality produces a character and way of life consonant with NT moral teaching.

________. *What Are They Saying About Scripture and Ethics?* Ramsey, N.J.: Paulist, 1984. This book examines six typical ways that Christian theologians use Scripture in ethics and evaluates each based on the premise that the diversity of thought is a necessary and positive result that comes from taking the living Word of God seriously.

Swartley, W. M. *Slavery, Sabbath, War and Women*. Scottdale: Herald, 1983. This is a historical and hermeneutical study of four ethical issues which tries to draw out general implications for Christian readings of the Bible with respect to ethics.

Swartley, W. M., ed. *The Love of Enemy and Nonretaliation in the New Testament*. Louisville: Westminster/John Knox, 1992. Included as part of a series on peace and Scripture by the Institute of Mennonite Studies, the essays in this volume look at Jesus' commands to love enemies and not to retaliate against those who do evil. An extensive bibliography gives resources on this topic from the last 70 years.

Verhey, Allen. *The Great Reversal: Ethics and the New Testament*. Grand Rapids: Eerdmans, 1984. This major study examines the ethic of Jesus, how the memory of Jesus' ethic was handed down in the early church, how that tradition came to be expressed in the NT, and how the NT has been and should be used in the continuing moral tradition of the church.

_______. *Remembering Jesus: Christian Community, Scripture, and the Moral Life*. Grand Rapids: Eerdmans, 2002. Verhey's intriguing book seeks to discover the moral life through the memory of Jesus in Scripture and in the context of the Christian community. From this framework Verhey begins with the continuing tradition of moral discernment in the church, then explores sickness and care for the suffering, liberation and chastity in sexual ethics, justice and generosity in economics, and theocracy and politics.

Volf, Miroslav. *Exclusion and Embrace: A Theological Exploration of Identity, Otherness, and Reconciliation*. Nashville: Abingdon, 1996. This acclaimed and important work was written out of the context of ethnic conflict between Croats and Serbians. Volf uses the metaphor of embrace to create a theology based on one's willingness to welcome and reconcile with the "other" rather than exclude a person based on otherness. The author works with the three central ideas of the self-giving love of the Trinity, Christ on the cross, and the embrace of the father in the parable of the prodigal son. From this framework, Volf examines identity, oppression and justice, deception and truth, and violence and peace.

Wenham, G. J. "The Gap Between Law and Ethics in the Bible." *JJS* 48 (1997): 17-29. An essay on the difference between law and ethics in the Bible.

Wheeler, Sondra Ely. *Wealth as Peril and Obligation: The New Testament on Possessions*. Grand Rapids: Eerdmans, 1995. Wheeler begins with a critical review of six methods of relating the Bible and ethics, then applies her own methodology to four particular NT texts dealing with wealth and possessions. Thorough exegesis of the NT texts is followed by a summary of the larger canonical context and a practical challenge to apply these ethics to the church with a series of relevant questions.

White, R. E. O. *Biblical Ethics*. Atlanta: John Knox, 1979. White traces the historical development of Christian ethics through the Bible beginning with the legacies of the OT and focusing on the NT canon. Attention is paid to Jesus' ethical themes, ethics of the primitive church, Paul's moral theology and ethical directives, and ethics in the Petrine and Johannine epistles. Another section looks at "sub-apostolic" writings, including James, Hebrews, the pastoral epistles, Matthew, Luke, and Revelation.

_______. *Christian Ethics*. Macon, Ga.: Mercer University Press, 1994. This volume includes two works: a reprint of *Biblical Ethics* (see above) and *The Insights of History*, which traces the history of Christian ethics through the earliest apologetics, Augustine, Abelard, Aquinas, Erasmus, Luther, Calvin, the Enlightenment, the social gospel and Christian social theory, Barth, Brunner, and Bultmann. This helpful resource concludes with a discussion of the "Christian norm" and situation ethics and an examination of the relevance of historical heritage for Christian ethics.

Wilder, Amos Niven. *Eschatology and Ethics in the Teaching of Jesus*. New York: Harper & Brothers, 1939. In this important book concerning the relationship between eschatology and ethics, the author seeks to answer those who claim that Jesus' ethical sayings only applied to his historical situation. He argues that the eschatological themes in Jesus' ethics do not point to an interim ethic but to the work of God brought about in Jesus Christ.

_______. *Otherworldliness and the New Testament*. New York: Harper & Brothers, 1954. This book seeks to uphold the transcendental nature of the NT as legitimate and important and argues that this aspect should not be divorced from common human experience. Biblical imagery and metaphor are analyzed to see how the world was viewed. The author critiques the charge of "otherworldliness," combats modern docetism, and examines resurrection faith.

Wright, Christopher J. H. *An Eye for an Eye: The Place of Old Testament Ethics Today*. Downers Grove, Ill.: InterVarsity, 1983. Wright seeks to provide a comprehensive framework for OT ethics and highlights OT themes such as economics and the land, law and the legal system, and society and culture. The book includes reflections on relevance for Christian ethics and application in the church.

_______. *God's People in God's Land: Family, Land, and Property in the Old Testament*. Grand Rapids: Eerdmans; Exeter: Paternoster, 1990. Wright's book on reading the Bible ethically focuses on issues of land and economics in biblical Israel.

_______. *Walking in the Ways of the Lord: The Ethical Authority of the Old Testament*. Downers Grove, Ill.: InterVarsity, 1995. Wright begins by introducing a method for using the Bible, especially the OT, in social ethics. The book includes a reflection on the nature of Scripture's authority and a survey of approaches to ethics in the OT from the early church to the present. An interesting chapter addresses the ethical relevance of Israel as a society. The second section presents essays on selected ethical issues in the OT, including the land, the jubilee year, and human rights.

Yoder, John H. *The Politics of Jesus*. Grand Rapids: Eerdmans, 1972. This classic treatment by a well-known Mennonite scholar still merits study. Yoder emphasizes the Jubilee as a foundation for understanding Jesus' ethical teaching, and like Bonhoeffer, seeks a radical following in the way of the cross.

WORKS TREATING THE ETHICS OF BONHOEFFER

Bethge, Eberhard. *Dietrich Bonhoeffer*. Rev. ed. Edited and translated by Victoria Barnett. Minneapolis: Fortress, 2000. This monumental volume by Bonhoeffer's closest friend is indispensable for any person who is seriously studying the martyr's life and legacy. It is a new translation from the original German and includes some sections that had been excluded from the first English edition (which was edited by the British Bonhoeffer scholar Edwin Robertson).

Bonhoeffer, Dietrich. *Christ the Center*. San Francisco: Harper Collins, 1978. This text is drawn from lectures originally given at the University of Berlin in Hitler's first year in power, 1933. It was reconstructed from the notes of Eberhard Bethge and other students. The book is indicative of the high Christology that permeates all the received writings of Bonhoeffer.

_______. *Creation and Fall: A Theological Exposition of Genesis 1-3. Dietrich Bonhoeffer Works*, Vol. 3. Edited by Martin Rüter and Ilse Tödt. Translated by Douglas Bax and edited by John E. de Gruchy. Minneapolis: Fortress, 1997. *Creation and Fall* first comprised lectures at the University of Berlin in the winter semester, 1932-33. It was published at the request of students who heard them. The lectures represented Bonhoeffer's first attempt to do theology in direct dialogue with the Bible. At this time he was generally following Karl Barth's model of expounding Scripture theologically.

_______. *Discipleship. Dietrich Bonhoeffer Works*, Vol. 4. Edited by Geffrey B. Kelly and John D. Godsey. Translated by Barbara Green and Richard Krauss. Minneapolis: Fortress, 2001. Originally entitled in the first English edition, *The Cost of Discipleship*, this new volume in the *Dietrich Bonhoeffer Works* series includes a detailed Editors' Introduction, which sets the 1937 publication in its precise context. It provides theological commentary on the Sermon on the Mount, as well as on Pauline metaphors for the church—the Body of Christ, the Saints, the Image of Christ, etc.

_______. *Letters and Papers from Prison*. Edited by Eberhard Bethge. Touchstone edition, Simon & Schuster, 1997. During his many months of prison captivity by the Nazis, Bonhoeffer wrote to his family, his fiancée Maria, and especially to his closest friend Eberhard Bethge. The letters serve as keys for following Bonhoeffer's spiritual journey, especially in his daily encounters with Scripture and the living Christ.

_______. *Life Together/Prayer Book of the Bible. Dietrich Bonhoeffer Works*, Vol. 5. Edited by Geffrey B. Kelly. Translated respectively by Daniel W. Bloesch and James H. Burtness. Minneapolis: Fortress, 1996. *Life Together* contains Bonhoeffer's thoughts about the nature of Christian community rooted in the common life that he and his seminarians experienced at Finkenwalde Seminary and in the "Brothers' House" there. The book is crucial for considering the conviction of Bonhoeffer that the Scriptures constitute an indispensable charter for the Christian's daily life, as well as for the community of faith.

_______. *Sanctorum Communio. Dietrich Bonhoeffer Works*, Vol. 1. Edited by Clifford J. Green. Translated by Reinhard Krauss and Nancy Lukens. Minneapolis: Fortress, 1998. An opening sentence in Clifford Green's introduction encapsulates the significance of this early Bonhoeffer writing: "Understanding the theology of Dietrich Bonhoeffer requires a thorough understanding of *Sanctorum Communio*, his doctoral dissertation from the University of Berlin and first published work." For the first time the reader can see the entire text in this English edition.

de Gruchy, John W., ed. *The Cambridge Companion to Dietrich Bonhoeffer*. Cambridge: Cambridge University Press, 1999. In this collection the essays of special relevance include those by F. Burton Nelson ("The Life of Dietrich Bonhoeffer"), Andreas Pangritz ("Who is Jesus Christ for us today?") and Geffrey B. Kelly ("Prayer and Action for Justice: Bonhoeffer's Spirituality").

Green, Clifford. *Bonhoeffer: A Theology of Sociality*. Rev. ed. Grand Rapids: Eerdmans, 1999. "This brilliant book is a refreshing indication that Bonhoeffer studies have indeed moved far beyond the earlier faddish phase into an era of serious scholarship . . . . All serious researchers into Bonhoeffer's theology must now somehow come to grips with Green's interpretations." (Geffrey B. Kelly)

Kelly, Geffrey B. *Liberating Faith*. Introduction by Eberhard Bethge. Minneapolis: Augsburg, 1984. In the preface one can find the author's rationale for this book: "My experience in giving countless talks, workshops, and courses on Bonhoeffer dictated the type of book I wanted to write. Where I had lectured on Bonhoeffer, I encountered a hunger for the liberating word of the Sermon on the Mount and the Gospel of Christ's sufferings for us as these were embodied in Bonhoeffer's career and in his extensive writings."

Kelly, Geffrey B., and C. John Weborg. *Reflections on Bonhoeffer: Essays in Honor of F. Burton Nelson*. Chicago: Covenant Publications, 2000. Includes essays by Richard Bliese ("Bonhoeffer and the Great Commission"), John D. Godsey ("Dietrich Bonhoeffer and Christian Spirituality"), Geffrey B. Kelly ("Bonhoeffer and Jewish-Christian Relations"), James Patrick Kelley ("Christological Concretion and Everyday Events in Three of Bonhoeffer's Sermons"), and John W. Matthews ("Responsible Sharing of the Mystery of Christian Faith: *Disciplina Arcana* in the Life and Theology of Dietrich Bonhoeffer").

Kelly, Geffrey B., and F. Burton Nelson. *A Testament to Freedom: The Essential Writings of Dietrich Bonhoeffer*. San Francisco: HarperSanFrancisco, 1990, 1995. This hefty volume takes readers on a historical and biographical journey that follows Bonhoeffer through the various stages of his life: teacher, pastor, preacher, seminary director, ecumenist, prophet in the terrorist Nazi era, and, finally, as martyr in the pursuit of peace and justice. One scholar's evaluation: ". . . destined to be the definitive text in English for all who wish to study the life and theology of Dietrich Bonhoeffer in depth."

Kuske, Martin. *The Old Testament as the Book of Christ: An Appraisal of Bonhoeffer's Interpretation*. Translated by S. T. Kimbrough. Philadelphia: Westminster, 1976. This volume is one of the few studies devoted to analyzing Bonhoeffer's methodology in relationship to Scripture. Here and there one finds an essay which illumines the connection. It will, however, remain a yeoman's job to write a comprehensive perspective. By 2005, it is expected that the English edition of the sixteen volumes in the *Dietrich Bonhoeffer Works* will be completed. That should then be the opportune time for such an effort.

NORTH PARK THEOLOGICAL SEMINARY

SYNPOSIUM ON THE THEOLOGICAL INTERPRETATION OF SCRIPTURE

SEPTEMBER 27-29, 2001

BIBLICAL ETHICS

THE PRESENTERS

M. DANIEL CARROLL R.
Denver Seminary (Old Testament)

CLARETTA DUPREE
University of Wisconsin (Nursing; Palliative Care Specialist)

PETER RHEA JONES
McAfee School of Theology, Mercer University (Worship Leader)

GEFFREY KELLY
La Salle University (Systematic Theology)

F. BURTON NELSON
North Park Theological Seminary (Ethics)

JOHN F. O'GRADY
Barry University (Systematic Theology)

IAIN PROVAN
Regent College (Old Testament)

MARION SOARDS
Louisville Presbyterian Seminary (New Testament)

GRAHAM STANTON
Cambridge University (New Testament)

SONDRA ELY WHEELER
Wesley Seminary (Ethics)

THE RESPONDENTS

ANDREW BURNETT
Prairie Hills Covenant Church and University of Minnesota

KARL CLIFTON-SODERSTROM
Loyola University

BRUCE FIELDS
Trinity Evangelical Divinity School

STEPHEN HALL
University of Chicago

PETER RHEA JONES
McAfee School of Theology, Mercer University

ALAN LENZI
Brandeis University

JEFF NELSON
North Park University

K. K. YEO
Garrett Evangelical Theological Seminary

NORTH PARK THEOLOGICAL SEMINARY

SYNPOSIUM ON THE THEOLOGICAL INTERPRETATION OF SCRIPTURE

SEPTEMBER 27-29, 2001

BIBLICAL ETHICS

PERSONS IN ATTENDANCE

James Amadon
Linda Belleville
Martha Berg
Robert Boehme
Paul Bramer
Linda Braun
Jim Bruckner
Andrew Burnett
Richard Carlson
M. Daniel Carroll R.
Mary Chase-Ziolek
Karl Clifton-Soderstrom
Michelle Clifton-Soderstrom
Jo Ann Deasy
Claretta Dupree
Rebekah Eklund
Bruce Fields
Linda Forbes
Stephen Graham
Stephen Hall
Bob Hubbard
Everett Jackson
Geffrey B. Kelly
Karl Klockars
Paul Koptak
Matt Kronberg
D. Brent Laytham
Alan Lenzi
David Moffit
Arthur Nelson
F. Burton Nelson
Jerome Nelson
David Noreen
Kathleen O'Donoghue
John O'Grady
John E. Phelan
Jennifer Pope
Iain Provan
Jerry Reed
Peter Rhea Jones
Phillis Sheppard
Klyne Snodgrass
Phyllis Snodgrass
Marion Soards

Esther Stanton
Graham Stanton
Norma Sutton
Fred Van Kamecke
John Weborg
Lois Weborg
Wayne Weld
Sondra Wheeler
K. K. Yeo

EX AUDITU

VOLUMES AVAILABLE

EX AUDITU Vol. 1 (1985) consists of selected articles presenting the issues inherent in the theological interpretation of Scripture.

EX AUDITU Vol. 2 (1986) discusses the theme: "Church and State Relationship." In addition there are two lead articles, one by Peter Stuhlmacher on "EX AUDITU and the Theological Interpretation of Holy Scripture," and the second by Ben F. Meyer on "The Primacy of Consent and the Uses of Suspicion."

EX AUDITU Vol.	3 (1987)	The theme: "Creation."
EX AUDITU Vol.	4 (1988)	The theme: "The Church and Israel (Romans 9-11)."
EX AUDITU Vol.	5 (1989)	The theme: "What is Salvation?"
EX AUDITU Vol.	6 (1990)	The theme: "Prophetic and/or Apocalyptic Eschatology."
EX AUDITU Vol	7 (1991)	The theme: "Christology and Incarnation."
EX AUDITU Vol.	8 (1992)	The theme: "Worship."
EX AUDITU Vol.	9 (1993)	The theme: "Resurrection."
EX AUDITU Vol.	10 (1994)	The theme: "The Church."
EX AUDITU Vol.	11 (1995)	The theme: "Biblical Law and Liberty"
EX AUDITU Vol.	12 (1996)	The theme: "Holy Spirit"
EX AUDITU Vol.	13 (1997)	The theme: "What is a Human?"
EX AUDITU Vol.	14 (1998)	The Theme: "The Theological Significance of the Earthly Jesus"
EX AUDITU Vol.	15 (1999)	The Theme: "Idolatry and the Understanding of God
EX AUDITU Vol.	16 (2000)	The Theme: "The Task of Interpreting Scripture Theologically"
EX AUDITU Vol.	17 (2001)	The Theme: "Biblical Ethics"

EX AUDITU Vol. 18 (2002).
The theme will be: "Spirituality"

To be published in April 2003